Victims and Values

A HISTORY AND A THEORY OF SUFFERING

Joseph A. Amato

with the assistance of
David Monge

FOREWORD BY
Eugen Weber

 PRAEGER

New York
Westport, Connecticut
London

Library of Congress Cataloging-in-Publication Data

Amato, Joseph Anthony.
 Victims and values : a history and a theory of suffering / Joseph
A. Amato with the assistance of David Monge ; foreword by Eugen
Weber.
  p.   cm.
 Includes bibliographical references and index.
 ISBN 0–275–93690–2 (pbk. : alk. paper)
 1. Suffering. I. Monge, David. II. Title.
B105.S79A52   1990a
128—dc20   90-7410

A hardcover edition of *Victims and Values* is available from Greenwood Press
(Contributions in Philosophy, Number 42; ISBN 0-313-25903-8).

Library of Congress Catalog Card Number: 90–7410
ISBN: 0–275–93690–2

First published in 1990

Praeger Publishers, One Madison Avenue, New York, NY 10010
An imprint of Greenwood Publishing Group, Inc.

Printed in the United States of America

The paper used in this book complies with the
Permanent Paper Standard issued by the National
Information Standards Organization (Z39.48-1984)

10 9 8 7 6 5 4 3 2 1

VICTIMS AND VALUES

In memory of my father
Joseph Amato
(1912–1989)

Contents

Foreword

On a hot summer morning, a prisoner hears himself condemned to death. He spends the next few weeks in the condemned cell, hoping for reprieve, but learns that there will not be any. On his last day, he is driven across Paris in an open cart, to his execution. Victor Hugo published *Le Dernier Jour d'un condamné (The Last Day of a Condemned Man)* in 1829, a tale of the sufferings of a man who hopes to avoid death, then learns he cannot do so and cries out against the injustice of having to die so young, so painfully: "They say it doesn't hurt. Have they ever put themselves in the place of the person who is *there*?"

"They" are the judge, the jury, the crowd who will watch him die. (The last public execution in France took place in 1939.) In the last resort, "they" are society, ready to punish, torture, inflict pain. It is society that Hugo addresses, hoping to inspire horror of the death penalty. In 1818, at age 16, he had passed, in a public square, a young woman being branded for "domestic theft." Her dreadful scream, when the red hot iron bit into her flesh, stayed with him. In 1820, two years later, chance made him cross the path of a murderer being led to the guillotine. It was Louvel, who had stabbed the heir to the throne of France. The horror and the pity of it shook him to the core. In his first novel, published when he was 21 years old, the demonic bandit, *Han the Icelander,* and his executioner, would be presented as equally murderous. In 1834, the story of *Claude Gueux,* whom injustice drives to murder and hence to death, a less elaborate forerunner of Jean Valjean in *Les Misérables* (1862), stated Hugo's case. It is misery that leads to crime. Give people, *the* people, schools for children and work for men, and crime will fade away. Until then, "Who is really guilty? Is it he? *Is it we?*" The debate continues to this day.

But the nameless hero of *The Last Day* does not seem to have been deprived. He describes himself as "refined by education," and demonstrates a knowledge of Latin available only to a privileged few in an illiterate age. In prison, while awaiting the outcome of his appeal, he gets pens, ink, and paper to note all the reflections that we read. His notes are all about himself, his imagination, his intellect "so young and rich," his moral torments while he awaits his doom. Only one topic never enters his mind, or that of his creator: the victim. The condemned man has committed premeditated murder (preceded probably by theft or attempted theft), but there is not a peep about the person he killed. He grieves about his little daughter: "Poor little girl . . . if those jurors had seen her, they would have understood that one should not kill the father of a three-year old child." The reader is moved, as one is meant to be. The murderer, however, forgets to ask: Had his victim been a father, or a mother? Had *his* crime left orphans in its wake? In 153 pages of self-pity, such questions do not arise. Alleged humanity dehumanizes, alleged morality demoralizes. The only victim in the book is the man about to die and, of course, those whom his death will victimize in turn. Compassion is selective.

One of Hugo's critics pointed out that *The Last Day of a Condemned Man* should have been entitled "The Last Day of a Murderer," then went on: "Abolish the death penalty by all means, but why not let murderers take the first step?" *(Que MM les Assassins commencent)*. Not an unreasonable suggestion.

Although Hugo cleans up his criminals to serve his ends, reading his novels reveals Claude Gueux as a repeat offender, violent, brutal, vain; Gavroche, the gay, heroic little guttersnipe of *Les Misérables,* as a juvenile delinquent whose death on the barricades saves him from jail, or worse; the *condamné* of 1829 as a self-pitying member of the privileged classes whose mind turns only to himself. Why, then, raise such a fuss about their passing? Because the idea of their suffering made Victor Hugo suffer? Just like his privileged hero, the privileged author's feelings were at stake. Indeed, at the stake. In the preface that Hugo added in 1832 to a new edition of *Le Dernier Jour,* he listed arguments against the death penalty. Of these, "sentimental reasons" are declared "the best." The possibility of judicial error, still the strongest argument against death, is not even considered. There is no distracting mention of a victim. Inflicting pain, let alone death, on one's fellows is a horrible thing to do. The upper classes must be persuaded to spare such experiences to the others and, above all, to themselves. It was egoism, not altruism, that moved Hugo. That may be why he was never moved to ask, as did New York State Senator James Donovan, quoted in the *Washington Post* of April 7, 1978, where Christianity would have been today had "Jesus got 8–15 years, with time off for good behavior."

When Hugo wrote, Romantic sensibility was taking over from Enlightened reason, which had argued—among other things—against excessive penalties and excessive pain. Utility suggested, with Beccaria, that punishment, swift, sure, appropriate, should fit the crime. Now, it was not waste, but the pain of others, that became hard to bear: the pain of selected others, because justice became a game of pick your victim.

In a more sensitive age, those who transgress appear more interesting than those who conform. Many societies have preferred those who sin to those who are sinned against. After Hugo, to take him as a benchmark, our society reflected growing doubt about just who sinned against whom. Or whether the idea of guilt, let alone sin, made any sense. Sociology, biology, psychology, and criminal anthropology nibbled away at notions of responsibility. Hugo's confusionism has become the norm. Are terrorists victims, or are their victims the victims? Who can tell? Better still, who can hazard an assertion that would not be forcefully challenged? The view of individuals as moral agents is outdated. Self-compassion masquerading as compassion counsels self-indulgence. And beliefs that do not correspond to facts are called principles.

All of which suggests that my friend, Joseph Amato, hazards himself into a minefield. Yet he does not flinch. He marches into Plato's cave determined to read the flickerings on the wall, and sometimes actually catches a glimmer of the fire. Angels grope forward where fools fear to tread. Joseph Amato is decidedly on the side of the angels.

Which does not mean that we always agree. I find it hard, for instance, to share Joseph's impression that suffering and tragedy have, in our time, been cheapened and banalized. We are far from Hugo's end, but we have gone a long way toward it. Suffering of a public nature (and little escapes our public notice) is more rare today than ever in the past, hence far less banal. But suffering because of others' suffering and, indeed, because of personal experiences once considered banal—blows, humiliations, insults, injuries—is rife. As Amato argues, as imagination expands, sensibility expands with it: Children, animals, women, plants, and "lesser breeds without the law," once undeserving of attention, claim and obtain access to empathy, sympathy, compassion—which is simply suffering with others, or with one another. Human rights have progressively expanded to mean rights for all humans, and even for non-humans: animal liberation and rights of the earth. Against this happy background, minor snags like reconciling the right to preserve and the right to exploit, the rights of producers and those

of the destitute, a woman's right over her body and the alleged rights
of her fetus, the right to live and the right to die, are considered secondary. To generations convinced of their constitutional right to have
their cake and eat it too, the priority of principle over practice poses
no problem, except the problem of avoiding the problem.

This book is also about claims and contradictions of this sort. Above
all, though, it charts the battles of rival sufferings and claims to suffering: a politics of suffering, curiously waged in an age when moral standards wane, and moral arguments do not get far beyond public rhetoric. Not so curiously, when you think of it, self-interest is, quite literally,
interest in ourselves. Like anxiety about cholesterol, self-interest represents the chief of our public passions. Guilt about the smarts and
stings suffered by others can cause discomfort, heartburn. Compassion,
like jogging, contributes to mental and physical hygiene. Like dieting,
it too is subject to changes in fashion; it hangs on the latest bulletins
from a fluctuating front. This, too, and how it came about, Amato
chronicles.

His analysis is profoundly original, not only in joining history and
religion, but in assuming—outside the province of theology—that religion has things to say to late-twentieth-century folk. Religion, of course,
is *religio:* that bond of common beliefs, assumptions, views of the world,
that colors the mindset of groups or times that it holds together. I hap-
pen to believe that the kind of communion, bond, morality, and code
of values, that religion used to provide or impose is distinguished in
our time largely by its absence. Hence, to assume its existence marks
Amato's nonconformist stance. A stance as rare today as that of Beccaria when, in 1764, the jurist from Milan suggested that punishment
should fit the crime. And perhaps as welcome.

Another anomalous aspect of this book is provided by the anachro-
nistic terms that Amato often uses: loyalty, fidelity, honor, sacrifice (for
worthwhile suffering turns into sacrifice). But loyalty is a high actuarial
risk; the promises of faith, like any other, engage only those who believe in them; honor has given way to Andy Warhol's 15 minutes' fame;
and sacrifice appears most evident in the national sport of sawing off
the branch on which we sit.

The gist of my mild objections will by now be clear. Amato is both
too sensible and too high-hearted to fit into today. Is it his Catholicism
(with its long realist tradition) or his sagacity that makes him recognize
with George Kennan the gap between what we dream and what we can
actually do? Is it my scepticism that makes me admire both, yet doubt
that this will be heard?

The book, an admirable essay, ends with a paean in praise of stories:
the stories that we tell about ourselves, whether we call them folklore
or history. Or literature. If stories, as he says, are the moral center of

our human experience, then, surely, we have no moral center left. It has been structuralized, analyzed, criticized, reified, and deconstructed. Tales, like history, had not so long ago been reconstructions of experience, designed to shape experience. When experience accelerates too much, our tales no longer can keep up with it. When experience shatters, history and our other stories shatter too. Irrelevance is the wages of progress, or, else, indifference. And yet Amato does not surrender his right to tell a story. He has told his wisely, movingly, stubbornly. For, what but stubbornness will maintain our honor?

—Eugen Weber

Acknowledgments

I depend on a lot of people to live and write. I hope this work honors them.

My indebtedness is first to my wife, Catherine, my children, Felice, Anthony, Adam, and Ethel, my parents, Ethel and Joe, and my wife's parents, Adam and Catherine. They have continued to support me in my compulsion to transform insights into books. Revealing my familialism, I always hope that if my grandparents were alive they would like this work. I am sure they would agree with one of its main assumptions, that we value ourselves by the stories we tell about our sacrifices.

I am grateful to many colleagues who, in this small college on the prairie, have been a family for me during the last twenty years. In the case of this book, I especially owe thanks to anthropologist Jim Hayes and fellow historian Ted Radzilowski. Ted's contributions to this work, especially to the last two chapters, were so great and so varied he could be considered, along with David Monge, to be a coauthor of sorts.

David Monge, friend, theologian, minister, and novice historian, continued to believe in this work when at times I did not. He helped me think my way through parts of it and he labored over several drafts of this work to improve it. Some of his writing on the Reformation and American thought was directly incorporated into the work.

Many others at this university have helped me in a variety of ways. While raising her son Brandon and going to school full time, Patty Schmidt, who confesses to being a fellow "workaholic," did a fine job in preparing the multiple drafts of this manuscript and the index to this work. Jan Louwagie, Jan Christenson, and Dorothy Frisvold were helpful in a variety of ways, as was the entire Southwest State University Library Staff, particularly Don Olsen, Mary Jane Striegel, and Frank Shindo. The university's administration and the Faculty Association's Faculty Improvement Committee also supported this work.

I must express also my gratitude to friends and colleagues at other universities who made critical comments on early drafts of this work. Jeffrey Russell of the University of California Santa Barbara, forced me to rethink whole parts of this work, especially the section on the relation of late medieval to Reformation thought. Professor Obayahsi, of Rutgers University, furnished an admirably sensitive and keen critical review of the manuscript, which had the consequence of forcing me to rethink my argument at a few points and even reorganize sections of the work. This work proved, felicitously, an occasion to renew my friendship with Professor Steven Tonsor of the University of Michigan and his wife, Caroline, both of whom were generous and helpful. Professor John Eyler of the University of Minnesota and Doctor Robert Meyerson of Atwater, Minnesota, offered useful insights to this work. I remain always beholden to the recently deceased Professor A. W. Salomone of the University of Rochester who, along with his wife, Lina, truly opened to me the door to his home and the discipline of history. I give special thanks to Professor Eugen Weber, who has written the foreword to this book. In unexpected, angering, and thus insightful ways, he has led me to see that in many cases the essence is nothing other than the function.

Also, my special thanks go to Ross Corson and Scott Perrizo, two young men who continue to lend me their energy, sympathy, and enthusiasm. Ross continues to recommend good books and articles to me. Scott, of Westview Press, and his wife Myra, also of Westview Press, have designed several of my books, and with labor and affection they continue to hold out the promise that there is a place for books, even mine, in the world.

Finally, my thanks go to Marilyn Brownstein, James Sabin, Margaret Brezicki Maybury, Catherine Lyons, and Mary Wolf of Greenwood Press. They have been as friendly and cooperative as they could be. Marilyn liked the idea of this work, encouraged my submission of it in outline, helped secure its acceptance, and humored and coaxed me along to its completion.

Introduction

The claims of suffering confuse and divide us. They have become greater in number, more extreme in demand, and increasingly complex in implication during the past two centuries. We do not know which sacrifices we should make and which we should honor, as our worlds of family, village, neighborhood, and religion are subsumed by the powers of market, government, party, and national and international causes. We debate the value of suffering. We contend over the worth of sacrifices. We selectively listen to the stories of preferred victims.

Paradoxically, our era, which proclaims happiness as a universal goal, not only preoccupies itself with—even invites despair over—certain forms of suffering, but also on an ever escalating scale it recognizes, ideologizes, and politicizes some forms of suffering and victims, making them valid, fashionable, and even official. At the same time, other forms of suffering, sacrifice, and victims are disregarded and even negated. Indeed, if the central contention of this work is correct, the conflicting claims of suffering increasingly have come to threaten identity, conscience, and public discourse in recent history.

Some types of suffering, it could be argued—although not easily or entirely successfully—take hold of us simply because we are human or yet, more specifically, are people of goodwill. Our nature, at least in the highest and most empathetic forms especially as cultivated by religion and a modern philanthrophic sensitivity, disposes us to respond to some forms of suffering. For instance, we read in the paper of a child who was beaten by his own parents until his buttocks were turned to a jelly-like pulp. Or we read of a child torn to bits by two pit bulls. Unless we lack sensitivity altogether, we are compelled, at least on some interior level, to react to this suffering—to its waste, stupidity, unfairness, and cruelty. There seems to us something so unfair, so outrageous, about the manifestly purposeless suffering of these children that we are tempted to say that anyone who remains unmoved in the face of such suffering does not belong to the human community.

We rebel against the idea of purposeless suffering. It seems unjust and intolerable. Furthermore, it threatens us as much as the unburied dead do. It argues that we have no final place in the order of things, that our individual person, actions, and prayers merit no special and exceptional treatment. Purposeless suffering, when generalized, denies life all meaning. Against it we throw up words and theories, we create religions, and we invent elaborate explanations of nature and society.

The senseless suffering of others particularly challenges our contemporary understanding of the world. In its worst forms, that of gratuitous evil (suffering caused for the fun or hell of it or for no reason at all) threatens to impeach our ability to impose a human order and meaning on life. The gratuitous evil act, like the murder of a child for no other reason than to see if one could murder a child, forces us to ask the extreme questions: Do we suffer, not because of nature's perversity and the limit of human order, but because of the will of an evil force, the Devil, Satan, Lucifer? Or yet, to tread one step further into the irrational, we ask whether or not God himself delights in our misery, anguish, torture, and destruction.[1] Are we a matter of indifference to him, or are we for him merely a source of entertaining stories? Whole cosmologies and theologies, as well as millenia-long practices of witchcraft and demonology—things which the modern mind had hoped long ago to set aside—arise in the presence of purposeless and senseless suffering.

Other forms of suffering that carry with them some sense of purpose test us less severely. Many of us have no difficulty believing that adulthood is attained only at the price of pain, success requires work, and wisdom has a cost in suffering. Others of us altogether naively believe that suffering, rather than ambition and meanness, is the door to greatness. Our peasant and working class ancestors, who still inhabit quarters of our mind, contend that to be alive is to hurt, to eat is to work, to choose is to risk and sacrifice. Even the most secularized among us believe sacrifice and martyrdom are necessary to purchase the good and consider their causes as religious ordeals worthy of devotion and holy stories.

Our identities join us to communities of suffering. Being Jewish or Christian, for instance, is a manner of suffering and a way of valuing one's suffering. Veterans of wars as well as veterans of labor struggles have traditions of suffering and sacrifice that insist on respect and compensation. Sacrificial suffering is a moral entitlement that constitutes a claim upon society at large.

In contemporary society there are multiple and conflicting claims based upon unjust suffering and sacrifice. They shape politics and conscience. Matching our suffering against that of others has become an abiding act of contemporary conscience in changing democratic societies. This is done—and this done naturally—in an era when happiness and well-being are official expectations of the great majority and even the old of modern society.

As members of modern national societies, who wish to be secure in our home and justified in our individual conscience, we constantly confront abstract assertions that the suffering of others has purchased and continues to purchase our happiness. We cannot live free of or practice our politics separate from the widely circulated claims of suffering and sacrifice that call for our reciprocity, gratitude, and duty.

In modern society our indebtedness is controversial and abstract. It is no longer a specific matter of what we owe our own family, neighbor, local community, or God, but our indebtedness is intertwined with vast public issues and rhetorics and ideologies about groups owing groups, classes owing classes, citizens owing nations. Hence, our senses of indebtedness and responsibility—keys to our conscience and politics, which themselves are profoundly associated—turn on complex historical debates about who did what to whom, abstract and contested sociologies that define and invent classes and their relations, and all pervasive ideologies that invariably argue not just about rights and duties, but insults, resentments, vindications, and revenge.

Suffering and victims have become a central political preoccupation and identity in modern society. Most academics from an array of disciplines—including literature, sociology, political science, folklore, and history—make preferred victims the moral spine and justification of their labors. Claims of suffering have invaded and, in measure, overwhelmed contemporary conscience and political rhetoric, which themselves are not easily distinguished. One need only think of the ideological functions of the Holocaust throughout the West, the uniquely powerful claims of blacks, women, and homosexuals in the United States, or the common view of the third world as a vast territory of suffering and victims.

Our view of the third world is never free of our view of slaves on ships or at work on sugar and coffee plantations and peasants who starve on the land or who flock to cities by the millions to become the helpless poor of countless barrios. This view of third world suffering and the developed world's guilt for it (which has a variety of sources including Lenin's view of international capitalism) argues, in a variety of popular and academic modes, that the world is a matter of victims and victimizers. More than an argument, it is a self-censoring and even morally dictatorial sensibility that contends that we are directly or indirectly responsible for all the world's victims, regardless of how distant they are or have been from our interest, influence, and acts. It assumes that we—the powerful and happy people of the West—have, through our agents or the force of interests or pleasures, done wrong against all the world's victims. From this point of view, the elemental moral notion of wrong by virtue of harm and injury to others is not only internationalized and universalized but fantasized, taking the form of unlimited, perpetual, and exaggerated self-accusation. Blood is always assumed to be upon our hands. This view is only mitigated by the belief that individuals and peoples are free and hence responsible for their own condition.

Victims have a powerful moral claim upon us. The victims' claim is the powerful ancient injunction that the rich should help the poor, and the strong aid the weak. It also conveys the newer and more democratic judgment that it is not fair for some to have so much, while others have so little. Perhaps more powerful are the aesthetic and sentimental conceptions of the poor (whoever and whatever they are) as deserving of our care and duty.

Increasingly during the past two centuries, thanks to natural unification and mass media, we of the literate upper classes of the democratic West judge ourselves by a comparison to distant others. (Resentment and diffuse guilt are the inescapable consequences of knowing, as humans since time immemorial have known, that there are those above us and those below us.) Out there, in our nation and the world at large, there are others who suffer, as we do not. We are never entirely free of them, however much we want to be and however removed our lives are from theirs. Our conscience is formed by continuous spectacles of suffering. An uninterrupted parade of images of distant victims as chosen and shaped by the media appear before us. We look out into the world—which is most often seen on the screen of our own televisions—and see victims, and they, as given face, look back at us. They become the eye of our political conscience and political drama. This is new in the twentieth century.

One of the primary goals of this work will be to suggest in outline the genesis of a conscience that increasingly knows itself in relation to the suffering of distant others. This will involve tracing in outline how a new social sympathy (empathy, if one prefers) has grown and expanded during the past two-and-a-half centuries. The genesis of this sympathy is found in Christianity and humanism, and more recently and powerfully in Enlightenment ideals and Romantic sensitivity; its great expansion from the late eighteenth century onward is not without relation to the rise of global markets, powerful states, and democratic nations. It also is inseparable from an immense social transformation marked by the replacement of the traditional individual, who was attached by life and imagination to a single locality, by the modern individual, who by thought, opinion, and empathy is joined to a changing world.

Analyzing the genesis of contemporary conscience requires examining a broadening sense of responsibility for the nation and world at large—not always matched by a responsibility for self, one's own family, or locality—which has increasingly characterized significant sectors of upper class Western society. As a consequence of the West's expanding power and knowledge, the modern Westerner increasingly considers humanity lord of the world. Correspondingly, God, fate, and nature less and less suffice as valid explanations for the suffering of the world. One can no longer argue that human suffering is certain and preordained without being judged conscienceless, even inhuman.

For all citizens of contemporary democracies there is a plethora of the world's suffering to be seen. There is no doubt that there exists "a 'market' in images of horror, and it is undeniable that 'commodities' are made out of other people's pain."[2] The suffering of strangers becomes an important part of contemporary media and public rhetoric. Individuals are asked to feel responsible for the world's suffering. It is often impossible for the great majority of us (who hear so much and digest so little) to separate the truth and justice of any particular case of suffering from an immense array of discourses, rhetorics, ideologies, orchestrated propaganda, and calculated lies that form the tissue of world communications. Indifference, in one of several forms, is a common reply to a world of information that pains, confuses, and seems always to be there in one form or another.

The convergence of our growing senses of sympathy and responsibility constitutes a new conscience—a great conscience of reform—that makes the suffering of others a political matter of the highest order. This conscience has extended itself to include the suffering of animals and the plight of nature. Emancipated from our own backyard, many of us now have feeling for the ecology of the entire world. No longer needing to live side-by-side with the animals, we include our chosen pets in our strongest sentiments of domesticity and lend our hearts to the plight of distant, wild animals.

This conscience, the source of so much reform and social good in the modern world, also confuses us as individuals and divides us as communities. Composed of unlimited and uncontrolled senses of sympathy and responsibility, this conscience peoples our inner dialogues and public rhetorics with countless victims. There are more victims at our door than our front steps can hold. Frequently we are numbed by the intensity, urgency, and contradictory nature of the remedies multiplying victims and their representatives propose. Victims threaten to overrun our reason and our politics.

Taking the side of victims, which has been so important for the advance of decency, justice, and well-being in the world, has also been an exploitative moral rhetoric in modern history. At its extremes this rhetoric elevates the claims of suffering beyond all other claims, even those of justice and fairness. Transformed into ideologies on the one hand, yet understood to be embodied in specific groups of victims on the other, this rhetoric, in the hands of its proponent, lays claims to such lofty responses as compassion, mercy, forgiveness, and love. None of these responses belong to the natural emotional perimeters of everyday morality and work-a-day politics.

Along with the banalization of suffering, there are other destructive elements associated with the politics of victims. The simple act of naming and identifying victims becomes a substitute for conscience and public discourse. Identifying oneself with the "real suffering" of a chosen class, people, group, race, sex, or historical victim is the communion call of the twentieth century secular individual. It is his sincerity, his holiness, his martyrdom. Objectivity, noncommitment, and indifference measure types of wrong corresponding to the Christian graduated judgment of the sin of not loving.

Furthering the threat that victim politics poses to public discourse are multiplying numbers of representatives and powerful advocates and agencies of victims. They contend that their victims alone matter: their victims alone are worthy of compensation. Such exclusive claims to suffering's right morally undercut the whole political community. They deny all claims to indifference, neutrality, autonomy, or independent judgment; no person, by either experience or reason, is exempt from being judged. Once having been classified as belonging either to the party of victims or that of victimizers, one is judged morally good or bad regardless of what he has done or is doing or however much he has suffered or sacrificed.

The claim to the exclusive status of being an owed victim constitutes one of the great moral nihilisms of this century. This claim on both the political right and the left is murder's accomplice, for it asserts the unquestionable moral superiority of one group over another. It negates the common values all individual and human groups associate with their own experiences of work, suffering, and sacrifice.

Ironically, to underline what is to be a major axis of this work, battles over the value of suffering intensify in the contemporary world precisely at the same time peoples in ever greater numbers discard the notion that suffering is an inevitable part of human experience. If any one thing distinguishes the modern Western mind from the traditional mind, as I have suggested, it is our doubt about the inescapability of suffering. Ambivalence about the place of suffering in human life characterizes the modern mind. The need to suffer is no longer universally conceded to be the price that God and nature put on all things in an absurd world. Accordingly, to a great extent, family and society have been stripped of their right to demand suffering.

As the benefits of modernity permeate greater and greater sectors of society, it is increasingly assumed by larger and larger numbers of people that it is wrong not to be happy. As suffering becomes less and less expected in one's personal life, paradoxically it plays a greater and greater role in shaping the moral rhetorics of the public order. Suffering becomes a moral identity and a basis for political entitlement. The greatest tragedies and the most banal causes adopt, exploit, and thus cheapen the moral rhetoric of suffering owed. Hunger fasts, which Gandhi himself first turned into a political instrument, have become, along with other nonviolent means, a common device for "suffering innocence" to have its way.

Adding to our confusion about victims' claims upon us is the increasing erosion of boundaries between the religious and secular, the private and public, the local and national, the nation and world. In democratic and mass industrial national society, we are more uncertain than ever about to whom we are connected and how, who are our friends and who are strangers. In this world, we are asked to define our selves and our society. Our traditional faiths and cultures, themselves not without confusions and conflicts, taught us to whom we were subordinated and to whom we were allied, who was familiar and who was strange. Now in our world an elemental part of our moral compass is broken beyond repair. We are unsure who our neighbor is and about the extent of our responsibility for his or her suffering. By virtue of belonging to a modern nation-state, especially a most powerful one, we are led at times to feel responsible for all suffering and victims in the world. At other times, given the size and profound diversity of our society, we feel absolutely powerless to change and thus not responsible for anything that happens at home or abroad. This makes more perplexing the questions: To whose suffering do we respond? What stories of suffering and victims do we honor?

In this work, I hope to do what few writers currently do: I seek to join philosophy and history. More specifically, I attempt to integrate reflection on ethics with insights drawn from intellectual history.

Also, I attempt to find some sort of middle ground between those who identify seriousness and truth with a willingness to be loyal to victims and unforgettable experiences of suffering, and those who dismiss the claims of suffering as matters of fashionable affectation and self-

serving political rhetoric. Because I do look critically at the matter of
suffering as a good and a right, my critics may argue that what this
century of suffering and victims needs is more empathy and commitment and less "cold and rational analysis." With such critics as these, I
can only disagree and ask them to read what I wrote rather than to
recite what they have long known and that of which they are morally
certain.

I assume that we know ourselves, in feeling and thought, aspirations
and contradictions, by knowing our history. History, I believe, is the
most specific and ultimately economical way to know ourselves. As the
book's subtitle asserts, I seek to delineate both a history and a theory
of suffering. My interest is not without relation to anthropology and
comparative religion insofar as this work is concerned with culture and
values, sacrifice and victims, and it has relation to political science in its
central examination of modern political ideology.

As I make clear in chapters 1 and 2, much of this work takes form
around the irreducible dilemma or the uncircumventable paradox that
human cultures must give meaning to suffering, yet they cannot. They
must, that is, value human work, sacrifice, tribulations, agonies, and
deaths, yet this necessity is forever thwarted by men and women's position in reality and by the nature of suffering itself. We are in suffering; we can't get beyond or around it. And suffering itself is heteroge-
nous: its sources range from coarse physical pain to the subtlest spiritual
anguish over death's inescapability. Suffering is pervasive: no aspect of
individual or collective life is free of what can be called suffering. Suffering cannot be isolated. It is inescapably connected with pain, death,
evil, and so much else that forms the elemental experiences of human
life.

In chapters 2 through 7, I join history and theory. In chapter 2 I
look at sacrifice as a fundamental means for humans to convey and
trade suffering with the gods, and I examine classical philosophers' failed
attempt to raise reason and will beyond suffering and sacrifice. In chapter
3 I underline how Christianity elevated the principle of self-sacrifice to
God himself and suggest how the church through doctrines (like the
Communion of Saints and the Treasury of Merits), sacraments (especially penance), and views of the afterlife (particularly purgatory), gave
form to an elaborate and, no doubt, abstract theological system of judging the earthly and heavenly value of suffering. It created a civilization
in which individual lay members, in imitation of Christ, fostered and
cultivated their own suffering and extended a new empathy to the
suffering of others. Of course, I do not assume that either Catholic or
Protestant Christianity brought the mentality of noble or peasant Europe fully into service of its elevated supernatural sacrificial views.

In chapter 4, where I reach the modern mind and its relation to suffering and victims—which is the primary focus of this study—I treat the eighteenth-century philosophers and Jeremy Bentham and his utilitarianism (an attempt to reduce suffering and happiness to rational calculations of pain and pleasure) as the expression of an increasingly confident civilization whose intellectual elites (the philosophes) dedicated their reason to solving the problems that impeded humanity from attaining earthly fulfillment and happiness. In chapter 5, I characterize romanticism as a profound revolution in Western sensibility, which focused and cultivated individual and group suffering for ever greater parts of the middle class and, thus, had the consequence of further putting human suffering and victims at the center of Western discourse. In chapter 6, I treat the First World War and the beginning of our contemporary world. In that chapter and the following two chapters, I explore our divided conscience over suffering and its worth. We question not only what we suffer, whether we should suffer, but even if we really suffer or not. Out public debates, increasingly ideological, are associated with the question of who suffers what at whose hands; the major moral axis of our public discourse has become the line drawn between victims and victimizers: hence, the title of this work, *Victims and Values.*

In an earlier work, *Guilt and Gratitude: A Study of the Origins of Modern Conscience* (Westport, Conn.: Greenwood Press, 1982), I explored our confusions and ambivalence over the matters of what we were given and what we owed. I argued that much of the modern debate over our consciences turned increasingly on a politicized gratitude (essentially in the service of the nation), which would define our obligations by virtue of what has been given, and a contradicting guilt, which progressive forces (usually opposing the status quo and often international in focus) use to enroll us morally in progressive causes. By seeking to analyze the contradictory claims of guilt and gratitude, I sought to help free our reason and judgment from the excessive claims and contradictions of prevailing sensibilities of guilt and gratitude and the ideologies that they support. Like *Guilt and Gratitude,* this work, too, has self-knowledge as an end. It also assumes that we must clearly hear the contradictory voices speaking within us and the world around us to free ourselves from their bondage, or at least, weaken their hold upon us.

Judging suffering and victims may seem like a cold and unsympathetic business, but nevertheless, it is necessary for the sake of conscience and politics unless we are to be bullied out of our reason, conscience, and politics and left with no stories of our own to tell. Furthermore, judging suffering's value is an ancient and well-practiced art. When have humans not measured loves and hates and not known friends and enemies by reference to sacrifices made and sacrifices betrayed? After all, is not choosing victims also an old human business? And are not our best and most important stories about suffering, sacrifices, and tragedies?

NOTES

1. A very useful introduction to evil and the problem it poses for human understanding is found in the introduction to Jeffrey Russell's study of evil, *The Devil: Perceptions of Evil from Antiquity to Early Christianity*, 4 vols. (Ithaca: Cornell University Press, 1977), 11–35.

2. Anthony Smith's discussion of Michael Ignatieff, "The Influence of Television," *Daedulus* 114, no. 4 (Fall 1985): viii.

1

Pain and Suffering, Currencies of Value

The most pressing human costs are in terms of physical deprivation and suffering. The most pressing moral imperative in policy
making is a calculus of pain.

Human beings have the right to live in a meaningful world. An
assessment of the costs of policy must also include a calculus of
meaning.

The history of mankind is a history of pain.

Three ideas from Peter Berger, *Pyramids of Sacrifice*

Pain and suffering are inescapably part of human life. We live with
them, we flee them, we resign ourselves to them, we embrace them, we
use them to control each other, we accept them to spare each other
hurt. We trade and commerce in them. Sacrifice, understood as concentrated suffering, is, along with prayer, our primary means to exchange with the gods and higher powers; victims represent what we
owe and also are who we owe.

We value our pain and suffering. Each life owes and is owed so much
suffering. Each class or station of life has its own pain and suffering.
In one of their many forms, which can range from menial labor to high
tragedy, pain and suffering (which we will distinguish later in this
chapter) define our consciousness, pervade our memories, incite our
conscience, and are the substance of our best stories. They are at the
core of our moral lives.

Expressing the Greeks' certainty about the inevitable need for man and woman to hurt, Aeschylus wrote "Who, except the gods, can live time through forever without any pain?" Voicing Christianity's equal certainty about the human need to suffer, Saint Bernard declared "It is misery to be born, a pain to live, and trouble to die." Buddhism teaches that pain and suffering pervade all life; wherever there is want, there is pain.

The fossil record of millions of years reveals the irreducible place of pain and suffering in life. As the first plants and animals emerged on the earth, parasitic microorganisms were waiting for them.[1] In addition to pain from hunger and injuries from battles, the most gigantic reptiles and their mammal successors suffered bone infections, arthritis, and pyorrhea. (Dinosaurs with aching teeth!) The considerable number of fossil vertebrates found with rigid limbs and necks radically curved backwards (which today is associated in humans with lockjaw, abscesses of the brain, severe middle-ear infection, meningitis, or strychnine poisoning) suggest death by tetanus. The fact that tsetse flies lived millions and millions of years ago only further proves the truism that where there is flesh, there is hurt.

Man, animal that he is, has suffered ever since he came into being. Hunger, cold, injury, infection were always there; hunting, reproducing, surviving—almost everything man did had a cost in pain. Ache, hurt, misery, they were always among his constant companions. For instance, one human fossil of a Neanderthal type, dating from thirty to forty thousand years ago, dubbed "Rhodesia Man," no doubt suffered bitterly because of his teeth: "Of the fifteen teeth remaining in his fossilized jaw, ten exhibited severe cavities; three had progressed to abscesses, with two perforations situated in front of the left ear as a result of the abscessed petrous bone."[2]

Human language reveals how rich our experience in suffering is. We have hundreds of ways of talking about our woes and hurts, miseries and pains. Suffering requires a language of a thousand tongues to describe. There are dozens of words and metaphors to describe everything from our twitches and irritations to our convulsions and paroxysms. Words like *failure, despondency, despair, loneliness, sadness, misery, sorrow, anguish, agony, rage, torment, torture, affliction, travail, ordeal, displeasure, discomfort,* and *distress* reveal other orders of our suffering. *Crying, weeping, moaning, shrieking, lamenting,* and *mourning* express grief. We console one another, we extend condolences (we share pain), we commiserate, (share misery), and we sympathize (have similar feelings, literally, to translate the Greek). We morally judge and name people in relation to how they handle suffering, praising the courageous person for his ability to tolerate pain while condemning the coward, the crybaby, the bellyacher for their inability to withstand pain. Revealing the range of our experience with suffering, our language imitates the basic animal grunts and groans of hurt and serves the common social requirement to meet death with wailing and lamentation, yet crafts the highest tragedies about human suffering.

Human pain and suffering are mediated through culture. While this view of culture does not rest on the assumption that each culture forms a distinct and autonomous view of reality, thus precluding the possibility of universals, it does assume that knowledge, values and sensibilities are inseparable from cultural mediation. Culture tells what hurt is, who can hurt, and why they hurt, as well as which pains can be cured, by whom and how. Culture defines suffering—as purposeful or purposeless, ennobling or degrading, holy or profane, transitory or permanent—and it is culture that prescribes proper and improper responses to our individual and collective suffering. Finally, it is culture in its highest forms of art and religion that explores suffering for its earthly and heavenly meanings. Without culture's mediation of pain and suffering, we would lack a means to impose hierarchies of importance on our experience. We would be left marked, vulnerable to the rush of sensations, feelings, and moods that engulf all sensate creatures.

To state two additional and important premises of this work: First, to a degree, pain and suffering are experienced and explained differently by different cultures. Second, as suggested in the Introduction, the most powerful psychological experience of modern men and women has been an uninterrupted and increasing encounter with a world containing a plurality of asymmetrical and conflicting cultures, such as is suggested by the juxtaposition of traditional, popular, religious, and academic cultures (themselves not in agreement) with newly emerging scientific, technological, national, and mass cultures.[3] Not only the exhilaration and freedom of choosing between these cultures and the private and public lives that sustain them, but also the ambivalences, contradictions, and irreconcilable dichotomies associated with these cultures make the experience of modern men and women what it is. Their understanding and valuing of pain and suffering, so important to their identities and sense of community, is inseparable from this great collision of divergent cultures.

VIEWS OF PAIN

Believing that so much of the substance and understanding of suffering is determined by pain, I will first begin with a discussion of it. Pain can be defined as every unpleasant sensation. Pain is ache and hurt. It can also be associated with aversion, disgust, regret, fear, dislike, apprehension, annoyance, hatred, dissatisfaction, as well as travail, torment, grief, and agony.

In *Pain and Pleasure,* Thomas Szasz suggests usefully that pain can be distinguished at "three levels of symbolization," arranged in a hierarchy of increasing complexity: "the first concept of pain," which is most biological in association and exposition, "is that of a signal by which the perceptive part of organism (ego) registers the fact there is a threat to its structural or functional integrity."[4] The second concept of pain refers to the pain that we express to others or others express to us. This involves us fundamentally in asking for help and in trying to communicate what pain is. The third concept of pain, in Szasz's words, "refers to that group of phenomena in which the meaning of the pain lies predominantly in the communicative aspect." The words relaying the pain have undergone a symbolic transformation; the communication no longer refers to the human body but instead makes a generalized plea for help, issues a warning, or sets forth a complaint about being treated unfairly.[5] The language of pain, in its most symbolic and complex form, becomes part of a general discourse about human existence.

Pain pervades human life. At any one time in the United States, as elsewhere, there are millions of people whose lives and identities are encompassed by pain. For these people of pain *(homines dolorosi),* many of whom are the ever more numerous elderly, pain consumes their lives. Millions of people in this nation suffer pain that they cannot control but simply must endure. Millions more are driven by pain to alcohol and drugs, health regimes and diets of one sort or another, other cures, or the growing euthanasia movement. Pain arises from and is tied to every part of human existence, including our increasing expectations about the possibility of happiness and the leisure to think about one's condition and imagine another. Pain, which fills our consciousness and conversations, provides one common, if highly subjective, measure of how we and others are doing. Talking about pain constitutes a most important but imprecise type of conversation.

Describing even the most immediate physical pain involves us in trying to categorize it. Is it sharp, dull, or diffuse? Is it fleeting, intense, agonizing, or unbearable? How does one feel at its outset, peak, and subsidence? Pain is a major preoccupation of language. Using the right words to describe a pain—its characteristics, source, and remedy—involves patient and doctor in a major act of interpretation.

Pain is not easily understood. Strangely enough, common ailments, like certain types of stomach irregularity, exist for the people and doctors of one nation but not for those of another. "The French," Jonathan Miller writes in *The Body in Question,* "interpret their symptoms in light of a national fantasy about the liver and unconsciously reshape their sensations in terms of this phantom organ. The English, on the other hand, are obsessed with their bowels. When an Englishman complains about his constipation, you never know whether he is talking about his regularity, his lassitude, his headaches, or his depression."[6]

Frequently pain is ambivalently situated between body and mind—and, of course, neither body nor mind can be localized or considered separately from the language by which we describe them. During the last two decades pain clinics, with all sorts of specializations, have sprung up across the nation. Their very foundation includes the belief that we should and can medically treat pain, but also the recognition that we cannot successfully manage chronic pain because it lies beyond our ability to define it.[7]

Adding to the indecipherability of pain, as classical philosophers clearly recognized, there is ambiguity not only within pain itself, but also in the relationship between pain and pleasure. How often have young children, as when I was a boy, been cautioned, "If you laugh at supper, you will cry before you go to bed." This didn't compare in elegance but shared some of the substance of Shelley's commonly quoted dictum: "Joy too intense is turned into pain." While one school of philosophy essentially considers pain as bad—something to be removed as promptly as possible—a second school recognizes pain fundamentally as fulfilling a valuable function. Of this view Thomas Szasz wrote:

According to [this positive approach], pain and suffering indicate—both to the superego and to others—that we are good or are trying to be good. Pain and suffering . . . are readily substituted for realistic effort and accomplishment. The whole complex concept of masochism . . . deals with this aspect of pain. . . . In this connection, the importance of the influence of Judaism and Christianity and of a Protestant ethic is apparent. Some connections between pain and pleasure on the one hand and secular law on the other become also evident at this juncture. Thus pain is, among other things, a currency with which we repay damages done unto others.[8]

Witch doctors, psychoanalysts, priests, and medical doctors, contend over the nature, sources, and cures of pain. Treating pain may be the oldest, yet the least precise, of the human arts. One person takes his whiskey (in Spanish, brandy is called *quitapenas*), another flees to a doctor, a third goes to a health spa, while a fourth takes a pilgrimage.

For some pain is the essence of life. For them pain and life are nearly synonymous. My grandmother from Sicily used to remark, "Every day has its dog." Philosopher David Bakan wrote, "Pain is the common companion of birth and growth, disease and death, and is a phenomenon deeply intertwined with the very question of human existence."[9] "For the individual, as for mankind in general, life," commented Sigmund Freud, "is hard to endure."[10]

Some interpret pain as the wages of sin. Whereas others do not attribute pain to a necessary order of nature or the will of god or devil,
but rather ascribe it to a technical matter of neurology, anesthesiology,
psychiatry, or some other science. And yet for others, the sources of
pain matter little: what counts is finding the proper attitude to endure
it.

Whatever the case, pain goes to the center of human life and language. To be human is to be conscious of pain and to talk, if only to
oneself, about it. By virtue of having a body and mind, we interpret
and argue about our pain. Pain brings messages. All its messages cannot be repressed or set aside by a reflex such as pulling one's hand
away from a burning object. Many of pain's messages must be interpreted; they insist upon a meaning. As anyone who has been warned
about a heart condition knows, he is driven by fear, conscientious self-
concern, or some mixture of the two to interpret the slightest bodily
sensations. Likewise, anyone who has found himself in a rehabilitation
center after an accident, knows that numbness of an arm or the tin-
gling of the scalp often lead to discussions of such subtle matters as
deferred pain, deflected pain, phantom pain, and distorted pain.[11] In
the worst cases, our pain is never properly diagnosed and death ensues
before a cure is found: In fact, death can be a consequence of mis-
guided efforts to effect a cure.[12]

Our major biological systems, circulatory, respiratory, and digestive,
do not have clear languages of pain. Diseases do not universally have
clearly defined accompanying forms of pain. Great pains can express
disorders of minimal significance, whereas slight pains can be symptoms of deadly disease. So when a new and enigmatic pain occurs, we
only know that we have an unpleasant sensation for which we need a
cure and a meaning. Our dialogue with our own body can be terribly
imprecise.

Pain compels us to self-interpretation. We must decide what we have
got and what we intend to do, if anything, about it. "Almost invariably
it is the sufferer who shapes the experience of illness into an intelligible
situation. At some level or other suffering gives way to a personal diagnosis. In the end the victim becomes a patient because he guesses
that something is wrong or odd about him and that he is the unwilling
victim of the process."[13]

At some point the victim must decide whether to seek help and
whether to surrender himself to the predominant cultural form of
treatment or to choose an alternative form of therapy. The victim of
pain classifies himself and his condition by the very act of deciding by
whom and how he should be treated. His choices do not end once he
has delivered himself into the hands of the therapist of his choice. He

must continue to weigh his pain in light of such questions as whether or not he is in good hands, is making sufficient progress, and whether the prognosis of the proposed cure is worth the money it costs and the risk that it involves. In the case of prolonged treatment of elusive pain— the sort often associated with back pain—the patient may be asked in the course of his treatment to consider singularly or in combination a whole range of therapies, ranging from rest, physiotherapy, chemical agents, pain killers, tranquilizers, muscle relaxants, and surgical relief to hypnosis and psychological therapy.[14] In life-threatening cases, especially like those associated with cancer, the patient may have to choose, if he elects any therapy at all, between an array of radiation and surgical therapies, each of which inevitably carries its own forms of pain and may only promise, at most, a moderate prolongation of life.

One patient (a close fiend of mine), with a case of stomach cancer that was diagnosed to be without cure, was presented, by one of the nation's most prestigious clinics, the Mayo Clinic of Rochester, Minnesota, with the chance of entering a new experimental program in which he would not be told what treatment he would receive. He would either be given a new viral medicine, a chemical radiation, or a placebo. He would not know which. He was being asked to surrender himself to an experimental program more for the sake of the advance of medicine than for his own cure. (There was only a one-in-three chance that he might get the new treatment, the viral treatment, which he wanted but that was yet of questionable medical value.) His pain had led him into a world of choices and interpretations. A few months later from his death bed, having forgone the chance of entering the experimental program, he wrote a letter of condolence to a friend whose daughter had just been murdered, telling her to look to the victory of Christ over death amidst our suffering.

In interpreting pain, we seek to value it. There are, to be more schematic than one really can be in such matters, at least five basic interpretations of the value of our pain.[15] First, pain is a natural warning mechanism. For self-preservation, pain is necessary for all living creatures.

Second, pain proves that the world is senseless and absurd, defying our understanding and our sense of fairness. It visits all regardless of their condition, age, innocence, or prayers. Pain is the whip of the fickle gods.

Third, pain is what humans avoid. Humans in overwhelming majority do all they can to flee mental and physical pain, adopting whatever devices and beliefs relieve them of their misery. To paraphrase Pascal, we play to forget our misery. Those who lack the means to escape pain, belong to the lowest class. In French the man who did the most degrading chores of the household was *un homme de peines*.

Fourth, pain is the opposite of pleasure. All that is not pleasurable and all that inhibits pleasure is painful. From this point of view we know pain by what it is not.

Fifth, pain is the price we pay for things. In more abstract terms, pain is the sine qua non of being and having. We cannot be, nor can we have things, without experiencing pain. All we know, have, and cherish has a cost in pain. Not only does nature put the price of pain upon things, but so does man. We speak to one another in the language of pain. Pain measures the sincerity of an effort. We use it to punish, to test and to purify, and to measure ourselves. It is pain understood in this last sense, as a currency of value, that I, anticipating our discussion of suffering, now examine.

VALUES OF PAIN

As punishment shows, pain has its use as a fundamental part of human discourse. Pain, which derives from the Latin word *poena*, which means punishment, counsels paths of action. As the gods were long thought to use pain to teach man, so man uses it to instruct himself. Pain tells individuals and groups about who is strong and who is weak, what is right and wrong, what is reality and illusion. As suggested by the French expression *portionner la peine a la justice* (make the punishment fit the crime), justice requires that we make pain equal the wrong. Pain is among mankind's first and most legitimate forms of compensation.

The principle that pain suffered should equal pain caused is a composing element of the human moral economy. It, if not purely, is voiced in such widely divergent cultural artifacts as Hammurabi's law of an eye for an eye or the Corsican code of a life for a life. In traditional societies, pain constituted the foundation of retributive justice. The logic of punishment was the more heinous the crime, the more excruciating the punishment should be. For treason and regicide, the greatest crimes in the land, the worst punishments were found, for what was wanted was not only information, especially about fellow accomplices, but a *supplice*, the most powerful physical suffering, which would rebalance the moral universe by the pain and sorrowful repentance the victim would express as punishment for his crime. Clemency, which only the great could give the weak, was the rare gift of allowing forgiveness, instead of pain, to satisfy the balance of the moral order.

From the register of the Parlement de Paris in 1610, we learn of the torture and death of Francis Ravaillac for the murder of King Henry IV. According to John Swain's *The Pleasures of the Torture Chamber,* they tortured him to redeem him from the torments being prepared him in the afterlife and to persuade him to declare his accomplices. First, using the torture of *brodequin,* that is constraining his feet and legs in a strong wooden box, they drove a wedge between his knees, compelling him to acknowledge that he was a sinner, to beg God for mercy, and to ask God that he "receive this penance as expiation for the greater sins which I have committed."[16] He still named no accomplices. Then they put fire on his right hand, while they tore at his breasts with red hot pincers. Afterwards, while the crowd cried for uninterrupted torture, lead and scalding oil were poured upon his wounds. He was then drawn by four horses, for half an hour, by intervals. Yet he denied having had any accomplices. "At length," Swain wrote, "when he had been drawn for a full hour by the horses, without being dismembered, the people, rushing on in crowds, threw themselves upon him, and with swords, knives, sticks, and other weapons, they struck, tore, and mangled his limbs; and violently forcing them from the executioner, they dragged them through the streets with the utmost eagerness and rage, and burnt them in different parts of the city."[17]

Torture reveals much about our human discourse in the language of pain. A recent exhibition in Rome featured torture devices from the Middle Ages to the beginning of the industrial era. This diverse array of instruments, which revealed the technology of the period, were used by secular and religious authorities as well. They included a vaginal pear (an opening device), a chastity belt, and two special masks to link together the heads of quarrelsome women. Beyond those obviously sexist instruments of torture, other devices included breaking wheels, the saw, hanging cages, axes and swords (devices reserved for the best aristocratic deaths), garottes, racks, head crushers, cradles, thumbscrews, and iron maidens, as well as pincers and tongs, a breast ripper, and a rectal pear. The lengthy guide that described the collection noted:

These [instruments] became standardized throughout Europe. . . . But besides these orthodox and institutional devices . . . anything and everything was and is good for torturing. . . . Good torture [only] requires a well tied victim and any object: a pencil, a stone, an ashtray, a nail, a match, a splinter of glass, a door with hinges, a pin, a mouse, everything, everywhere, anytime, provided it be used with a bit of creative fantasy.[18]

Torture, of course, does not belong to one place, era, or people, even though there is no doubt that certain times and situations—especially war and revolution—and cultures invite torture. Torture plays too large a role in the human discourse with pain for us to conceive of it ever being banished entirely. Torture can be used to punish, to purify, to gain information, to break wills, to make example of, to display power, and, finally and most perversely, to explore the outer boundaries of human agony.[19]

The torturer conducts a discourse in pain with his victim. He aims his pain at the spiritual center of the victim, seeking dominance.[20] Contrariwise, the victim must resist the torturer. With all his will, memory, and hope, he must affirm that he holds secrets, loyalties, and fidelities that the torturer's pain cannot force him to surrender. As the torturer turns his screw, brightens his lights—does what he will—the victim must not only resist the torturer's pain, as subtle or immense, constant or erratic, and always endless as it seems to be, but he must battle against the despairing notion that he who causes pain is stronger and better than he who suffers pain.

PAIN PURCHASES THE GOOD

In addition to being punishment and torture, pain is a measurement human activity. As human energy is counted in calories, so human labor counts itself, at least on the negative side of the ledger, by pain. All actions involve repetition and strain, and risk unforeseen consequences. Invariably, actions are taken against the inevitable resistances that exist within the self, society, and nature. Even activities of pleasure and ecstasy require preambulatory efforts that are painful and can have hurting consequences. Everything that amounts to anything has a cost in pain. "Pain," Hesiod wrote, "is the price that God puts upon all things."

What is attributed as having a worth is revealingly called being "painsworthy." Humans lay claim not only to things that they have been given or that they have purchased, but also those things that they have paid for in pain. The greater the payment in pain for a thing, the stronger claim to possession. A near universal law of fairness and justice—one found in custom and recognized by formal law systems—is that men and women believe they own what they have worked for. In *The Little Prince*, Antoine Saint-Exupery has the fox explain to the Little Prince, "It is the time you wasted for your rose that makes your rose so important."[21]

Joined to the law that one purchases a thing or a right with pain, is the corollary that pain invested in things makes them valuable. For instance, one person claims ownership of an animal because he captured and tamed it while another bases his possession of a piece of land upon the fact that he cleared it. Far more universal and less dubious than the economic labor theory of a value (the value of a commodity is determined by the work invested in it) is the moral law that a person should possess what he has paid for in pain.

This abiding moral law that pain equals ownership (a law that does not go uncontradicted) underpins progressive ideologies of the modern political right and left. Representatives of the middle class attack the aristocrats upon the basis that the middle class alone produces society's wealth. In turn, representatives of the lower class claim they are the working body of society and that they should enjoy the fruits of their labor, while representatives of those at the top, especially those recently arrived, claim they merit their wealth by virtue of what they and their family did in business or in public service. (It is even common in India to hear one of the highest Brahmin explain that he feels no guilt over his well-being, given the poverty and misery that surround him, since he earned his well-being in this life by pain he underwent in previous lives.) Those who argue to justify property rights in the tradition of John Locke (which is the ultimate modern source of the labor theory of value) contend that individuals should be free and secure to shape the worth and value of their own lives, which they cannot do without property, while those who argue for equalization of wealth argue that every person should have a fair opportunity through effort, risk, and sacrifice to secure a good life in society. The principle that one should enjoy the fruits of one's labor is part of the ethics of much contemporary political discourse.

We react strongly when we believe this law is violated. Again to use a French phrase, *perdre sa peine* (to waste one's efforts) always carries with it a sharp sense of unfairness. To be robbed of what one has earned is always judged to be a great wrong. It is considered universally cruel to force a person to work at what he cannot accomplish and for the work to serve no other purpose than to cause the worker pain. In *House of the Dead,* Dostoevsky remarked that nothing so demoralized his fellow prisoners in Siberia as purposeless work, such as moving a pile of rocks from one place to another, only to return them to their original place; whereas, he found that even in the coldest weather men would take heart in the most difficult jobs—such as removing the wood from a ship frozen in ice—because they could see a purpose to their effort.

Also, in light of the law that pain gives value, it is understandable why it is repugnant to hear someone claim to have worked hard to achieve a good, when truthfully he obtained it with almost no effort. No one is more tedious than the braggart whose "great accomplishments" involved little effort and produced insignificant results. No complaints are as common, especially in peasant societies, as those aimed at the lazy and the do-nothing, who are understood to create no value of their own while taking that of others. They eat other men's bread. The moral indictment of parasites is not just directed against the do-nothing, who never shoulders his share of the burden, but it is extended to every brand of person who lives off the labors of others. This indictment is often especially aimed at the banker, who lives off money rather than work; the capitalist—especially the finance capitalist rather than the industrial capitalist—who makes his profit from manipulation of stocks rather than real goods; and the administrator, whose very

office inhibits rather than permits work. Not exempted from this indictment are intellectuals, who are understood to live by words rather
than work. And everywhere there is general moral agreement that no
person is as distasteful as one who reeks with moral judgments of other's failures, but is constitutionally, even perversely, unwilling to work
himself.

No accusations are as powerful as those of ingratitude. They voice
the moral claim, "I gave you my pain, I made my sacrifices for you,
and you did not recognize them." Ingratitude is about this gift betrayed. It arises from the sense that what one has given—be it by a
single and free act or through a lifetime of sacrifice—has not been re-
spected. At the core of the charge of ingratitude, is the moral complaint that the beneficiary of pain and suffering does not recognize
what he has been given. Accusations of this sort form a significant part
of the moral language of the household, the neighborhood, the work-
place, and the political order, and give resentment an abiding place in
all moral discourse.

PAIN, THE MEASURE OF A PERSON

Pain is not only necessary for creating things, but it also is essential
for the building of good character. Human life is possible only upon
the condition that we learn to live with, despite, and beyond certain
pains. In all things, even death, a certain composure and decorum are
required and idealized. A minimum requirement for a person with integrity is a capacity to endure and over overcome a range of pain. A
person who cannot stand pain is considered to be characterless. The
complainer, the whiner, the crybaby, and the hypochondriac are all
judged to be morally inferior; the coward, even more reprehensible, is
considered to be the most despicable type because he is dominated by
pain.

Different ethnic groups experience and express pain differently. As
Mark Zborowski showed in his classic study, *People in Pain,* individuals
of Jewish, Irish, and Italian heritage (the groups he chose to study)
feel, express, and interpret their pain in different ways.[22] Also the
members of different social classes experience and are expected to experience pain differently. For example, the aristocratic code of life, which
held powerful sway in Europe up to the First World War, prescribed
that a member of the upper classes should willingly bear mental pain
and accept death rather than dishonor, nevertheless aristocrats were
permitted to complain bitterly about the slightest personal inconve-
niences. Contrariwise, the lower classes, who were conceded great rights
to act out mental anguish, were expected to endure both insult to their

person and everyday pain, as if that was the natural thing for them to do.

The different sexes have been traditionally expected to experience and to express pain differently.[23] The woman's natural and proper pain was that associated with childbirth, nurturing, and the maintenance of the everyday life. The pain, which was understood to define and ennoble the woman, was essentially biological and domestic. Kathryn Holme described the husband's praise of his wife for having given birth to a child. " 'And, for the twentieth time,' he exclaimed, 'I don't know *how* you did it all alone!' His admiration for her bravery sent a glow of happiness through her. It was a new kind of tribute from him. It was a payment in full for all the terrors of her lonely ordeal."[24]

The pain that elevates and ennobles a man is still widely conceived to be more noble than that of the woman. A man's pain arises from his duty to test the physical and mental limits of the human condition. He confronts and battles beyond the boundaries of the household, the village, and the city, at the perimeters of life. He fights other men, nature, and even the gods.

The great tests of humanity are often tests of pain. In miniaturized form, rites of passage inflict pain that allows individuals to pass the important boundaries of life. Hinduism makes all of life a journey across pain, which if well taken, permits one to pass from one order of life to another. To a large extent men and women of all places and times define and value themselves in reference to the ordeals they have undergone.

We respect the person who conducts himself well, but we revere the person who has mastered great pain. This person has brought human strength out of pain. Even more revered than the person of strong character is the person who in spirit has survived tragedy. He stands beyond the pain that no ordinary person can conceive of, or imagine himself, enduring. He affirms that the human spirit prevails against the greatest tests. He lives beyond what we take to be boundaries of human life. He forces us to examine our own capacity to affirm the values we hold most dear, despite everything. As Elie Wiesel wrote, "Everyone in his or her own destiny, has a certain relationship with pain."[25]

At this point, pain turns us to the question of suffering. As pain first invites us to look for discrete and localized explanations, so, in the end, it confronts us with the matter of life itself, which is inseparable from the question of suffering.

SUFFERING DEFINED

Religious thinkers are quick to draw radical and sharp distinctions between pain and suffering. They make the former a matter of body and medicine, the latter, a matter of spirit and faith. Everyday language, however, does not entirely concur in making such a sharp distinction. We commonly use the two words as synonyms. They so much appear to be each other's causes that the very act of distinguishing one from the other appears an unnecessary act of abstraction. As great pain, common sense argues, almost always equals suffering, so suffering almost invariably entails pain. Also supporting their identification is the fact that they commonly occur together; we attribute to them many similar functions such as to purify, to punish, and to make worthy.

Also, like pain, suffering's heterogeneous forms, if nothing else, account for our inevitable debate about suffering's value. Revealing some of the most basic arguments that surround suffering, some writers contend that suffering is essential for human character, greatness, and wisdom. Romantics like Dostoevsky and Baudelaire argued the case of suffering's worth contending that suffering gave man a unique nobility and that suffering itself was the source of consciousness.

However, others argue that suffering is nothing other than a curse. In standard books of quotations we read that suffering lacks all therapeutic value. George Santayana quipped "If pain could have cured us we should long ago have been saved," while Homer long ago warned in the *Iliad*, "There is not any advantage to be won from grim lamentation," and Goethe cautioned those who would find good in prolonged suffering, "Man can only endure a certain degree of unhappiness; what is beyond that either annihilates him or passes by him and leaves him apathetic."

Without assenting to relativism as a philosophical doctrine, it must be acknowledged, as is the case in pain, that suffering is both experienced and judged differently by different people in different nations. Rarely does one value the suffering of others as one's own. (A pimple on one's own nose is felt more than the starvation of a whole people of a distant nation. An old Sicilian proverb reminds us, "Woe to those who die, the living are easily consoled.") Additionally suggesting the variable nature of pain and suffering are expectations of how different groups should bear them. In the Middle Ages, a soldier was expected to suffer differently than a civilian, a noble differently than a commoner, a peasant differently than a city dweller. The peasant, whose suffering was considered to be the least worthy, was expected to bear the toil and pain of working for man's food. His suffering was considered to be the closest to that of the animals. The middle class's hard work, self-discipline, and risk taking were, in the Middle Ages, not considered human activities worthy of the aristocratic heroic test of aims or the Christian saintliness of self-martyrdom.

Some ages are more lachrymose than others. During certain epochs, as the Dutch historian J. Huizinga demonstrated in his *Waning of the*

Middle Ages, whole groups are moved by feeling and sentiment. They cry easily and a lot and bemoan many things.[26] We smile when we read of the fifteenth-century preacher who cried a great deal in his sermons and threw at his audience the tears he collected in a small cup from his own eyes.[27] But when the representatives of contemporary victims shower us with their tears we do not smile so knowingly and condescendingly for we do not so easily separate ourselves from the claims of our own world's suffering. It is even fair to say (especially in reference to the upper class and literate heirs of romanticism) that sensitivity to suffering is not only learned but in some instances culturally contagious, fashionable, and even economically profitable and politically advantageous.

Culture profoundly shapes what we consider suffering to be. It indicates whose suffering counts, what kinds of suffering are valid, and what can and should be done in response to different types of suffering. For instance, in traditional cultures a woman is expected to suffer well in matters of sexuality, reproduction, and child rearing, yet she is exempted from having to suffer other types of pains, like those resulting from a blow, with equal dignity. The elderly, to choose another example, are almost universally conceded to have won their right to express grief in a manner no younger person is permitted to display his feelings.

However many similarities in language, argument, and interpretation there are between suffering and pain, there are also significant differences between them. By its first definition, pain is understood to belong to a part of a body. It inflicts itself upon a specific person at a given time for a definite reason. Pain, in other words, occurs in finite conditions and forms, and as a negative part of a whole. We turn to magic or medicine for particular remedies so that the ailing part be restored to the whole.

Contrariwise, suffering by first definition, deals with spirit rather than body. Suffering is greater and more comprehensive than pain. Suffering describes a general condition, person, group, or society. While not impossible, it would be unusual to speak of the many sufferings of a person's pain, whereas we commonly speak of suffering as if it is composed of many pains. Suffering does not invite specific and immediate remedies. Even if it is considered curable, it is understood to elude the particular acts of healing by doctor and magician. Its cure, in contrast to pain, requires diverse and protracted human treatment or great and special powers of the gods. Accordingly, as pain seeks its relief almost exclusively in magic and medicine, suffering directs us for help to philosophy and religion and, also, more recently to social work and psychoanalysis.[28]

Suffering, in opposition to pain, engulfs the whole person, group, or era. Suffering, unless trivalized of its meaning, can be understood to be a matter of wholes. Unlike pain, which is most commonly understood to be singular, specific, limited, and homogenous, suffering pertains to totalities of life.

Even though, as in the case of pain, we can make a range of distinctions between types of calculable suffering, such as labor that achieves a goal, sacrifice that permits a creation, and even martyrdom that secures a friend's life, most suffering involves what seems to be an irreducible and only problematically comprehensible and mythically explainable part of human existence.

Flaubert's phrase, *Le bon Dieu est dans le détail* (God is in the detail) can be translated for our purposes to mean that every act of suffering is a unique world in itself.[29] A separate and unique universe of meaning can exist in each person's suffering. Each experience of significant suffering is worthy of a story, and each story insists upon its own telling. While men and women feel anguish and die in the millions, suffering the same accidents, famines, diseases, plagues, and wars, each of their lives and deaths merits a singular story.

Equally resistant to our attempts to articulate an understanding of suffering is the degree to which certain forms of suffering appear absolutely senseless. They defy not only our calculations and sense of meaning, but negate all purpose and justice themselves. The slaughter of the innocent, the unnecessary agonies of the old, and unexpected deaths of the mature suggest the host of forms of suffering that defy our understanding and compel us to consider the possibility that there is no meaning whatsoever to our lives. As suggested in the Introduction, suffering opens up the possibility that the gods, if they exist at all, are fickle and perhaps evil. Purposeless suffering confronts us with an entirely random universe or a universe in which evil has a radical place. In the words of Polish poet, Alexander Wat, "There is no bottom to evil."[30]

Once we associate suffering with evil, we are led to try to explain what we cannot. We must consider the most perplexing assumptions: All who suffer deserve their suffering. We suffer to placate our collective wrong. God wills suffering to test us or save us or for his pleasure. God does not wish us to suffer, but cannot restrain the adversary's desire to cause us to suffer. Each of these assumptions leads us to realms in which our understanding and logic fail; we are left with only our metaphors, myths, and faith.

So suffering tends to engulf our lives, encompass our meaning, and drive us toward ultimates that we name but do not understand. Thus, we forever are in suffering; we do not stand beyond it.

As suggested by its Latin roots, suffering implies being weighed down under. (*Su[b]* in Latin means to be under and *ferre*, to bear.) Suffering is something we must bear; it can claim whole lives, reaching from birth to death. Only in fairy tales, where magic and luck are in full force, is suffering banished in the twinkling of an eye.

Suffering fills us with ambiguity. Suffering, even the suffering of animals, compels us to turn away. At the same time, it invites us to look at it and question it. Suffering enticingly reveals men and women in agony, caught up in tragedy, exposing what stuff we are made of. We also ask whether a given instance of suffering is real or feigned. We ask if the suffering is the bellyaching of the chronic complainer, the paid-for sadness of the professional mourner, the histrionics of the melodramatic egotist, the sympathy mongering of the hypochondriac, or even the more bizarre illnesses of the Munchausens who fake sickness to receive care.

Suffering interrogates us. It asks about the important subject of who is lucky and who is not. Suffering often is about the loss of health, beauty, wealth, power, skill, and cunning. To paraphrase Shakespeare, "Some men seek suffering; others are born to it; still others have it thrust upon them."[31] Suffering often announces our fate; it unveils the most important chapter in our lives.

As thinkers from Pascal to Freud testify, we have a great number of psychological mechanisms to avoid suffering, especially the suffering of others. Nevertheless, we can no more ignore severe suffering than we can live with an unburied body in our midst. Somehow we must try to explain suffering. It is too elemental and pervasive to be ignored.

Like the voice of a crying child, suffering issues a claim upon all who experience it: it is a summons for help or pity. And if the suffering is innocent, free of guile and calculation or the consequence of clearly chosen wrong, the claim upon us is all the stronger. Suffering that can awaken disdain, is indeed a claim upon the world; suffering gives one the status of being owed. It is a kind of moral entitlement; it is a demand (as the beggar's craft so well illustrates) for the attention, sympathy, and aid of others. Suffering calls out to the world, seeking compassion, forgiveness, and mercy. With our cries, wails, supplication, lamentations, and victims (who are envoys of our suffering and need) we make claims upon the gods.

Suffering asserts earnestness of intention. Suffering, the highest currency of pain, purchases forgiveness. (One thinks of Holy Roman Emperor King Henry IV. Ill clad, he stood in the snow at Canossa asking Pope Gregory VII to lift his ban of excommunication and restore him to his kingdom. Gregory VII, Christ's vicar, forgave Henry. Henry's sorrow was worth a kingdom.)

People use suffering to prove their sincerity. They renounce pleasures, undertake dangerous journeys and pilgrimages, undergo great ordeals to prove their worth, or receive forgiveness. In addition to the wager of judicial combat that equated justice and victory, a whole range of ordeals that tested truth and character through suffering by fire and water were developed in the Middle Ages.

Suffering also allows us to cross important borders of reality. In one of its many forms, suffering pays for the tariff of passage for seer and warrior alike. Of the hero, who is the great border crosser, Joseph Campbell wrote, "[He] ventures forth from the world of common day into a region of supernatural wonder; fabulous forces are there encountered and a decisive victory is won: the hero comes back from this mysterious adventure with the power to bestow boons on his fellow man."[32] "The deed accomplished," Campbell wrote elsewhere, "life no longer suffers hopelessly under the terrible mutilations of ubiquitous disaster."[33] All heroes, having met the test, can say like those heroes of Euripides' *The Cretans*, who challenged Olympus, "I have endured his thunder-cry; / Fulfilled his red and bleeding feasts."[34]

We make our claims upon each other not only in reference to the suffering we bear and cause, but also in terms of the moral patrimony of past suffering, which either as the children of innocent toiler, hero, or martyr victims, merits us benefits or as the children of thiefs, persecutors, assassins, or other violators of the innocent implicates us in the fruits of their wrongdoing and thereby indebts us. The tradition of moral suffering, which morally judges us as belonging to the owed or owing, is not only a matter of individual deeds but concerns acts of person against person, class against class, people against people, nation against nation. For instance, no theft, even that of the most precious and holy gift, is considered more heinous than the theft of an object, however humble, in which a whole family or group has invested their live's sufferings. Thus is not an attempt to support Marxian labor theory of value or yet the earlier Lockean middle class theory of property ownership as derivative from work but is, on the contrary, a critique of any and all theoretical traditions that would reduce and homogenize—and ultimately politicize and ideologize—suffering, and what I call "a suffering theory of value," to labor and a labor theory of value. As we will see later, suffering, which gives rights and claims, is a much greater, variegated and, if one wishes, spiritual act than work. Suffering is much more about sacrifice.

Each person has some claim, however tenuous or spurious, to innocent suffering (in the form of toil, self-abnegation and saving, heroism, martyrdom, or victimization of one form or another). In the name of innocent suffering, we tell stories about ourselves and others. At the core of these stories is the moral matter of victims and victimizers—who suffered and who caused suffering. These stories—explicitly or implicitly—are about justice, equity, fairness, compassion, mercy, forgiveness, resentment, grudge, revenge—in effect, the most powerful words of moral language.

While there is no doubt, as pointed out in the Introduction, that our public world, both national and international, is aswarm with moral stories of suffering, sacrifice, and martyrdom, it would be a mistake not to recognize the degree to which human affairs at every level have always turned upon the issue of suffering's entitlements. The peasant, for instance, claims land to be his, not just by the use he has of it or his title to it, but because of the work he and his family have invested in it. A family's claim to rights is often based upon a tradition of sacrifice. And, to chose a more diffuse example of the connection of suffering and right, both our criminal and civil laws render many of their judgments in reference to suffering invested and caused.

From a personalist point of view (as well, but not exclusively, articulated by twentieth-century French Catholic thinker Emmanuel Mounier), human life itself is understood to be composed of hierarchies of values, each of which in measure has and receives worth by virtue of us suffering and being willing to sacrifice for it.[35] We build up ourselves (our persons) and the communities that we most value out of our sacrifices. Revealing the obvious Judaic-Christian influence of his thought, Mounier composes our highest communities of action and faith of sacrifices. For Mounier, the highest and fullest act of the whole person is the sacrifice of life itself for the good we affirm.

Thus, we arrive at the paradox: We must think about suffering and live by sacrifice even though, as I will suggest again later in the discussion of Bentham, there can be no calculus of suffering. Suffering cannot be reduced to pain; we cannot establish a homogeneous language to discuss it and, while no doubt, we are able to understand some of it along a spectrum (marked frivolous and serious, commonplace and singular, bodily and spiritual), we cannot escape the fact that each act of significant suffering belongs to individual lives and stories. Furthermore, suffering compels us to the most perplexing questions of life, evil, creation, and the nature of God. Paradoxically, suffering forces us to seek to understand what, at least rationally, cannot be understood.

Suffering also exceeds our capability to give it definition because of its inseparable connection to our mortality. As Michel Montaigne wrote, "It is . . . our inability to stand the idea of death that makes us unable to stand pain, and we feel pain doubly painful because it threatens us with death."[36]

Death, adding to the pain of our suffering, puts mortality in all physical and mental suffering, but it threatens to undercut the values we attribute to our suffering. Death jeopardizes human labor, ordeals, sacrifices—all the suffering by which individuals give themselves worth and bind themselves to one another. A person can die on the eve of completing a lifetime's work. An heir can squander in days the patrimony laboriously gathered by generations. Death does not honor human senses of fairness and justice.

Death ruptures our ethical world. It creates a discrepancy between what is intended and what is achieved, between what is offered and what is accepted. Death makes injustice permanent. Sacrifices are betrayed; the legacy of heroes, perverted. Death throws up a boundary human exchange cannot cross.

Death forces a discourse between the living and the dead. Unpaid debts of love and hate, respect and disrespect, insist upon this discourse. Death does not separate the living and the dead from the chain of the giving and taking that joins them. The dead speak to us. They demand justice, complain of their incompleted lives, or call for us to avenge their suffering. And we reply to the dead. We take up their cause, judge them, assign them to heavens and hells, or even submit them to cycles of endless reincarnations or purgatories.

Death, which in many ways forms the essence of suffering, compels us to carry on discourse that reaches beyond our lives. Death awakens questions of eternal life and the gods that people, at least through ages, have felt compelled to ask and cannot answer.

Nevertheless, however rationally warranted, the skeptical position that we cannot value our sufferings cannot be lived on a day-to-day basis. We have no choice other than to judge the value of our own suffering and that of others. We are forced to value and trade in sufferings and sacrifices by virtue of the simple fact that we choose one act, one victim, or one moral story in preference to another. Every day we calculate what is not calculable—and so we will continue as long as life requires humans to weigh things in the cost of pain and suffering. We must continue to carry out sacrifices and reason about an existence whose boundaries are known only by faith, metaphor, and myth.

NOTES

1. Corinne Sherwood, *Human Sickness and Health: A Biocultural View* (Palo Alto, Calif: Mayfield, 1979), 4.

2. Ibid., 15.

3. The theme that contemporary conscience and sensibility are shaped by a plurality of asymmetrical and conflicting cultures is central to my *Guilt and Gratitude: A Study of the Origins of Contemporary Conscience* (Westport, Conn: Greenwood Press, 1982), as well as my *Ethics, Living or Dead?* (Tuscaloosa, Ala: Portals Press, 1982 and Marshall, Minn: Venti Amati, 1982), esp. 1–10, 111–18.

4. Thomas Szasz, *Pain and Pleasure: A Study of the Bodily Feelings* (New York: Basic Books, 1975), 103–4.

5. Ibid.

6. Jonathan Miller, *The Body in Question* (New York: Random House, 1978), 44.

7. For instance, the lack of a taxonomy of pain led the University of Washington Pain Clinic to articulate the SAD Index for pain. This index conceives of pain as a mixture of somatic factors, anxiety, and depression, which, in conjunction with social environment, cultural factors, and gains from compensation (from the injury) provide a pain profile, essential for the management of chronic pain; Richard Black and C. Richard Chapman, "SAD Index for Clinical Assessment of Pain," *Advances in Pain Research and Therapy* 1 (1976): 301–5.

8. Szasz, *Pain and Pleasure*, 249.

9. David Bakan, *Disease, Pain & Sacrifice: Toward a Psychology of Suffering* (Boston: Beacon Press, 1968), 57.

10. Sigmund Freud, *The Future of an Illusion* (New York: Liveright, 1953), 27.

11. For a range of articles on the diagnosis and treatment of pain, see Matishou Weisenberg, ed., *Pain: Clinical and Experimental Perspectives* (St. Louis: C. V. Mosby, 1975), 45–49.

12. Thomas P. Hackett, "The Surgeon and the Difficult Pain Problem," in *Pain*, 279.

13. Miller, *The Body*, 45.

14. For a list of therapies see Richard Serjeant, *The Spectrum of Pain* (London: R. Hart Davis, 1969), 119–49; also see Hackett, "The Surgeon and the Difficult Pain Problem," 279.

15. For a lengthy essay on interpretation of pain, see Ferdinand Sauerbruch and Hans Wenke, *Pain: Its Meaning and Significance* (London: George Allen and Unwin, 1963), 100–148.

16. John Swain, *The Pleasures of the Torture Chamber* (London: Dial, 1931), 10–11.

17. Ibid., 13.

18. Roberto Held, *Guida Bilingue all mostra di Strumenti di Tortura Chamber dal Medioevo all Epoca Industriale* (Florence: Qua d'Arno, 1983), 13.

19. For a short but useful survey of torture in the Western World, see Edward Peters, *Torture* (Oxford: Basil Blackwell, 1985).

20. Elaine Scarry *The Body in Pain: The Making and Unmaking of the World* (New York: Oxford University Press, 1985). Scarry develops the thesis of the torturer's search for total dominance with single-mindedness and she does it with the tortured language of a deconstructionism, which ironically has the effect of making the most obvious matters seem impenetrably profound.

21. Antoine Saint-Exupery, *The Little Prince* (New York: Harcourt, Brace & World, 1943), 70–71.

22. Mark Zborowski, *People in Pain* (San Fransisco: Jossey-Bass, 1969).

23. S. L. Notermans and M. M. Tophoff, "Sex Difference in Pain and Tolerance and Pain Apperception," *Pain*, ed. Weisenberg, 111–16.

24. Elaine Partnow, ed., *The Quotable Woman* (New York: Facts on File, 1982), 272.

25. Elie Wiesel, "Messenger to the Ten Thousand," *Commonweal* (October 24, 1986): 555.

26. In Dutch historian J. Huizinga's 1919 classic *Waning of the Middle Ages*

(New York: Doubleday, 1954). See especially chapter 2 "Pessimism and the Ideal of the Sublime Life," 31–56. For a recent study of how the religious values of the elite of an age shape their perception theory and public policy, see Boyd Hilton's, *The Age of Atonement: The Influence of Evangelicalism on Social and Economic Thought, 1795–1865* (Oxford: Clarendon Press, 1988).

27. Cited in Michael Baxandall, *Painting and Experience in Fifteenth Century Italy* (Oxford: Clarendon Press: 1972), 65.

28. For a single discussion of the similarities and differences between religion and magic, see E. O. James, *Comparative Religion* (London: Meuthen, 1961), 61–77.

29. Cited in Italo Calvino, *Six Memos for the Next Millenium* (Cambridge, Mass: Harvard University Press, 1988), 69.

30. Alesander Wat, "From Persian Parables," *Mediterranean Poems* (Ann Arbor: Ardis, 1977), 6.

31. Barrington Moore paraphrased Shakespeare in *Injustice: The Social Bases of Obedience and Revolt* (New York: M. E. Sharpe, 1978), 64.

32. Joseph Campbell, *The Hero with a Thousand Faces* (New York: World Publishing, 1956), 30. Campbell had added emphasis to this entire paragraph.

33. Ibid., 29.

34. Ibid., 27.

35. For a preliminary discussion of personalism and Mounier, see my *Mounier and Maritain: A French Catholic Understanding of the Modern World* (Tuscaloosa, Ala: University of Alabama Press, 1975), and Emmanuel Mounier, *Personalism* (Notre Dame, Ind: University of Notre Dame, 1970).

36. Michel Montaigne, *The Complete Essays of Montaigne*, 3 vols. (New York: Anchor Books, 1960), vol. 1, 49.

2

Sacrifice, All But the Philosophers' Way

"When we go to the center of the hoop we shall all cry, for we should know that anything born into this world which you see about you must suffer and bear difficulties. We are now going to suffer at the center of the sacred hoop, and by doing this may we take upon ourselves much of the suffering of our people." Each of the men then declared which of the sacrifices he would undergo, and Kablaya made his vow first: "I will attach my body to the thongs of the Great Spirit which comes down to earth—this shall be my offering."

Black Elk, *The Sacred Pipe*

Wisdom is a crime against nature. . . . Socrates' great Cyclop's eye—that eye which never glowed with the artist's divine frenzy—turned upon tragedy.

Frederick Nietzsche, *The Birth of Tragedy*

As medicine treats pain, so religion cares for suffering. It does this by currying favor with the gods, propitiating wrongs, and performing the correct rituals in order to maintain the proper order of things. Religion also justifies good fortune, for if it is not justified, suffering is due. Max Weber wrote

The fortunate is seldom satisfied with the fact of being fortunate. Beyond this he needs to know that he has a *right* to good fortune. He wants to be convinced that he "deserves" it, and above all, that he deserves it in comparison with others. He wishes to be allowed the belief that the less fortunate also merely experience his due. Good fortune thus wants to be "legitimate" fortune.[1]

Since religion cannot successfully ward off all suffering, religion does what is second best: it consoles people. Hinduism and Zen Buddhism, for instance, teach an enlightenment that frees their followers from the suffering of this earth, whereas Judaism and Christianity find in faithful suffering itself the means to redeem the individual and ransom humanity.

Religion's role to minister to suffering and death is not, especially in traditional culture, easily separable from that of culture at large. Traditional cultures, embracing a people's whole way of life, provided meanings for the various faces of suffering. They explained the uneven distribution of suffering, prescribed who should suffer, what they should suffer, when, how, and why they should suffer. They furnished rituals for grief, ways of mourning, the songs of lamentation. They also provided ways to dispose of the corpse, evade the wrath of the dead, and secure the remarriage of the widow.

Sacrifice was religion's primary means to concentrate and transvalue suffering in a world in which pain abounds and good fortune and happiness are scarce. In either a formal sense (public and ritualized) or informal sense (personal and spontaneous), sacrifice is based upon the premise that nothing is for free: it is necessary to give up one thing for the sake of another. Social life too demanded sacrifice. Some slaved so others could be free. One child was sacrificed for the sake of others. Only in recent times, and then only in select urban quarters of the developed world, have significant numbers of people come to doubt this guiding principle of the old order that life must be traded for life.

Sacrifice, the need to offer life for life, still commands much interior discourse. Even the modern individual defines self and world in terms of sacrifices. Dorothy Rowe writes of contemporary people, "It is hard to give up our attachments, especially the attachments we have to our own suffering."[2] Modern personal social relations are conducted in reference to exchanged suffering: "I suffer this for you, on the condition that you suffer that for me." Friendships and marriages, although rarely with perfect equality, proceed on the assumption of shared burdens. Without some sort of reciprocity of mutual suffering and sacrifice, they dissolve. Mutual sacrifice is a necessity and an important test of sincerity and fidelity as well.

It should be pointed out however, lest cynicism appear to control this work, the prominent places that self-interest and reciprocity occupy in human exchange do not abrogate the fact that people do sacrifice themselves without expectation of return. Seeking to deny this, leads to postulating a world of extrarational self-interests and subconscious motivations in order to try to explain away countless manifest instances of apparent altruistic and self-sacrificing acts.

Individuals carry on the most complex discourses about sacrifices. Sacrifice and its claims to respect, mutuality, reciprocity, gratitude, and love form the moral housing of human relations. The moral claim of "I have suffered for you," charges human relations with great demands, which left unmet, as in measure they always are, charges society with feelings of disappointment, resentment, grudge, and revenge.

There is little wonder, especially in times when misery is so bountiful and good fortune so scarce, why people believed they had to appease the gods with the most serious gifts: sacrifices of life itself and suffering and blood, which most represent life. Sacrifice, as concentrated and dedicated suffering, was the means to make exchanges beyond those of everyday life. For example, the mortification of the flesh, a form of self-sacrifice, for the sake of vision played an important role in the practices of such disparate groups as Christian monks, Jewish Essenes, Buddhist hermits, and Islamic whirling dervishes.[3] Regarding the ecstatic, I. M. Lewis remarked, those "whose lives flow smoothly without much difficulty or distress are rarely summoned by the spirit," while those who have a claim to vision "must indulge in extremes of violently self-imposed suffering to validate their calling as shaman."[4]

Ritualized self-sacrifice, which made oneself temporarily a victim (an offering to the gods) imposed a kind of first death upon the initiate so that the gods would allow him to be reborn. Mircea Eliade commented that the ascetic practices joined to North American initiatory rites "pursue the annihilation of the initiate's secular personality."[5] E. Hoebel described the self-inflicted and voluntary torture of young Cheyenne warriors in the sun dance (an earth renewal rite) in order to receive pity, good fortune, and, not to be forgotten, social prestige.

The self sacrifice in the dance lodge is known as "hanging from the center pole." One who has vowed to do this asks a medicine man who himself made the same sacrifice to help him. The medicine man fastens the end of two ropes to the crotch of the center pole, adjusting them so that they will reach just to the breast height of a standing man. He next punches or cuts two holes in the skin just above each nipple. A small skewer is pushed through each pair of holes so that a narrow strip of skin laps over it and holds it against the breast. The free ends of the rope are fastened about the skewers. The sacrificer may then dance, fastened to the pole, all through the night, and if by morning he has not succeeded in tearing the skin loose so as to free himself, his medicine man cuts the skin off, and his ordeal is ended. Or, if the sacrificer wishes to achieve his end in one sudden burst, he may suddenly strain back on the ropes in an effort to tear the skewers free at once.[6]

Although a self-imposed test of this sort must be considered extreme even in the past, it testified, as many other rites do, like self-scarification, to the belief that sacrificial suffering was to be the unique medium by which a man can pass from the ordinary to the extraordinary. In *Tristes Tropiques,* Claude Levi-Strauss remarked how North American Indian youths had themselves cast off alone and without food on a raft for long periods, exposed themselves in the wilderness to the greatest dangers, or amputated one or more of their fingertips, in order "to break through to the world beyond."[7]

Sacrifice was among our first and most important currencies of transaction with the gods and higher powers. (Myths of many peoples reveal how they believed that even the gods themselves had to offer sacrifices to achieve their own ends.) In several cultures, children were buried in the walls of houses and cities to secure the walls. Agamemnon sacrificed his daughter, Iphigenia, to obtain favorable winds to cross the sea to the battle of Troy. Abraham's faith in God was proven by his willingness to sacrifice his only son, Isaac. Not all sacrifices were oblivious to practicality and self-interest and required extreme measures or death. Sometimes sacrifices were only partial and symbolic, such as taking vows or substituting a finger, hair, or blood for the person himself. Strangers, scapegoats, or effigies were often substituted for real victims. Other gifts could speak for the community as a whole, such as honoring the dead by pouring blood on their graves, leaving them food, or holding games in their honor.[8]

Sacrifice, in its myriad forms, constitutes human discourse with the gods and ancestors, as well as forces of nature. It served a range of functions such as homage, praise, thanksgiving, abnegation, supplication, propitiation, sacralization of places, maintenance of the cosmic order, sending of messengers to the world beyond, and even furnishing of future guides and servants for the dead. Sacrifice arose both out of conscious and unconscious senses of violation.[9] Expiatory sacrifices were commonly accompanied by confession, as remains the case with the Catholic mass.

In their classic study, *Sacrifice: Its Nature and Function,* H. Hubert and Marcel Mauss specifically defined sacrifice "as a means of communication between the sacred and profane worlds through the mediation of a victim."[10] Recognizing their explicitly or implicitly inferior place in the order of things, people made offerings for things that were beyond their power to secure. They sacrificed first offerings (first crops and firstborn animals or children) for continued favors and fertility. They offered up animal and human sacrifices for specific favors, such as ending violence and expiation for serious wrongs. Assuming that the gods want significant gifts in return for what they gave, or were expected to give, earlier peoples frequently believed that only a living human would be a satisfactory victim.[11] Since the victim was the measure of the community's sincerity, nothing but the best should be sent as a messenger.[12]

Accordingly, the human victim, in many instances, was treated well, even honored, until sacrificed. Holy victims were at one point the gold standard of humanity's transactions with the gods.

BLOOD, THE RIVER OF LIFE

Blood, whose redness signifies life's passion, intensity, and suffering, was "the perfect symbol of sacrifice. All liquid substances (milk, honey, and wine, that is to say) which were offered up in antiquity to the dead, to spirits and to gods, were, it is argued, images of, or substitutes for blood, the most precious offering of all."[13] Sacrificial blood obtained from the sheep, the hog, and the bull in classical times and from human sacrifice in early Europe, parts of Asia, America, and Africa above all else, had the function of appeasing the gods.

Blood was the divine water of life. Blood alone expiated wrongs and mollified the gods' wrath. Folktales suggested that even the sun and moon were animated by human blood sacrifice. Blood was understood to have the power to contaminate and purify, clean and remain indelible, make fertile and sterile, reveal guilt and innocence, as well as to drive people to mad acts, demonstrate fidelity, form people into a community, and assure sacred vows. The headhunters of the Central Celebes in the East Indies drank and ate human blood to become brave, as did Norwegian, German, and Hottentot warriors, to mention a few others.[14] The Vikings ran their long ships over the bodies of their prisoners so that their bloody keels would pay tribute to the gods of the seas. (An analogue to this custom is preserved symbolically in the ship-christening ceremony of today.[15])

In many folktales blood is the magical water of life. It heals wounds and restores the dead to life. In the folktales "Two Brothers" and "Faithful John," a bath in blood reanimated men turned to stone. One twelfth-century legend told how the blood of Thomas Becket, placed on the eyes of a blind woman, restored her sight.[16] Other beliefs in the efficacy of blood were abundant in the Middle Ages. Blood was used to cure mange and epilepsy. It was poured into graves in order to free the dead.

To be literally or figuratively bathed in blood, put one at the center of life and sacrifice; it set one aside, made him special, holy; it gave one a special power. "When you bleed, you bless," wrote a contemporary poet.[17]

Blood also meant community. Blood defined the most compelling obligation. In *The Nuer*, E. Evans-Pritchard pointed out that within a tribe blood wealth was paid in compensation for homicide, whereas with outsiders the cost of spilt blood had not been regularized.[18] Blood sealed bonds; by signing in blood, sharing it through drinking, joining it in

mutual wounds, and other blood rituals people consummated agree-
ments, made blood covenants, formed blood brotherhoods, and even
made kinships between individuals who were not related.[19]

One's own blood had to be avenged. According to William Graham
Sumner, "Blood revenge was almost universal among American aborig-
ines," and there are few, if any, primitive and traditional peoples who
still are not moved by the law of revenge.[20] In some cultures, sons cannot inherit until they have avenged their fathers; in others, blood feuds
go on across generations. According to Sumner, "the greatest duty known
to the Arabs was blood revenge. (Blood was, in their view, more holy
than anything else.)"[21] Even the modern state and modern criminal law
(whose very origin is aimed at ending blood revenge) have not succeeded in suppressing the belief that blood defines primary communities and first responsibilities.

The shedding of blood, either spontaneously or in a ritual, still marks
a significant moment and opening in the human order. The shedding
of blood indicates serious times: times of birth, death, violence, murder, and martyrdom. When blood spills, we move out of ordinary time.
Bloody sacrifice is our means to special territories. The victim, the essence of bloody sacrifice, is our messenger to the dead and the gods.

KINGS AND PRIESTS ALL

When humankind moved from small tribes to the more centralized
life of civilizations, priests and kings became the heads of sacrifice. Priests,
who existed in all the great religions of ancient civilization, but whose
particular functions could vary from civilization to civilization, ad-
dressed sacrifices to oracles in hopes of receiving answers, affecting ex-
piations, and, in the guise of magician priests, curing the suffering of
their followers. Priests were responsible to try either to obtain the good
or to forestall or mitigate the bad.

Kings often shared with and even, as was the case in Egypt, contested
the priest's function of making sacrifices. In Rome, the king was head
of the state religion; he was *rex sacrorum*. At Athens, he was high priest,
archon basileus. Unlike the priest, the king is at the center of society and
is the symbol of totality.[22] The king, who mediated for all society, connected the earthly and heavenly orders. His election and powers determined the group's fate.

The king, above all others, was the arbitrator over human life. He
determined who prospered and who suffered in society. The king's
peace stood above the law of blood revenge.

Divinity encircled the king. For many cultures, he was man-god. Like
god on earth, he gave and took all, showing either mercy and clemency
or wrath and vengeance. The weather, the crops, and the whole social

order depended on him. The group looked for its well-being in his powers.

In many cultures, like those of early Greece, rephrasing a central insight of James Frazer's *The Golden Bough,* the king was periodically slain.[23] He was put to death either at the end of a fixed period or whenever his health or strength began to fail or when some public calamity such as drought, death, or defeat in war occurred indicating that the power of his magic and sacrifices was at an end. Or to choose Frazer's favorite case, the king-priest lost the kingship, which he himself killed to gain, when he was slain by his successor.

The king's role as symbol of the group's luck, as well as mediator between the human and the extrahuman spheres, placed him in the category of superior humans. Accordingly, his real and symbolic powers were never carefully distinguished. Serving as the intermediary between humanity and the gods, the Germanic kingship, for instance, was based on "the indissolubility of its religious and political functions. . . . [The king himself was] "the charismatic embodiment of the 'luck' of the folk. . . . [He was] leader of the folk and the guarantor of their *heil* who acts so that the gods may bless them."[24]

In early societies, the king was god, first father, founder of the law, establisher of the order, and symbol of all things. "In some societies (especially in sub-Sahara Africa) the king may be ritually killed if he loses his vigor. . . . Some ancient mythologies present a mythical king as a sacrificial victim. In some Indo-European traditions a first king, who is often a 'first man,' is the victim of the first, cosmogonic sacrifice and the world is created from his dismembered body."[25]

In early Greece, the king himself was sacrificed for his people; he was king and victim. In certain Semitic traditions of the first millennium B.C., during a crisis the king offered his own son, the future king, as a victim to the gods for their help. Standing for the community at large, the king, or the mock king, is sacrificed for the whole.

In some sense, if only by empathy, each of us is both king and victim insofar as all humans must measure the worth of life by their sacrifices. We, like the king, must make sacrifices, deciding what we will give the dead and the gods and what we will ask from them in return. Knowing that suffering—at least in some of its many forms—is necessary and that good luck is not permanent, we seek to sacrifice wisely and efficaciously. Often for us all that remains of former rituals and ceremonies of sacrifice are worn superstitions and lingering reflexes.

Sacrifice is the language we speak to the gods. (In his *Essays,* Montaigne described how a king who was dissatisfied with God took revenge and ordered that for ten years no one should pray to God or speak of him or, as far as the king's authority could prevent it, believe in him.[26]) Like blind Oedipus and broken Lear, kings we all are, and suffer we will. While knowing we cannot establish a final value to our suffering, we must hope that we can give it a meaning. We can only hope our sacrifices are heard. We can only repeat Heracles' remark to Molorchorus before undertaking his first labor of having to slay the Nemean Lion: " 'Wait thirty days,' he said. 'If I return safely, sacrifice to Saviour Zeus; if I do not, sacrifice to me as a hero!' " [27]

There were very few people in the primitive or ancient world who dared or even imagined that man could live by anything other than sacrifice. The Greek philosophers constituted such an exception. They responded to their suffering and fortune not with prayer and sacrifice, but understanding and reason. In this sense, they were the first of the moderns.

REASON AND THE PHILOSOPHER'S WAY

As sacrifice was archaic man's way to order his world, philosophy emerged as a unique attempt to transcend suffering and secure self in an environment established by human reason. Since philosophy took full form in fifth century B.C. Greece, it was alien to the worlds of suffering and sacrifice.[28] Classical philosophers could be considered to be irreverent and impious by definition, since they carried on their activities independent from the array of gods, spirits, shrines, rituals, customs, and observances that made up the religious order of antiquity.[29] The philosophers were not the proponents of family worship, the first religion of antiquity, nor were they the servants of the countless local deities and shrines that marked the classical landscapes.

Since the earliest Ionian philosophers of the sixth century, the philosophers' primary interest was explaining the natural order of things. They gave neither suffering nor its victims a unique meaning, exempt from the laws of nature. They carried out their work with words, numbers, explanations, arguments, and logic, not with rituals and sacrifices.

Voicing the rational humanism of the emerging urban order, philosophers in the fifth century B.C. affirmed the desirability of a rational order. They left questions of fortune and matters of suffering to others: to priests, whose sacrifices and victims might relieve human misery, and to the tragedians, whose art explored the tantalizing questions of suffering as a consequence of the intersection of human life and the cosmic order.

The philosopher was, in some altogether unpredictable sense, a new type of warrior. As Homer's heroes lived by their honor—they were what they were willing to suffer—the philosophers lived by their words and wits. Homer's warriors lost face, which alone mattered to them, when they, as Alasdair MacIntyre points out, did not boldly meet their fate, which inevitably meant even for the strongest defeat and death.[30]

Inflicting and enduring suffering was their calling; defeat alone resulted from failing to play the role to which their honor called them. At Troy, Homer had the Greeks play out their first moral code. Contrary to Homer's warriors, the philosophers proposed another moral code, which was also combative. They would struggle to live by mind. Their battle was to understand the laws that controlled all things. Their science, which they believed higher than the priest's ritual and magic, would deal with what was certain. They would teach the new order of all things.

As Werner Jaeger explained in his *Paideia*, it is impossible to pinpoint the origin of philosophy: "It is hardly possible to separate 'mythical thinking' in the epic from the rational ideas with which it is interpenetrated."[31] He further explained, "There is no discontinuity between Ionian natural philosophy and the Homeric epics. . . . There was already . . . much rational thought in what we call the 'mythical age,' and there was still a large mythical element in what we call 'rational thought.' "[32] M. I. Finley found the presence of rational thought in the earliest expression of Greek literature; he depicted Greek rationalism as a demythologizing spirit. "Mystery rites (literally 'orgies,' a word which does not appear in the poem) and blood rites and human sacrifice and everything else that dehumanized the gods were ruthlessly discarded. Thus, the important story of the sacrifice of Agamemnon's daughter, Iphigenia, was omitted, and the many gross atrocities in the prehistory of the gods were toned down radically."[33] Like men, Homer's gods, neither the creators nor the caretakers nor the moral guides of the world, acted in the world. With Homer, Finley concluded, "Having made the gods into men, man learned to know himself."[34]

From the beginning of their activity, the first Greek philosophers, the Ionians, showing the same courage the poets did in depicting human emotions and actions, applied logic to the universe.[35] Such thinkers as Thales, Anaximenes, Anaximander, Heraclitus, and Parmenides boldly pushed philosophy in pursuit of knowledge of the origins, composite elements, abiding forms, and structural changes of the universe. These philosophers sought knowledge of the laws that governed all things.

For the philosophers, fate *(moira)* was not blind and senseless. Instead, it was the moral decree that ruled all existing things, natural and man-made alike. What was destined and what was right were not easily distinguished by the Greeks, according to F. M. Cornford.[36] Fate set an inescapable moral requirement upon everything, determining in all instances what was due: *what one thing owed another.* Contradicting so much of the essence of religion, philosophers denied the power of sacrifice and victims to create specific happenings and a unique order. Heraclitus, an early philosopher, "used legal and moral concepts to express the inviolability of the physical order."[37] Voicing how much Greek philosophy in its formative stage unified natural and moral concerns in its speculations, the early philosopher Anaximander saw strife and suffering themselves as necessary compensation in a changing world. Anaximander saw "the process of coming into being and passing out of being in terms of *dike* and *tisis,* 'justice and reparation' (a sort of *lex talonis*), and by proclaiming that if the sun were to overstep his measure, the Erinyes, the handmaids of justice *(Dike)* will find him out."[38] Elsewhere Anaximander wrote, "It is necessary that things should pass away into that from which they are born. For things must pay one another the penalty and compensation for their injustice according to the ordinance of time."[39]

The rationality of the philosophers' universe both mirrored and was a consequence of the newly emergent urban civilization. Philosophy voiced a new environment, in which man, to an unprecedented degree, became self-determining. As Greeks in cities had come to control their own environments, so the philosophers (who thrived on the increased leisure and cosmopolitan circumstances) correspondingly turned their attention to discovering the order of the universe. The philosophical, political, scientific, literary, and moral proceeded hand in hand as the new order of the Greek polis took form. Remarking on the interplay of the religious and the political, Jaeger suggestively wrote: "The idea of the cosmos is even now one of the most essential categories of man's understanding of the universe. . . . It conveniently symbolizes the whole influence of early natural philosophy upon the culture of the Greeks. Solon's ethico-legal conception of responsibility and retribution was derived from the epic theodicy."[40] Philosophy's rationalism voiced a world in which men had become self-legislating beings. Politics and laws had eclipsed sacrifices and ritual; philosophy was born out of the polis.

Philosophy, however, was not content to be the handmaiden of the polis. Philosophy supported an individualism that ultimately—as in the case of Socrates in specific and the sophists in general—could prove to be antithetical to the religion of the polis. The philosopher elevated his reflective consciousness beyond the temples and altars of the polis; philosophy would equal in mind the efficacy of victims on pyres and armies on fields. The philosophers, according to Eric Voegelin, placed "the order of the human psyche beyond the order of the polis and articulated their discovery in the symbolic form they called philosophy."[41] The Greek philosophers' deepest discovery was "an internal cosmos," making each philosopher, in some final sense, a king. Assessing this revolution, Jaeger, subscribing to Hegel's view of the Greeks, wrote:

The soul of the Orient weighed down by religious yearning, sinks into the abyss of emotion, and finds no firm foothold in it; but the Greek spirit, trained to think of the external cosmos as governed by fixed laws, at last searches for the inner laws that govern the soul, and at last discovers an objective view of the internal cosmos. It was chiefly that discovery which, as the crisis of Greek history, made it possible to follow Plato's ideal and develop human character in a new way—on the basis of the philosophical knowledge. . . . The lofty speculations of the early Ionians were not intended to educate Greece; yet they were, in the midst of the chaotic growth of a new society, and the collapse of the old mythical conception of the universe, a fresh attempt to solve the deepest problem of Being itself.[42]

The philosophers' identification of self-consciousness, reason, and the good life reached its first full form with Socrates, who found human happiness not in success or honor, but in what "he called the perfection of the soul."[43] Man's first duty, as now idealized by the philosophers, should be the ordering of himself. Equating the good life to the life guided by reason, the philosophers judged the realm of feelings and passions to be transitory and therefore inferior to requirements of the good life.

To use the dichotomy that Nietzsche used to characterize Greek life, the philosophers sided with Apollo, the god of reason, against Dionysus, the god of life. They chose, that is, the principle of the heavens and the emerging order of the newly formed city-states against the forces of earth, the body, fertility, passion, and the countryside. The philosophers allied themselves with control and order against frenzy, passion, suffering, pride, honor, and vengeance—all that was irrational and that drove people destructively beyond their place in the world, and their nemesis, a just and inevitable retribution by nature and the gods. As typified by the works of Plato and Aristotle, the philosophers sought to create within and around man orders that would allow man to best fulfill his nature as a social and rational creature. Suspicious of the poets as mythmakers, the philosophers strove to insulate man from the powerful demands of honor and vengeance, sacrifice and victim.

The philosophers contended, in direct opposition to the warriors' and priests' codes, that no coherent ethics could be based on the worth of human suffering or the power of human sacrifices. They believed suffering and sacrifice belonged ultimately to the irrational territories of passion, violence, and mystery. The philosophers knew the tragic fates of men and women; they knew that pain and suffering would always remain forever particular, asymmetrical, and unfathomable by human reason. They chose to leave the matters of pain, suffering, and fate to the priests, poets, and prophets.

As the Italian philosopher of history Giambattista Vico so correctly judged in his 1725 *New Science,* the philosophers marked a new age: the age of humanity, philosophy, and prose; the age of poetry—that of myths, gods, and Homeric heroes—was over. The order of reason, at least for a small minority in cities, replaced the efficacy of sacrifice.

Classic philosophical systems, from Plato and Aristotle to the Stoics and Epicureans, consistently praised strong character formed by virtues like courage, patience, and perseverance, all of which presupposed the experience of suffering and the need to withstand. None conceded any intrinsic good to suffering itself. Believing suffering to be a source and consequence of disorder, the philosophers thought that humanity's good was found in fulfilling its highest place in nature. Inspired (as we have seen) by the aspirations of an emerging scientific cosmology, the philosophers conceived man, like all things, had a nature and that it was the good of his reason and will to attain the fulfillment of his nature. The philosophers believed that no one could be happy who lived in violation of his highest potential as a rational creature. Certainly the person victimized by circumstances and fate was neither idealized as holy nor as given any special wisdom.

Asserting that pleasure and pain were mixed and, thus, confused, Plato argued that the good required a criterion beyond pleasure and pain themselves. Anticipating the thrust of Christian mysticism, Plato directed man to seek an end that transcended earthly experience and was predicated on the final unity of the true, the beautiful, and the good. Aristotle believed that the virtues of a good man, especially his reasoning, led him to attain his full nature, whereas the vices of the incontinent man moved him in an opposite direction toward a disordered character. Vices, according to Aristotle in his *Nicomachean Ethics*, made a man's life like a ship without a captain. In their most pernicious form, they denied man the use of his reason and will and the virtues of the soul.

While the intellectualism of Plato and Aristotle was indisputable, neither concluded that reason and virtue were sufficient to make a person happy. Both assumed that a good polis was important for the formation of a good person. Carrying this belief to the extreme, Plato proposed a thoroughgoing tyranny as the ideal city in his *Republic*, in which everyone was assigned a fixed place in class and social function, poets were banished, and a knowing but reluctant philosopher was made king.

Aristotle also did not conceive of happiness as depending on the individual alone. Aristotle understood that happiness, in large measure, was a matter of good fortune. He wrote of the happy person,

[He] needs the external goods as well; for it is impossible, or not easy, to do noble acts without proper equipment. In many actions we use friends or riches and political power as instruments; and there are some things the lack of which takes the luster from happiness . . . ; for the man who is very ugly in appearance or ill born or solitary and childless is not very likely to be happy, and perhaps a man would be still less likely if he had thoroughly bad children or friends or had lost good children or friends by death.[44]

Aristotle conceived of ethics and politics as joined: a good person, if not necessarily a happy person, would more than likely arise out of a good city, for there would be good examples to be imitated and proper laws to be followed.

Contradicting Plato and Aristotle, Epicurus (342–270 B.C.)—an Athenian philosopher—altogether abandoned the political ideal. In the spirit of the sophist, Epicurus put his philosophy exclusively at the service of the rational and autonomous individual: an individual who was no longer intent on helping to define the world (the polis), but who must discipline himself to survive it. As boldly as any philosopher, Epicurus in a single stroke sought to redefine philosophy by reducing happiness and suffering to being no more or less than matters of pleasure and pain.

For Epicurus, pleasure was the only intrinsic good; pain the only intrinsic evil. Articulating what Jeremy Bentham would make the first premise of modern utilitarianism (as we will later see), Epicurus argued that happiness, which for him was the good, was solely a matter of maximizing pleasure and minimizing pain. Giving philosophy a decided therapeutic role, Epicurus contended that philosophy that doesn't help humanity is useless. "Vain is the word of a philosopher which does not heal any suffering of man. For just as there is no profit in medicine if it does not expel the diseases of the body, so there is no profit in philosophy either, if it does not expel the suffering of the mind."[45] So defined, philosophy became the enemy of suffering.

Articulating the therapeutic intention of his philosophy—and voicing one of the dominant mental attitudes of our era—Epicurus made the aim of the blessed life a sound body and serene mind. Epicurus counseled simplicity in all things. "It is better for you to be free of fear lying upon a pallet, than to have a gold couch and rich table and be full of trouble."[46] Since all pleasures are not the same and it could be argued that there must be a higher criterion for preferring one pleasure to another, Epicurus affirmed that one should choose the passive, sustainable, and enduring pleasures, like friendship and the pleasures of the mind, rather than the short, active, and intense pleasures most frequently associated with the body.

Epicurus, whose philosophy was not without influence on Bentham and other philosophers of the eighteenth century, tried to destroy what he understood to be the two great sources of human suffering: the fear of divine retribution and the fear of death. He did not go as far as the Buddhists, who, in order to free us from suffering, attack the self at the root of desire and craving. Epicurus argued that the idea that fortune befalls the good and misfortune the bad has no basis in our experience. It is simply a false supposition, as is the notion—a notion so fundamental to Judaism and Christianity—that god would be moved by emotion or interest to concern himself with causing good or ill to any lesser creature. Equally bold, Epicurus claimed that death should not interest us, for, while all that is good and evil involves sensation, death by its nature is the deprivation of sensation. Death, indeed, is the absence of consciousness. "It takes away all craving for immortality."[47]

According to Epicurus, ideas about supernatural beings and an afterlife only increase human suffering by magnifying fears and confusing reason. Destiny, fate, tragedy, death, and divine punishment, as well as all human efforts to mitigate these powerful forces, which are so inextricably tied up with suffering, should have no place in human understanding or practice. Believing that the gods are deaf, Epicurus taught that humans should concern themselves with nothing beyond their power. He counseled people to abandon their sacrifices, to forsake the high callings of truth and the stormy realities of politics, and to find abode in the philosopher's garden where friendship and reflection, the highest and most enduring of human pleasures, thrive.

The impulse to use reason to sustain humanity against suffering was carried to the extreme by the Stoics, as typified by the first century A.D. Stoic Roman philosopher Epictetus (336–264 B.C.). Starting with the familiar classical assumptions that everything in nature obeys laws and that man was "an individual rational being" ("a fragment torn from God," to use his poetic language), he sought to teach control and self-discipline: "Remove aversion then from all things that are not within our power and transfer it to things undesirable, which are within our power."[48] "Chastise your passions that they may not chastise you. . . . It belongs to a wise man to resist pleasure; and to a fool to be enslaved by it."[49] Epictetus taught that we can maintain order by learning to diminish the passions that give birth to desires and the aversions that give rise to the perturbations, sorrow, lamentations, envy, tumults, misfortunes, and calamities that render us incapable of following our reason and carrying out our social duties.

Epictetus argued that what is essential is an attitude that allows one to confront pain and suffering with dignity. "It is our attitudes toward events, not events themselves, which we can control. Nothing is by its own nature calamitous—even death is terrible only if we fear it."[50] Confronting what must be taken to be one of the ultimate sources of human suffering, he wrote: "Death is not terrible. But the terror consists in our notion of death, that is terrible."[51]

Assuming that we live in a world in which calamities are as real as our prayers and sacrifices are futile, Epictetus counseled: "Take then away aversion from all things which are not in our power."[52] Ignore the body; forget the opinion of others; and finally "neither wish for anything, nor . . . avoid anything which depends on others."[53]

Second-century Roman emperor and philosopher, Marcus Aurelius, who embraced the main tenets of Stoicism, contended that pain and pleasure themselves should have no hold on our spirit. According to Marcus Aurelius, life and death, honor and dishonor, and pain and pleasure come equally to all; they make us neither better nor worse; consequently, they are neither good nor evil.[54] Marcus Aurelius would have us express the highest and most godlike spirit within ourselves: He wrote, "[Be] uncontaminated by pleasure, unharmed by any pain, untouched by any insult, feeling no wrong, a fighter in the noblest fight, one who cannot be overpowered by any passion, dyed deep with justice, accepting with all his soul everything which happens and is assigned to him as his portion."[55]

Stoicism, as articulated by Aurelius and Epictetus, would make individuals godlike in their autonomy. They would be passionless creatures. They would be indifferent to their own suffering and that of others. They would not concern themselves with the question of why they were lucky or unlucky. They would not carry out special pleadings with the gods through sacrifices. They would serve neither egotism, nor altruism; their sole end—an end so resembling that of Kant's categorical imperative—would be to serve the universal moral order of the cosmos.

Stoicism and Epicureanism express a type of resignation to which only a rare person can consent and no living culture can permanently adopt. They expressed philosophy's original and continuing distance from the living interests of humanity at large. Philosophy affords no discourse between man and the gods about the all-important matters of fortune and misfortune, happiness and suffering. The philosophers' gods are remote, distant, indifferent—ultimately like the ideals of those who describe them. They are idle entities who, at most, moderately indulge themselves as they too obey the necessary laws of things. Philosophy essentially counsels indifference to what is beyond, calling us to a happiness that is found in what Socrates called "perfection of the soul."[56]

Reasoned discourse, the philosopher's first and last promise, does not satisfy the majority. It offers no hope of controlling fortune. Most people cannot even conceive of the desirability of bearing one's suffering alone and dispassionately. Contrary to the philosophers, the majority will not live by mind alone. They insist on what has been bred in bone: taking one's fortune and misfortune seriously. They insist that their prayers, lamentations, supplications, and sacrifices be heard by the gods. They want their pains and sufferings to have a meaning greater than

simply benign resignation to an all-powerful and unalterable order of
things. Right from its beginnings, philosophy failed the tests of popular
interest; it proved no substitute for sacrifice for most people.

The passion of the majority of Greeks themselves was not for philosophy but for theater. Tragedy was "a spectacle of suffering that explained but necessarily justified."[57] Joining themselves as audience to
the point of view of the chorus, they could suffer with pity and fear
the fortunes of men and women, who in one way or another fell afoul
of the gods. Tragedy was the way for them to ask the question that
preoccupied them in the fifth and sixth centuries, "Why does God send
suffering into the life of man?"[58] With tragedy, according to Jaeger,
"The force of this question was now intensified in the presentation of
human suffering to the eyes and ears of the spectators at the tragic
festivals by the emotional ardors which the chorus expressed through
dance and song, and which through the entrance of several speakers
developed into the presentation of a complete episode of human fate."[59]

Tragedy was the way the Greeks chose to ask passionately about man's
relation to suffering. They could ask whether insight came from it,
discuss, as Sophocles did so well, the inscrutability of the gods, voice
the irony that they knew cut across so much of human fate, and express their darkest pessimisms that it was "better man was never born."[60]
They could counsel moderation of desire, avoidance of risk, excess in
nothing. They could teach manly endurance of hardship, or even teach
that "wisdom may come through suffering."[61] Through tragedy they
examined the jealousy of the gods, the consequences of hubris, the flaws
of character, the inevitability of retribution (nemesis), and the circle of
fortune that controls every family across the generations.

On the stage of the amphitheater, which often (as was the case in
Segesta, Sicily) stood above the temple itself, the Greeks asked themselves about their suffering—a suffering that, unlike ours, had no technological or medical promise of cure or relief. They passionately identified with the protagonist the tragedians created. The tragic person—
often a king, queen, or member of the royal family—reaching heroic
heights of endurance, agony, and strength, rose to a far loftier humanity than had ever existed before.[62] They were heirs of Prometheus, and
having defied Zeus's will, they suffered his revenge. In an atmosphere
heavy with religious awe and sacrifice, in an epoch when the people
looked to the luck of their kings for their own well-being, tragic individuals were yet another living revelation of man's place in the order
of things. Their suffering went beyond both myth, ritual, and philosophy. The tragic individual—neither priest, warrior, nor philosopher—
was the concentrated human point of flesh and spirit upon which the
cosmic-moral order turned. His suffering expressed the irreducible Greek

awareness that men and women belong to an order whose forces are intent on greater things than human happiness.

NOTES

1. Max Weber, "The Social Psychology of the World Religions," from *Max Weber: Essays in Sociology,* ed. H. H. Gerth & C. Wright Mills (New York: Oxford University Press, 1958), 271.

2. Dorothy Rowe, *The Construction of Life and Death* (New York: John Wiley & Sons, 1984), 184.

3. Peter Farb, *Man's Rise to Civilization* (London: Paladin, 1971), 128–29.

4. I. M. Lewis, *Ecstatic Religion: An Anthropological Study of Spirit and Possession and Shamanism* (Baltimore: Penguin Books, 1971), 67.

5. Mircea Eliade, *Rites and Symbols of Initiation: The Mysteries of Birth and Rebirth* (New York: Harper & Row, 1958), 68.

6. E. Hoebel, *The Cheyennes: Indians of the Great Plain* (New York: Henry Holt, 1960), 16.

7. Claude Levi-Strauss, *Tristes Tropiques* (New York: Atheneum, 1969), 41.

8. Forms of sacrifice can vary depending on who offers what to whom, by what means, and for what reasons. These distinctions are found in a very useful and recent article, Joseph Henninger, "Sacrifices," *Encyclopedia of Religion,* 16 vols., ed. Mircea Eliade (New York: Macmillan, 1987), vol. 12, 544–57. Additionally, useful pieces on sacrifice include "Sacrifice," *Encyclopedia of Religion and Ethics,* 12 vols., ed. James Hasting (New York: Scribner, 1961), vol. 11, 1–40; "Sacrifice," *Encyclopedia Britanica;* 802–5; and Annemarie De Waal Malefijt, *Religion and Culture* (London: Macmillan, 1968), 209–15. For a recent study, see René Girard's, *Violence and the Sacred* (Baltimore: John's Hopkins University Press, 1977), which narrowly but insightfully identifies sacrifice with the need of the community to offer a scapegoat up to deflect internal violence from revenge.

9. Henninger, "Sacrifices," vol. 12, 549.

10. H. Hubert and Marcel Mauss, *Sacrifice: Its Nature and Function* (Chicago: University of Chicago Press, 1964), 97.

11. In common agreement with many other scholars, Farb argues, "Human sacrifice never occurs in societies beneath the level of chiefdom, because in simple societies almost everyone is in a relationship to everyone else through marriage alliances, sodalities, or economic partnerships," *Man's Rise to Civilization,* 185. Agreeing, Edward Norbeck contends that small societies proved infertile ground for human sacrifice, since relations were personal and a matter of kinship, *Religion in Primitive Societies* (New York: Harper & Row, 1961), 65. William Howells adds that "the most spectacular cases [of human sacrifice] are provided by three peoples arriving at an early stage of full civilization: the Aztecs, and the early Bronze Age dynasties of Mesopotamia and China," *The Heathens: Primitive Man and His Religions* (Garden City, N.Y.: Doubleday, 1962), 228.

12. A central thesis to Girard in his *Violence and the Sacred,* the best victim is

someone marginal to society, since his death does not threaten the group with the perpetration of retaliatory violence, esp. 250–73.

13. Useful for sacrifice and other related elements in antiquity is ed. Harry Peck, *Harper's Dictionary of Classical Literature and Antiquities* (New York: Cooper Square Publishers, 1965); also useful is eds. N. G. L. Hammond and H. H. Scullard's *The Oxford Classical Dictionary*, 2nd edition (Oxford: Clarendon Press, 1970).

14. See Eric Maple, "Blood," in *Man, Myth, and Magic*, (24 vols., ed. Richard Cavendish (New York: Marshall Cavendish, 1970), vol. 2, 291.

15. Ibid., 291.

16. Ibid.

17. Florence Dacey, "She Comforts a Bleeding Child," *The Necklace* (Minneapolis: Midwest Villages and Voices, 1988), 19.

18. E. E. Evans-Pritchard, *The Nuer* (Oxford: Oxford University Press, 1969), 121–22.

19. Maple, "Blood," 292.

20. William Graham Sumner, *Folkways* (New York: New American Library, 1940), 422.

21. Ibid., 425.

22. See Cristiano Grottanelli's "Kingship: An Overview," *The Encyclopedia of Religions*, 313–17.

23. James Frazer, *The Golden Bough* (New York: Macmillan, 1963), 319–30.

24. William Chaney, *The Cult of Kingship in Anglo-Saxon England* (Berkeley: University of California Press, 1970), 11–12.

25. Grottanelli, "Kingship," 314.

26. Montaigne, "How the Soul Discharges Its Passions on False Objects When True Are Wanting," *The Complete Essays of Montaigne* (Garden City, NY: Doubleday, 1960), Vol. 1, 17.

27. Robert Graves, *The Greek Myths*, 2 vols. (New York: Penguin Books, 1960), vol. 2, 104.

28. Useful for examining the interrelationship between man, nature, and the gods in the preclassical Ionian philosophy is Henri Frankfort and H. A. Frankfort, "The Emancipation of Thought from Myth," in *Before Philosophy* (Baltimore: Penguin Books, 1949), 237–63. For a collection of texts from the early Greek philosophers, see Jonathan Barnes, ed., *Early Greek Philosophy* (New York: Penguin Books, 1987).

29. In *The Ancient City* (Garden City, N.Y.: Doubleday, 1956), esp. 15–39, Numa Denis Fustel de Coulanges, offers a useful guide to the mentality, beliefs and rituals of ancient Greece and Rome.

30. Alasdair MacIntyre, *After Virtue: A Study in Moral Theory* (Notre Dame, Ind.: University of Notre Dame Press, 1981), 114–22.

31. Werner Jaeger, *Paideia: The Ideals of Greek Culture*, vol. 1 of *Archaic Greece, The Mind of Athens* (New York: Oxford University Press, 1965), 151.

32. Ibid.

33. M. I. Finley, *The World of Odysseus* (New York: Penguin Books, 1979), 137.

34. Ibid., 141.

35. Jaeger, *Paideia*, 154–55.

36. F. M. Cornford, *From Religion to Philosophy: A Study in the Origins of Western Speculation* (New York: Harper and Row, 1957), 13.

37. Willian Greene, *Moira: Fate, Good, and Evil in Greek Thought* (New York: Harper & Row, 1963), 225.

38. Ibid.

39. Jaeger, *Paideia*, 159.

40. Ibid., 161.

41. Eric Voegelin, *The World of the Polis*, vol. 2 of *Order and History* (Baton Rouge: Louisiana State University, 1957), 168–69.

42. Jaeger, *Paideia*, 152–53.

43. F. M. Cornford, *Before and After Socrates* (Cambridge: University Press, 1960), 35.

44. Passage from Aristotle, *Nichomachean Ethics*, bk. 1, 1099a 33–1099b 6, cited in *Great Traditions of Ethics*, eds. Ethel Albert et al. (Belmont, Calif: Wadsworth, 1984), 37.

45. Epicurus, *Fragments*, cited in *Great Traditions of Ethics*, 51.

46. Epicurus, Letter to Menoeceus, cited in *Great Traditions of Ethics*, 59.

47. *Ibid.*, 57.

48. Epictetus, *The Enchiridion*, 1, 2, cited in *Great Traditions of Ethics*, 76.

49. Epictetus, *Fragments*, 4, 106, cited in *Great Traditions of Ethics*, 78–79.

50. Epictetus, *Discourses*, bk. 1, ch. 18, cited in *Great Traditions of Ethics*, 69.

51. Epictetus, *Enchiridion*, 5, 8, cited in *Great Traditions of Ethics*, 77.

52. Epictetus, *Enchiridion*, (Los Angeles: Henry Regnery, 1956), 157.

53. Epictetus, *Enchiridion*, 162.

54. Marcus Aurelius, *Meditations*, (Los Angeles: Henry Regnery, 1956), 14.

55. Aurelius, *Meditations*, 21.

56. Cornford, *Before and After Socrates*, 35.

57. Greene, *Moira*, 96.

58. Jaeger, *Paideia*, 251.

59. Ibid.

60. For a useful survey of Greek tragedy, see Edward Ballard, "Sense of the Tragic," in *Dictionary of the History of Ideas*, 4 vols., ed. Philip Wiener (New York: Charles Scribner's Sons, 1973), 411–17.

61. Greene, *Moira*, 5.

62. Jaeger, *Paideia*, 267.

3

Christianity, Suffering's Worth

That I may know him, and the power of his resurrection, and the
fellowship of his sufferings, being made conformable unto his death.
Philippians 3:10

Tanto il bene ch'o aspetto ch'ogni pena me diletto. (So great the
good I await that each pain brings me pleasure.)
St. Francis

It is necessary to earn paradise, but everyone can't become a monk
to win his salvation. Thus, one at least must practise charity to redeem his faults. Charity unburdens our sufferings.
Jean-Louis Goglin, *Les misérables dans l'occident médiéval.*

Christianity defines our Western sense of suffering. Even our most
contemporary and secular ideologies of suffering resonate with the story
of the God who made himself man and sacrificed himself for humanity.

Christianity went beyond representing Christ as a sacrificial scapegoat who atones for wrongs. Instead, it invited its believers to embrace
Christ, to make themselves one with this king of victims, who chose not
to defend his friends like John the Baptist, his followers like Peter and
Paul, or even himself from injustice, humiliation, and death. Defiant of
so much that constitutes human nature, Christianity called its believers
to abandon the identities and values they had accumulated through
their own pain, labor, suffering, and sacrifices and to join themselves
to the single redeeming sacrifice of Christ.

Christianity made self-sacrifice the first principle of the moral world.

Christianity made suffering and sacrifice the primary means by which man and God carry on their discourse. Sacrifice is the essence of God's love. Believers can only reciprocate God's love by transforming their inner selves into an altar upon which they perpetually offer themselves in all things to God.

In the first part of this chapter, I treat the central place of sacrifice in Christian thought. In the second part, I stress how early and medieval Christians believed themselves to belong to a community of suffering that joined Christ to the church, believer to believer, the living to the dead. In the third part, I examine how Reformation thought, especially as represented by Luther and Calvin, undermined notions of the church as a community of suffering, sacrifice, and grace.

SELF AS ALTAR

Christianity spoke of suffering as the classical world did not. For Christians suffering is never meaningless. There is suffering that people bring upon themselves by their self-abuse; suffering that comes from the first sin; suffering by which people test and educate each other; and finally truly redemptive suffering, the innocent and saving suffering of prophet, messiah, or believer, which renews God's promise to his people. While Christian thinkers have never been free from wrestling with the insoluble dilemma of the existence of an all-powerful God and the reality of innocent suffering, they have never abandoned the notion that human suffering is worthy of human prayer and God's mercy. On this point, Christians are children of the Old Testament.

The Jews of the Old Testament considered that God was singularly interested in their well-being: God suffers Israel's tribulations. When given a choice between the more pure theological desire to emphasize the transcendental nature of God and the desire to have a God who is more concrete and directly interested in human affairs and sufferings, Jewish thinkers traditionally preferred a personal God, a God who rewarded, punished, and tested them.[1]

Judaism had ample rituals and sacrifices to maintain their relationship with God. The Hebrews lived by sacrifice. They were controlled by the law that something had to be given for something to be received; something had to be offered in order for something to be permitted. Even when they abandoned human sacrifices to conduct their most serious affairs of reproduction, war, and agriculture, they continued to utilize a whole range of vows and promises, as well as a host of elaborate rules that allowed sacrifice to permit the commutation of an owed action or the redemption of an animal, house, or field already pledged to God. (For instance, rates of redemption usually set by a priest, and usually including a one-fifth surcharge for the priest, even drew distinctions between the quality of tendered animals.) Ritualized sacrifices of this sort, however, did not express the depths of Judaic spirituality, which proclaimed with its most dramatic stories of Jacob's vow, Abraham's sacrifice, or Job's test, the principle of faith that God, who gave his people everything, rightly asked everything of them in return.

The Christian's God proved equally insatiable. Christ, the apostles taught, took vicariously upon himself all human suffering.[2] At one and the same time, he is man and God, victim and priest, the crucified one and king. He raised the principle of innocent suffering to the Godhead itself.

Christ's death was in conformity with the Hebrew idea of sacrifice. He was the firstborn and unblemished, the perfect victim; he substituted for all others; he was the ransom to be paid for punishment owed. As the new Adam, he propitiates God's wrath, expiates humanity's sins, freeing them from death itself.

Christ consciously took upon himself the tradition of David's line. He would save the faithful remnant of the people; he was the suffering servant predicted by Isaiah who would raise up the people by being brought low. Christ was the lamb of God—the lamb who, in the words of Isaiah, was led to slaughter;[3] the unblemished lamb of the Passover feast; the lamb in the book of Revelation who receives the praise of the twenty-four elders; the Lamb.[4] Iconographically, Christ is the elevated lamb from whose side blood flows, filling the chalice of communion.[5]

Like a gigantic *Wergild,* the debt ancient Germans were required to pay to satisfy a crime, so Christ's blood was the cost of the sins of the human race.[6] Christ's blood, as the old spiritual declares, not only washes us clean, but opens a new covenant for us: as the shedding of Abel's blood led God to direct his covenant from the many to the few, so Christ's blood returned the covenant from the few to the many.[7]

The cross, the very principle of the power of sacrifice, forms the heart of Christian faith. Christians believed that all things are harmonized on the cross with the crucified Christ.[8] In both Eastern and Western Christianity the cross became a magic talisman. The sign of the cross opened locked doors, silenced barking dogs, purified water, and among other things cured cancer while "the ordeal of the cross" (*judicum crucis)* settled disputes and assured oaths. Additionally, the cross cured diseases, healed wounds, and quenched bleeding, and in the folklore of the Slavs and Transylvanians, had powers against vampires and is reported to have raised the dead.[9] The church used the cross to bless goods, to control the profane, to mark its holy spots, to begin and end its services, and to lay hold of knighthood, putting its strong arm in the service of the faith.[10] ("True" relics of the holy cross multiplied throughout the Middle Ages, becoming in the words of one contemporary cynic of such abundance that they would have been sufficient to rebuild the city of Jerusalem.[11]

During the high Middle Ages, the crucifixion, which has received more attention than any other event in Christ's life, came to play a prominent part in the veneration of the medieval church.[12] In contrast to the art of the early Middle Ages, whose object of attention was the risen Christ, Lord of judgment, later medieval art, demonstrating a turn in the humanistic direction, focused on Christ the man and Christ who died on the cross. Revealing a new and increased willingness to focus on human life and suffering, churchmen and artists of the twelfth and thirteenth centuries turned their attention to Mary and her sorrows. The pietà, the dead Christ on Mary's lap, became a favorite theme. The religious and artistic leaders of this age were cultivating and refining suffering and forming a sensibility that, supported by faith, was open to earthly suffering. Art was helping create what art historian Erwin Panofsky calls "faith by empathy."[13]

While the ethical command to join Christ on the cross has unequally motivated Christians, taking up one's cross has been the general requirement of Christianity. Throughout the New Testament, Christ consistently suggested that there was no way to God except through self-sacrifice. "This is my commandment to you," Jesus taught his apostles, "that you love one another as I have loved you. Greater love has no man than this, that a man lay down his life for his friends."[14] Paul testified to this sacrificial impulse when he appealed to the Romans, "to present your bodies as a living sacrifice, holy and acceptable to God, which is your spiritual worship."[15] While theologians quarrel whether the requirement to suffer has its roots in our need to imitate Christ, to express gratitude to him, or to participate as victims in his suffering, Christianity found all earthly things an occasion for sacrifice. Conscience became the altar on which self and world were sacrificed. Hence, the good for Christians, as Nietzsche so bitterly commented, arises out of transformation through renunciation instead of will.[16]

The crucified Christ put on Christians' conscience an unlimited obligation to sacrifice self in all things. No single act of sacrifice (not even the sacrament of the mass itself, which perpetually reenacts Christ's sacrifice) sufficed the Christian his obligations to God. Even the Reformation proposition "faith alone saves" (sola fides) did not free Christians from the principle of unlimited sacrifice.

MARTYRS AND THE COMMUNITY OF SACRIFICE

Christian martyrs and saints also testified how powerfully the impulse to sacrifice operated in the Christian conscience. Martyrs were, as the Greek meaning of the word suggests, special witnesses to Christ: they shed their blood for God. ('Martyrdom," according to Tertullian, "meant a second baptism since it removed all sin and assured the martyr of his eternal crown."[17]) Judged to be fanatics, as they were by some fellow believers, or praised, as they traditionally were for having seeded the church with their blood, martyrs made the measure of faith unlimited sacrifice.[18]

Martyriums—edifices honoring the grave or sight of death of martyrs, similar to today's memorials at the death camps of the Holocaust—sprang up during the first two centuries. In several instances, places where martyrs died became the sights of special shrines, which, in turn, eventually became new churches and urban centers. The tombs of martyrs were also gathering places for families, kin groups, and regions. Pilgrims came to the most important of these holy sights not just to testify to their faith and to seek forgiveness for their sins but to seek cures for ailments for which they could find no cures locally.[19] By the middle of the third century, there is evidence of a formal veneration of martyrs as part of Catholic worship.[20] Christian liturgy and more popular writings, such as Gregory of Tours's *Glories of Martyrs,* recognized the important place of the martyrs in the community of the faithful. From the middle of the fourth century, martyrologies containing thousands of names were compiled.[21]

Church fathers extended the halo of martyrdom from the actual giving of one's life to the inner willingness to give one's life for Christ. Clement of Alexandria claimed that "both the preparation for martyrdom and the martyrdom of passions were equivalent to the actual shedding of one's blood."[22] Origen acknowledged that there were many Christians who "suffered a daily martyrdom of conscience by willingly carrying their cross behind the Savior."[23]

Christians came to see the elevating principle of martyrdom as a description of a whole range of voluntary action, associated with the exemplary dedications of one's whole life to God and the church. Monastic life established its claim to serve God around the worth of self-elected suffering. Irish monks, among the most severe of the ascetics, distinguished a white and a green martyrdom. The former "amounted to giving up what one loved for God, while the latter consisted of suppressing the passions and doing penance ceaselessly."[24] Joining martyr and saint was the notion that the path to God was narrow, and self-denial and sacrifice were essential.

Christian communities gave rise to saintly ascetics, whose entire lives were dedicated to self-mortification. The most rigorous ascetics ate next to nothing and lived in the smallest and least hospitable shacks or caves, or, like the forerunners of the modern flagpole sitter, they perched on small platforms elevated above the ground.[25]

Other Christian saints of a more legendary sort, not without their counterparts in Celtic, Germanic, and even Buddhist literature, engaged in a range of heroic and miraculous deeds, including the winning of battles, the fighting of dragons, the breaking of spells, and yet other prodigious displays that demonstrated the presence of the supernatural. Appropriately, they were the spiritual warriors of this feudal age, when mortal combat measured the good. Also, they promised help and mercy in a cruel age, when feudal lords were brutal and justice was rare.

Christians associated suffering with goodness in several ways. First, suffering was considered necessary payment for a life that was less than perfect. Second, it appealed to God's mercy. Third, it emptied one's soul. Fourth, suffering that one submitted to voluntarily imitated Christ and his humiliation at the hands of man.

Even beyond this, some Christian traditions suggest the act of suffering itself makes one holy. For instance, in early Anglo-Saxon history, there is the tradition of the slain king who becomes a saint-martyr. In one case, even though the king was a heathen, his violent slaying itself made him a sacrificial victim and saint.[26] This belief has its counterpart in the Russian Orthodox church, in which extreme and emptying suffering (kenotic suffering) was commonly understood to make people saints. According to G. P. Fedotov, the Russian idea of holiness teaches that "every disciple of Christ is left in the world to suffer, and all innocent and voluntary suffering in the world is suffering in the name of Christ."[27] Independent of what social class they come from, Russian saints, Fedotov observes, had in common that they suffered and were murdered, testifying to the underlying idea of the redeeming merit of suffering. ("Children," he writes, "are particularly numerous in this group, their natural innocence adding to the purification by blood."[28]) Even though the suffering of many of these saint-victims was not willed and passive, and hence, not in full conformity with the suffering of Christ, nevertheless, they suffered, bled, and died. And their suffering itself as a victim made them holy and was considered reason enough to join them to the crucified Christ, who himself was defeated and humiliated on the cross.

A COMMUNITY OF SUFFERING AND
A TREASURY OF MERITS

Confident that the saints were risen with Christ in heaven, believers looked to them for efficacious intercession. Being on good terms with a saint amounted to having a "friend in high places." Indeed, in conformity with the practice of the Romans, early medieval Christians drew a network of invisible fellow human beings around themselves. They worked out a series of intense relationships modeled on what they considered to be good relationships in ordinary life.[29] In conformity with the principle of patronage, which pervaded the classical world, the saints became patrons, spiritual protectors of families, regions, and eventually whole peoples. Their suffering entitled them not only to special status, but made them benefactors of significant powers and even God's grace and miracles.[30]

Saint-martyrs were intercessors in a way no solely human hero could be. They were God's friends. While orthodox theology considered saints to be entirely dependent for their powers on Christ, the people commonly granted saints' discretionary powers to perform great and small miracles. Having no end of needs, men and women asked no end of miracles from their saints: to cure illnesses; make humans and animals fertile; find lost goods; end possessions; ward off fire, flood, and lightning; and protect against violence. No human request was considered to be too small or great for the saints' consideration. Collectively, the saints served as little gods, super priests, doctors, finders, psychologists, aids, and others whom a person might summon for help.

Saints developed particular functions. St. Anne, Mary's mother, helped make a woman fertile; St. Barbara protected against lightning; Blaise warded off throat problems; Christopher prevented sudden accidents; Denis stopped headaches; Vitus cured epilepsy; and Margaret treated insanity. Some saints served only certain classes: for instance, Leonard, Nicholas, and Rochus helped the peasantry. Other saints were singularly powerful in certain regions, such as St. Anthony and Rosalia in Italy and Boniface in Germany.[31] However, whether understood to be little more than local spirits, older pagan deities dressed in new clothing, or universally identifiable Christian personalities, saints had special powers because they belonged to a community in which all the believers, both the living and the dead, were understood to be alive and interconnected as part of the body of the risen Christ.

In the early church, Christians not only cared for their dead, as all peoples did, but they took up the novel practice of praying for the dead. According to Salomon Reinach, "Pagans prayed to the dead, Christians prayed for the dead."[32]

Believing that the living and the dead alike were alive in Christ, early Christians were prohibited from purposely excluding anyone from their prayers.[33] Convinced of the intercessory powers of those who had died in Christ, it was common practice among early Christians to address their own needs and the needs of others to martyred saints.[34]

The community of believers, for the medieval church, formed the Communion of Saints, which was composed of the church militant, comprised of earthly believers; the church expectant, comprised of those in purgatory; and finally, the church triumphant, comprised of those

in heaven. Between all three parts of the church, an interplay of supernatural energies was hypothesized, all partaking "in all stages of Christ's
life, from his lowliness in suffering and death to his risen glory."[35]

As the earthly representative of the Communion of Saints, the church
assumed that it was in control of the Treasury of Merits, based upon
Christian suffering and sacrifice. Certain of its access to the risen Christ
and his saints, it took itself to be the mediator between earth and heaven.
Through teaching, prayers, sacraments, and the faith and sacrifices of
its believers, the church assumed powers of petition and intercession.
Understanding itself to be the extension of the body of Christ, the church
believed itself to be the living continuation of his sacrifice.

As Paul claimed to complete Christ's suffering for the church, so the
church would help complete all redemptive suffering for humanity. It
did this with reference to Paul's statement, "Now I rejoice in my suffering for your sake, and in my flesh I complete what is lacking in
Christ's affliction for the sake of his body, that is the church."[36] As the
Old Testament Jew drew up and fortified his claim by reminding God
of everything Abraham and his people suffered for the sake of their
faith, so the church in its prayers and masses drew upon its own lineage
of holy suffering to petition God in the name of Jesus and Mary, the
apostles, martyrs, bishops, confessors, and saints. The church com-
merced in divine and human suffering, especially in the name of Christ,
victim of victims. "It is awful, though in the spirit of the New Testament," conceded Protestant thinker, Karl Löwith, "to think this reiter-
ation of acting and suffering through all the ages should be required
to complete the Passion of Christ."[37]

INDULGENCES, SUFFERING EXCHANGED

The church presumed to be the earthly regulator of God's grace.
Although the church was unable to provide what humanity most prefers, miracles upon demand, nevertheless, it did carry out its sacraments, which, though less spectacular and personal and specific, were
more dependable and efficacious than sacrifices.[38] With baptism, the
church reopened the gates of heaven, saving believers from the everlasting torment of hell. With the sacrament of the mass, the most important sacrament of all, the priest repeated Christ's sacrifice and nourished the believing community with Christ's body. With penance, the
most recently developed of the sacraments and the sacrament that most
interests us here, the church in Christ's name absolved sin and all the
punishment associated with it, which meant escaping certain imminent
and even unending suffering.[39]

While offering forgiveness in light of the penitent's true contrition,
the church at the same time assigned a temporal penance for the res-

titution of wrong. Prayers, acts of self-abnegation, almsgiving, all of which can be considered self-imposed suffering of one sort or another, as was the pledge to begin a new life, played a part in the penitent's restitution. (In the early centuries of the church, penance was not an act of forgiveness between penitent and priest, as it became in the high Middle Ages, but it was a public action by which one, who had separated himself from the believing community by sin, expressed his sorrow and desire to restored to the community.)

As bizarre as this seems, by the early Middle Ages, the length of penance for such sins as murder commonly exceeded the expected life of the penitent. For the penitent to meet the terms of his penance, he would need either special acts of remission or the help of others to fulfill his assigned penance. This was one possible source of indulgences. Another was the church's growing willingness to forgive pain owed through an array of varied actions, such as vows, fasts, almsgiving, prayers, attending special masses and devotions, and visits to a rapidly multiplying supply of relics. The church increasingly defined a world of significant works by which one could avoid the sufferings of hell and eventually win the happiness of heaven. From this perspective, the church was already imposing a rational and predictable order upon suffering, human fate, and God's grace, leaving incalculable evil and unfathomable misery to the dark spaces of life and mind.

In the course of the Middle Ages, Peter's keys to heaven and earth were used ever more frequently. In promoting the Second Crusade, Pope Eugenius III (1145–53) offered not only to protect the crusaders' wives, children, and property, but canceled their interest on outstanding debts. Crusaders were free to mortgage their lands to representatives of the church and, most important of all from a religious point of view, were to receive "absolution and remission of sins, so that those who devoutly undertake and accomplish this holy journey, or who die by the way, shall obtain absolution for all their sins which they confess with humble and contrite heart, and shall receive from him who grants to each his due reward the prize of eternal life."[40] Innocent III (1198–1216), carried the principle of absolution a step further by reserving to the pope the absolution of many sins and religious crimes, making pardon, de facto, a matter of bargaining with him.

In no case was the church's manipulation of grace and forgiveness, thus to a degree eternal pain and pleasure, revealed as explicitly as in the matter of indulgences. Indulgences were an explicit part of the church's growing systematization of believers' spiritual lives. Derived from the bishop's power to forgive public penance en masse and responding to what had grown to be an elaborate system of penance, which reckoned each sin in days, weeks, months, or even years, indulgences took form in the eleventh and twelfth century with the purpose of forgiving earthly penance still owed.[41] Indulgences became ever more essential as the sacrament of individual confession and the corresponding assignment of penances took hold of Europe's urban believers. Forgiveness of penance, which indulgences promised, became a major preoccupation of the age as the church and its growing armies of priests articulated an ever more elaborate scheme to weigh earthly sacrifices against heavenly gifts. In effect, five centuries before the Enlightenment and Bentham (the subjects of the subsequent chapters) the church had already established a primitive utilitarianism that weighed all grades of earthly pleasure and pain in light of the ultimate pleasures and pains of eternal life.

Already common in the eleventh century was the notion of gaining indulgences in advance of sin. The banking of such grace could be gained by indulgences assigned for participating in the consecration of a building, attending the festival of a venerated saint, transporting or visiting a relic, making a pilgrimage, giving alms, or contributing to the upkeep of a church, abbey, or hospital. A veritable network of indulgences, holy deeds, and good works was now regulated by the church. The exchange of prayer, vow, and deed sustained an active and swift commerce in suffering and grace across a trade triangle of the living, the dead, and God and his saints.

In calling for the First Crusade at the Council of Clermont in 1095, Pope Urban II announced the first full plenary indulgence: "The individual may count that journey in lieu of all penance".[42] With a good confession, the crusader was certain of heaven. As crusades of various sorts abounded in the twelfth and thirteenth centuries, knights were granted indulgences for fighting not only in the Holy Land, but also in Spain against the Moors, eastern Germany against the Slavs, southern France against the Albigensians, the Baltic countries against the pagans, Hungary against the Mongols, and elsewhere.

Revealing the rationalizing spirit of a new age, the knights eventually had no need even to risk their lives to win a full plenary indulgence, but could win their indulgences more safely by sending a representative or helping finance the project. No doubt, a new age of commerce was at hand. Suffering had been politicized and commercialized. Pilgrimages and crusades formed a new industry of salvation.

By 1300, the year when Boniface VIII offered a plenary indulgence for a pilgrimage to Rome, the church had a bountiful number of indulgences ranging from one to five years. Indulgences multiplied rapidly thereafter as they came to be attached to persons, places, and churches; objects like crucifixes and medals; and special prayers and devotions, such as the rosary and the stations of the cross. Having at its disposal in addition to the sacraments a host of indulgences, a sea of tolerated superstitions, and many specialized saints, holy places and

relics, the church was well, but not perfectly, equipped to channel human superstition and consecrate human suffering to higher purposes.[43] The church, when it chose not to stress how sinful humanity
was and how wide the door to hell was thrown open, could reward the
most modest human efforts, when supported by faith, with hope of
eternal happiness.

Already in the ninth century, popes and bishops frequently concluded their letters with an absolution grant and a solemn prayer that
through the intercession of Christ and his saints asked God to absolve
the sinner of all punishments due to sin. Their grants included the
dead as well as the living. By the end of the Middle Ages, the church
was explicitly offering to shorten the term of the suffering of the dead.
In 1476, Sixtus IV explicitly granted a plenary indulgence to the souls
in purgatory. At this point, the church was boldly offering its services
to help all the souls in purgatory. The church did, though, leave heretical attempts to free the dead from hell itself to folk stories, which most
illustratively include the story of St. Peter's aborted effort to save his
mother from hell.

PURGATORY, THE SUFFERING OF THE HOPEFUL DEAD

While the church fathers had the idea that one must pass through a
purging experience before entering heaven, purgatory took its imaginary form in space and time in the twelfth and thirteenth centuries
and was enshrined in doctrine between the middle of the fifteenth and
the beginning of the seventeenth centuries.[44] In *The Birth of Purgatory*,
Jacques LeGoff notes that each historical period from purgatory's doctrinal enshrinement had a purgatory of its own, thus it is useful to
speak of a Counter-Reformation purgatory, a baroque purgatory, a romantic purgatory, and Sulpician purgatory.[45]

Purgatory first was a place where the church could gather the souls
of the dead and with merits, sacraments, prayers, and indulgences,
minister to them, diminishing their pain and hastening their departure
for heaven. Presuming that the dead of purgatory were hers (believers
delayed on their way to heaven), the church claimed to have within her
power rights to limit the duration and intensity of their suffering and
speed their admission into heaven. The church here again was claiming
to tame the most uncharted areas of human destiny and happiness.

Furthermore, purgatory rested on the notions of the reversibility of
merit and the solidarity between the living and the dead. The living
could intercede for the dead, who, once free of purgatory and as-
cended into heaven, could reciprocally intercede for the living.[46] Hence,
purgatory not only permitted a full reciprocity between the living and

the dead but also satisfied a familialism that was older and culturally more universal than Christianity itself.

For believer and theologian alike, purgatory satisfied undefined points of their faith. It spoke directly to the believers' common sense assessment that their fellow believers, like themselves, would upon death neither merit eternal damnation in hell, nor be worthy of heaven. Analogizing from their world, a world in which pain was a cost of all significant transactions (whether for instance it be the tilling of a field or the fighting of a battle), they hypothesized that purgatory supplied the God-appointed amount of pain to purify a soul for heaven.[47]

Additionally, supplying a theological need not met by the New Testament or the church fathers, purgatory gave an answer to the question of where immortal souls reside between the time of their individual death and the Second Coming and Final Judgment of Christ. Indeed, purgatory amounted to what Jacques Le Goff considered not only an expansion of social imagination and religious certitude but an increase in "the geography of the beyond."[48]

As contradictory as this might seem, purgatory also provided unique testimony to the emerging individualism of the era. Rather than being a place of all-encompassing darkness, in which all are equally mired down in undistinguished misery and equal punishment, in purgatory unique individuals suffer unique punishment for their own acts.[49] Residents of Dante's purgatory, like the inhabitants of hell, are independent of God. They stand alone in their own suffering, being no more or less than what they spent their lives on earth making themselves. Erich Auerbach even went so far as to argue that in the work of Dante "the image of man eclipses God," and the notion of man's self-fulfillment in the beyond gives human reality a place of primacy it did not hold in classical literature.[50]

In the twelfth century, people, especially of the upper classes of the urban centers of northern and central Italy, began to be freed for the first time from the overwhelming sense of being stalked by a universal apocalypse.[51] Anticipating the young romantics of five centuries later, they began to attribute immense values to their own lives, making their own feelings, callings, sufferings, and deaths worthy of their own full preoccupation. Suggestive of what we see on vast scale in modern history, as individuals gained control of their own lives, they began to cultivate their own sensibilities, attributing singular value to what they and others suffer. As the church kept step with improving material and political civilization by providing a rationalizing ethic, so people gave expression to a new sensibility in which feelings and affections were given new value.

In the twelfth century, people started to assert the worth of their own spiritual lives. With the formation of guilds, philanthropic enterprises, and confraternities; the foundation of the lay orders; and the increased presence of itinerant preachers; lay piety became a valid notion.[52] Anticipating the Reformation, the lay ideal of piety asserted that imitation of Christ and holy suffering did not belong exclusively to the life of the cleric within the institutional church but was possible for all who would imitate Christ through prayer and especially through a ministry to the poor, the sick, the homeless, and the outcast. Empathy for the suffering of others already was becoming a defining characteristic of the good person.

"Christ's passion was no longer remote to the laity; the discovery of the apostolic life of the early Church was depriving the monasticism of its traditional primacy," wrote Marvin Becker.[53] Lay piety sanctified the new realities of urban life. "The pentitential life," Becker remarked,

was extended far beyond the bounds of the religious orders into the world of the everyday. Flagellation, once the preserve of the heroic ascetics, was soon to become a popular ritual. . . . Evangelical principles supported a break with an ancient realm in which gift, the benefice, the oath, and even the feudal glamour of the liturgy were to be renounced in favor of fraternal ties and more abstract bonds of association. Manual labor was to be valued more than lavish displays or liturgical pomp. As the norms of society became more impartial and judicial, the need for collective ideals heightened; a belief in the power of love, charity, and brotherhood found new forms in the guild, the confraternity, the festival, and philanthropic enterprises.[54]

In the relatively open and comparatively secure social order of this urban life, piety became more personal. Individuals and families dedicated larger amounts for private masses, altars, and the construction of chapels.[55] These "newly born individuals," to use a phrase of W. Ulmann, saw saintliness not as a single act of martyrdom, but as a process that took a whole lifetime.[56] They understood grace as acquired and developed rather than instantaneous. Correspondingly, they took into their own hands the matter of securing their own eternal well-being. In the teaching of this new lay spirituality, each person was considered to have a unique destiny with God. Purgatory conformed to the new personalization of the spiritual life and a new level of personal interest in individual vocations, death, and final destiny.[57] Purgatory provided the individual with an imaginary way to take measure of the ultimate value of his life and fill "the gap between his temporal trajectory of 70 years ([the Biblical] three score and ten) and the interests of the entire human race which reaches across multiple thousands of years."[58]

THE INDIVIDUALIZATION OF SUFFERING

The church did not claim to prevent suffering, instead it gave eternal significance to the pain, labors, ordeals, and miseries of individual lives.

Even lives that turned on the coarsest impulses and the pettiest calculations were made part of an all-encompassing salvation drama. Everything could be made a gift or a payment to Christ. As the lives of the
saints exemplified, life was an inexhaustible opportunity to sacrifice to
God.[59]

In reference to a distinct sacrificial ethic, the church blessed the primary activities of the three orders of life: the clergy who prayed, the
nobles who fought, and the peasants and laborers who worked. Each
order required a form of suffering; each harvested, when the suffering
was faithfully done, both earthly and heavenly goods.[60] Only the activity of the merchants and the financiers, the commercial order, was ini-
tially denied an intrinsic value by the church. Unlike the other orders,
this new order was judged ethically to operate by selfish calculation
alone: it risked nothing, it made nothing, and it was judged by church
and aristocracy alike to embody no principle of sacrifice. Even later in
the Middle Ages, when the church had accommodated itself to this new
class, it was still compelled to assert the primacy of its transcendental
transactions over and against the secular exchanges of this new order
and its growing rationalism, naturalism, and individualism.[61]

As the church grew more powerful during the Middle Ages and medieval civilization itself brought more and more lives under its rational
order, the use of suffering became more refined and internalized. There
was even, so to speak, a surplus of compassion. Contemplation was increasingly made a central object of spiritual devotion. In contrast to the
Eastern Orthodox church, the church encouraged meditation on the
suffering of Christ, his mother, and the saints. Saint Anselm prayed, "I
am myself the wound of your sorrow, I am to blame for your murder.
I have merited that you should die, I am the scourge of vengeance
upon you. I am the real malice in your Passion, the real suffering in
your Crucifixion."[62] St. Bernard exhorted believers, "As much as we
can, let us love our wounded Lord, let us give love for love, and embrace Him whose hands and feet and side wicked ploughmen have fur-
rowed."[63]

As believers were more intimately drawn to Christ the man in their
devotions, so Christ was imagined ever more as a man. Artists, whose
church paintings were the primary texts of the medieval understanding
of the world, reflected this new interiorization and personalization of
Christ's suffering. Christian believers, turning inward, used holy suffering to cultivate their spiritual lives. They devoted their attention to
the pictorial representations of Christ's suffering: Jesus a helpless babe
in the crib (most perfect innocence born to suffer); Jesus along the way
of the cross, his holy agony, as well as the sorrows of his holy mother.
Each of these motifs of suffering became a matter of popular devotion,

countless artistic representations, and sermons of the newly formed mendicant preachers of the thirteenth century.[64]

St. Francis, above all others, expressed as well as helped form this newly emerging spirituality of a rationalizing church and civilization.[65] This most joyous and outgoing medieval saint was austerely devoted to the suffering Christ. Francis was, according to Friedrich Herr, a man of extremes: a man of joy and sorrow, serenity and grief, quietude and turbulence. He was an ecstatic and a crucified man.[66] He gave up his inheritance as the son of a successful Assisi merchant and took up the role of beggar. He, who never became a priest, considered poverty his bride, ministered to the poor and sick, and preached that suffering born out of love was the way to God. Revealing his asceticism, St. Francis transformed a knight's poetic lines to his lover, "So great the good I have in sight/That every pain I count delight," into a long sermon on the religious life.[67] Francis was marked by the stigmata, the tangible signs of the crucified Christ. He was "convinced of the reality of endless suffering."[68] His life turned on his invocation, "We adore Thee, O Christ, and we bless Thee, because of Thy Holy Cross, Thou has redeemed the world." In an age when God's wrath and hell were still real, Francis spoke of most scarce and thus most cherished things: love, mercy, and forgiveness.

As Francis subdued the legendary wolf of Gubbio with the promise of food and a sermon, so the church analogously triumphed over suffering itself. It did this not by denying sufferings' existence, teaching resistance to it, or offering the hope of its elimination. Instead the church, like St. Francis, transformed suffering into the path of salvation. All suffering, except that which arose out of sinning, ideally could be borne in Christ's name. The church blessed the warrior's code of sacrifice, made the imperium holy, read the works of Plato and Aristotle as doorways to the eternal truth, and turned the love poetry of southern France into mystical poetry. It offered the hope that men and women were more than just miserable biological creatures. Thus, while conceding that humanity was *born into pain,* the church defied what the great majority of peasants believed: that man was *born for pain.*

Catholic historian Christopher Dawson maintained, "There has never been an age in which Christianity attained so complete a cultural expression as in the thirteenth century. Europe has seen no greater Christian hero than St. Francis, no greater Christian philosopher than St. Thomas, no greater Christian poet than Dante, perhaps no greater Christian ruler than St. Louis."[69] While historians of different persuasions might disagree over what ultimately were the refining and civilizing forces of the Middle Ages and certainly question how deeply these forces penetrated the hearts and minds of warring nobility on the one hand and downtrodden peasants on the other, there can be no doubt that the church provided ideals for the people of that period to tame their sexuality and aggression and give purpose to their sufferings. The church taught that misery, despair, evil, and all the senseless suffering associated with them, need not prevail: Christ, the victim, allowed all to rise beyond the prison of pain and suffering.

THE INTERNALIZATION OF THE
SACRIFICIAL COMMUNITY

The degree to which Protestantism radically transformed medieval Christianity is sharply contested in recent European historiography.[70] In any case, Protestantism presented a singular challenge to the church as a hierarchical community of holy suffering and grace and as the active mediator between man and God, the living and the dead. With their singular focus on Christ as humanity's sole savior and his sacrifice alone as redeeming, the reformers challenged a whole complex world associated with belief and practices about holy suffering, forgiveness, mercy, and salvation that the church had articulated over more than a millennium. Steven Ozment supports this view of the Reformation:

Viewed in these terms, the Reformation was an unprecedented revolution in religion at a time when religion penetrated almost the whole of life. The Reformation constituted for the great majority of people, whose social status and economic condition did not change dramatically over a lifetime, an upheaval of the world as they knew it, regardless of whether they were pious Christians or joined the movement. In the first half of the sixteenth century cities and territories passed laws and ordinances that progressively ended or severely limited a host of traditional beliefs, practices, and institutions that touched directly the daily life of large numbers of people: mandatory fasting; auricular confession; the veneration of saints, relics, and images; the buying and selling of indulgences; pilgrimages and shrines; wakes and processions for the dead and dying; endowed masses in memory of the dead; the doctrine of purgatory; Latin Mass and liturgy; traditional ceremonies, festivals, and holidays; monasteries, nunneries, and mendicant orders; the sacramental status of marriage, extreme unction, confirmation, holy orders, and penance; clerical celibacy; clerical immunity from civil taxation and criminal jurisdiction; nonresident benefices; papal excommunication and interdict; canon law; papal and episcopal territorial government; and the traditional scholastic education of the clergy. Modern scholars may argue over the degree to which such changes in the official framework of religion connoted actual changes in personal beliefs and habits. Few, however, can doubt that the likelihood of personal change increased with the incorporation of Protestant reforms in the laws and institutions of the sixteenth century. As historians write the social history of Reformation, I suspect they will discover that such transformations in the religious landscape had a profound, if often indirect, cultural impact.[71]

For the reformers, especially Luther and Calvin, everything that happened to the individual was understood to be part of God's providence and preelection. Suffering, accordingly, occurred only with God's knowledge and will. The reformers denied the existence of fate and destiny, the staples of every peasant's mental diet, and, in contradiction to many medieval thinkers, they denied chance any place in human affairs. For them, however commonplace, bizarre, or seemingly altogether unjust a happening, it was to be understood as God's providence. Anticipating the modern understanding of nature as directed by a set of rational laws, the reformers understood providence as the purposeful hand of God existing behind all things.

While people could pray, supplicate, and entreat God for mercy and relief from their suffering, the early reformers did not encourage them to expect miracles. They took all hope for favorable intercession on the part of angels, the dead, or saints to be heretical. They judged heretical any attempt by an individual to offer up his suffering to God on behalf of his good or the good of another. Likewise, they forbade the living from presuming that they could pay a spiritual price owed by the dead, or vice versa. Calvin stripped the church entirely of its role as sacramental mediator between man and God, the living and the dead, and saints and believers, whereas Luther retained the mediating powers of the sacraments of baptism and the Eucharist. Denying all salvational worth to human deeds, the reformer's consolation was faith, and faith alone. All that beats people down—despair, temptation, famine, death—had only one answer: faith in the saving grace of Jesus Christ who suffered, died, and rose. Nothing—no vow, deed, prayer, or sacrament—can substitute for nor merit this faith.

Luther defined faith as trust in the goodness of the *Deus absconditus,* who remains hidden even in Christ and in the church. The hidden God reveals himself as Word of God (scriptures and sacraments) in the visible world. Sacraments and prayer save us only to the extent that they reestablish the bond of trust.

The object of Luther's faith was the suffering Christ of the cross. Luther saw in the cross the single revelation of the hidden God: a saving Christ to whom suffering and mortal humanity must cling for salvation. The union of believer and Christ was not consummated in some glorious vision of a risen Christ, but achieved at the cross itself.[72]

Luther, who did not hesitate to encourage fellow believers to seek out apothecaries and doctors and to take whatever other practical steps they could to alleviate their pain and suffering, offered no promise of hope by intercession from saints, the offering of vows in exchange for cures, or the belief that the spiritual actions of others might prove to be efficacious. Luther advised his own sick mother, "First, dear mother, you are now well-informed about God's grace and know that this sickness of yours is his gracious fatherly chastisement. It is quite a slight thing in comparison with what he inflicts upon the godless, and sometimes even upon his own dear children. One person is beheaded, another burned, a third drowned, and so on."[73] Luther added that she should accept her suffering "with thankfulness as a token of God's grace, recognizing how slight it is (even if it be a sickness unto death) compared with the suffering of his own dear Son, our Lord Jesus Christ, who did not suffer for himself, as we do, but for us and for our sins."[74]

In a letter to a friend, Luther's consolation suggested that faith during illness is analogous to a good business deal. "The exchange [of illness for salvation] is to be accepted cheerfully. Christ is a good merchant and a gracious tradesman who sells us life for death, righteousness for sin, and lays a momentary sickness or two upon us by way of interest and as a token that he sells more reasonably and borrows at more favorable rates than the Fuggers and the tradesmen on earth."[75]

Luther gave a vast range of advice to the suffering flock of his new church.[76] He wrote one person to fear the Devil when he is sick, another to trust God, even if he suffers like Job, and yet another, to let Christ worry for him. He consoled others who were mourning by telling them to believe that their beloved is now with Christ.

Luther's consolation to others was of course the consolation he offered himself. He advised the scrupulous, among whose ranks he himself was surely numbered when a young monk, to abandon themselves to their small temptations, in which the Devil breeds the frustration and despair that leads to great sins. In counseling a young melancholic prince, Prince Joachim, in whom he in all likelihood saw himself, Luther advised, "Be merry . . . for gladness and good cheer, when decent and proper, are the best medicine for a young person—indeed for all people. I myself, who have spent a good portion of my life in sorrow and gloom, now seek and find pleasure wherever I can."[77] Elsewhere Luther counseled a believer, "Those who try to climb into heaven without the revealed Christ, and think that they have both feet in heaven, tumble down to Hell."[78]

At the heart of Luther's consolation to fellow believers was the message that saved him from despair and, more than anything else, the single spark that ignited the Reformation. The victim of a scrupulous conscience, the young Luther was filled with despair about his own sinfulness. Confession did not free him of his guilt and fear of his damnation. Only when he realized that Christ, and not we ourselves, saves did Luther feel himself to be freed of the burden of constant anxiety over his salvation and the never-ending treadmill of sin and confession. This insight first led him to an essential denial of the asceticism of monastic life and, finally, to a break with the church itself.

At the heart of Luther's revolt two fundamental, yet what might seem to today's readers obscure, theological propositions were in play. The first proposition, which was not without support in medieval theology, maintained that Christ's sacrifice alone satisfied man's debt. The second proposition, which took form in fourteenth-century theological circles, contradictorily affirmed that Christ's satisfaction is not to be measured by the pain, suffering, and agony he bore on the cross, but that the satisfaction belongs inscrutably to God's will to save man through his Son.[79] Furthermore, Luther turned away from the superabundant satisfaction of Mary, the saints, and the church, fixing the eye of his faith on the singular and saving powers of Jesus Christ, which expressed the unfathomable will of the Father. This concept of faith sharply denied the efficacy of suffering in the salvation plan and consequently, the church's power as head and mediator of a community of suffering and grace. This constituted the source of Luther's profound collision with the church.

Steven Ozment argued that the central issue of salvation for the medieval theologian was "*caritas*—love—not faith."[80] Faith was in the medieval theologians perspective only the beginning of the Christian life, whereas "love bound together the persons of the Trinity, the soul with God, and man with his neighbor," and even the living and the dead.[81] There could be no love, it followed, without passion and sacrifice—the sufferings of love. In contrast, for Luther, the central issue was not the matter of love but trust and belief.[82] Luther's faith answered in the affirmative the question of whether or not God could be depended on to save man.

Luther's war with Rome began with his criticism of indulgences and their practices. It developed to include a renunciation of the Treasury of Merits, the efficaciousness of saints' intercessory powers, the existence of purgatory, the worth of prayers for the dead, the value of works, priestly vows, monastic asceticism, ordeals, and pilgrimages.

In a single blow, Luther had challenged the communal sacrificial character of Christianity. Contradicting what in one form or another people had done since time immemorial, he denied the value of the informal and ritualistic practices of trading and haggling over sufferings with God. At the same time, Luther denied the most ancient of human institutions, the priesthood, and its powers to efficaciously work exchanges in holy matters. He reduced the number of sacraments to two, baptism and communion. At the same time he denied the supernatural powers of the mass as a living sacrifice by making the transformation of the bread and wine into the body and blood of Christ contingent upon the believer's faith in such a transformation. For Luther, priests could lead prayers and perform their two sacraments, but in so doing they only exteriorly formalized what faith made possible. From this vantage point, Luther was a theological reductionist, who transformed Christianity from a priestly into a lay religion.

In his work of 1520, "The Babylon Captivity," Luther argued all callings are equal in the eyes of God. He wrote "I would vehemently . . . dissuade anyone from entering an order or becoming a priest unless he recognizes that what he does . . . counts no more in the eyes of God than the work of a farmer in the field or a *Hausfrau* in the home [both of which Luther esteemed], because the eyes of the Lord look only onto faith."[83] In his treatise "To the Christian Nobility of the German Nation" (1520), Luther wrote, "My advice is to let the saints canonize themselves. Indeed, it is God alone who should canonize them. And let every man stay in his own parish; there he will find more than in all the shrines even if they were all rolled into one. In your parish you find baptism, the sacrament [Eucharist], preaching, and your neighbor, and these things are greater than all the saints in heaven."[84]

Calvin developed Luther's attacks against Roman Catholicism. Calvin was convinced that the fundamental error of medieval Catholicism was idolatry.[85] In *The Institutes,* Calvin accused the Catholic Church of losing sight of "the inestimable price of Christ's blood."[86] Calvin accused the church of having substituted the blood of saints and martyrs for the cleansing blood of Christ that alone washes believers of their sins. Calvin quoted Augustine, "No martyr's blood is shed for the forgiveness of sins."[87]

Following the spirit of Luther, Calvin elsewhere wrote in *The Institutes,* that "indulgences teach that the believers wash their robes in the blood of the saints." Indulgences make the salvation of souls "the object of lucrative trafficking."[88] Calvin also said that senseless and mandatory personal confession had been imposed between the believers' hearts and Christ's mercy. Good Christian lay callings had been distorted by self-defeating vows and unnecessary ascetic heroism to no purpose; faith in Christ had been weakened and confused by a belief in the very existence of purgatory. People attributed magical powers to sacraments, rather than seeing them as signs confirming faith in the power of God's grace and word.

Like Luther, Calvin found a spiritually edifying worth in suffering. In *The Institutes* he referred to the "cross as medicine" prescribed by "the heavenly physician."[89] He suggested that sufferings increased a believer's communion with Christ.[90] He even went so far as to conceive of suffering helping "in promoting salvation," by teaching patience and obedience.[91] Elsewhere in *The Institutes* he identified suffering as a matter of fatherly chastisement, a burden of righteousness, and, if borne in the Lord's name, a worthy honor. Finally, Calvin believed that suffering's most powerful therapy was to compel men and women to seek their refuge in God.

Calvin's comforting God was the risen God, who ruled all from the beginning to the end of time. Calvin's providential God, like Luther's, elected his saints before the creation of the earth. The gift of saving grace, was in Calvin's teaching as certain and inscrutable as God's will and foreknowledge. One could not work at one's election by making oneself meritorious by deeds or by suffering; one could only display one's election with confident faith. The believer's final comfort for Calvin could be understood to be most elemental and egotistic: he could believe that he was lucky, and know why he was so lucky; also, he could go happily about his affairs, chosen in them by God, certain to be spared the pains of hell and assured eternal bliss. To doubt this was to mar the gift of his good luck.

However, for Calvin election did not exempt one from suffering. Suffering must be accepted as part of God's providence: "If poverty, illness, childlessness, slighting and defeat are our portion and we attribute them to Providence, what comfort we receive in such adversity!"[92] Calvin defined the ideal and dutiful Christian as meeting adversity in the following spirit. "The cup must be drained therefore and the battle won by endurance with undaunted soul. You are God's tool. He wills to wear you out by use not idleness. Oh happy man, whom He calls to work!"[93]

Calvin allowed the believer only the comfort of his faith. He made himself the enemy of all "religious frills." In the words of Evelyn Underhill,

He cast away without discrimination the whole of the traditional apparatus of Catholicism; its episcopal order, its liturgy, symbols, cults. No organ or choir permitted in his churches: no colour or ornament but a table of the Ten Commandments on the wall. No ceremonial acts or gestures were permitted. No hymns were sung but those derived from a Biblical source. The bleak stripped interior of the real Calvinist church is itself sacramental: a witness to the inadequacy of the human over against the Divine.[94]

Underhill further wrote that Calvinism was magnificent in "its uncompromising devotion to God's glory . . . and total rejection of religious comfort and self-interested piety."[95] Yet, she reminded us that austerity concealed "a doctrine of predestination so ruthless that it sees and adores in all things and events—even man's damnation—the inscrutable action of the Divine."[96] Calvin was not alone in teaching that God's justice included eternal punishment for most, and he joined such loving souls as St. Bernard and St. Thomas Aquinas in holding that the contemplation of the suffering of the damned would rank high among the pleasures of the innocent.[97]

Calvin joined Luther in decisively defining the terms of a new lay spirituality.[98] For Calvin, faithful individuals alone constituted the church. As Luther found the faiths of the Hausfrau and the farmer equal to that of the priests and monks, so Calvin held that believers could serve God with righteousness and glory in their everyday calling, be that in army, government, or business. The clergy and the aristocracy were no longer the heroic actors of Calvin's lay world. Holiness no longer required retreat from the world or death in battle. Rather, faithfulness and steadfastness in one's affairs were signs of the highest Christian calling.

The reformers did not conceive any need for special orders of priests and monks, or special religious orders and places like monasteries and shrines. The church organized itself and its teaching to keep the faithful holy and to convert unbelievers. While laws, especially in Calvinist communities, could be rigorously enforced when challenged, such as the merciless murdering of Anabaptists and the prohibition of all profane things like dance, song, and gambling, there was no belief that men and women had to separate themselves from the world. God's glory could be praised by going about one's business in a well-ordered community.[99]

Luther and Calvin further helped articulate the lay spirituality that urban Catholics initiated in the twelfth and thirteenth centuries. While lay and church authority were not done away with, in Christ's name they freed men and women (especially of the urban middle class order) to be themselves in their own daily affairs. Important elements of modern democracy were inherent within the reformers' communities, especially those of Calvin. In these communities there was an essential equality between community members and institutions. No priesthood was acknowledged as having distinct and special powers to carry out human transactions with God on behalf of human suffering; all agents of superstition were rooted out, witches foremost among them.

Despite Luther's and, particularly, Calvin's intentions of returning Christians to the early church, they and their followers—in large part unintentionally—helped prepare believers for the new and emerging secular order of the modern world. For that order, history was profane and nonsacramental. Theology was suspect, speculation and concern about the afterlife was curtailed, and saints and angels became a matter of derision. Miracles became less and less frequent, and they finally stopped occurring almost altogether everywhere, except in the more remote areas of the Catholic countryside. Miracles, God's most dramatic response to human suffering, were considered—just as the reformers would have it—less and less likely means to be used by God.

They were increasingly allowed to exist, especially in rational, middle class, and urban forms of Christianity, only on the condition that they be personal and quiet, private answers to private prayers. All doctrines of the power of sacraments, the intervention of saints, intercessory powers of the church, or any other beliefs implying transactions between individuals and God other than those occurring directly between Christ and his followers were judged to be mere superstitious remnants of a past and dark order. Faith alone was the only legitimate cure for those many, many maladies of which science yet had no knowledge and before which medicine and pharmacy still were but clumsy and ignorant infants.

As an unintended consequence of their teaching, the reformers helped create a world in which holy spaces and sacred time vanished. Nature was no longer a repository of diverse forces and powers, but as everything else, was brought under the sway of a single and uniform providence, which, while concerned for humans, did not interrupt the regular course of things. On this count the reformers' Enlightenment doctrine of providence helped anticipate both deism and rationalism. God became as orderly as the nature scientists were in the process of creating. In this new secular world, Christ was increasingly confined to the heart of the individual and his providential "chair" in heaven, the church was stripped of its powers of mediation, the afterlife lost imaginary vividness, and the believer, with the help of the church and the Bible, must transact in the inner privacy of the self the ultimate meaning of suffering.

In one way, the reformers helped complete the Christian destruction of both primitive and classical views of the world. In the name of God, all other gods had been removed from nature. Now in the name of Christ's singular sacrifice, sacrifice itself was lost to man as the primary means for him to conduct his most important transactions with God. (A moving argument at the Council of Trent to continue to consider the mass as a sacrifice was, "If the mass were not a sacrifice, Christians would have no sacrifice at all, and so would be more unfortunate than the pagans, all of whom have had sacrifice."[100]) In the reformer's ideology, God and faith triumphed over all else.

However, what was true on the plane of ideas was not fully worked out in social reality. Despite the reformer's teachings, whole groups, especially the lower and rural classes, looked for the direct intercession of God, preached great miracles, and foresaw the end of the world and the installation of a whole new order. The majority insisted, no doubt believing in the miracles of the New Testament and all-too-well knowing the needs they had, that God responds more directly to suffering and prayer than Luther and Calvin taught. This separation of official teaching from the masses—a separation the Catholic Church experi-

enced throughout the Middle Ages and even after Trent—is understandable when it is recognized that Luther's and Calvin's message only
aroused short-term meaningful reactions among urban populations to
whom the reformer's messages were almost exclusively directed to the
new laity.[101]

Indeed, many Protestants, particularly in Lutheran lands, continue
to act like Catholics. In the late sixteenth and early seventeenth century, Lutherans were still found who practiced their faith as their medieval forefathers had. They commonly professed their faith in these
terms "I believe in the Virgin Mary, the Mother of God, and Jesus
Christ, her son." Also, they looked for intercession by saints, made the
sign of the cross, continued to believe in the merit of good deeds, prayed
for the dead, said the mass in Latin, insisted that their priests hear their
confessions, used exorcist formulae, rang their church bells to keep
away storms, and adamantly held to their icons and saint days.[102] There
are comparable instances in Calvinist lands of the dominance of medieval beliefs and practices that measure the distance between reformers'
theology and the religious ways of their followers. For example, in Vaud,
Switzerland, from 1630 to 1670, numerous complaints about believers
venerating a tree stump that reputedly cured gout, using a sacred
fountain that took away evil spirits, crossing the border to attend Catholic festivals and dances, and "even observing traditional holidays like
St. Bridle's Day, when no horses were supposed to be worked."[103]
Throughout seventeenth-century Protestant Europe, celebrations of
patron saints and Catholic holidays, as well as concerns for astrology
and witchcraft, had a prominent place. Protestants continued to bar-
gain with God and to expect his grace to display itself in more ways
than creation itself and the electing faith preached by both Luther and
Calvin.

Remarking on how historical change is seldom straightforward and
is often ragged, causing successive historical periods and classes to
overlap, Jonathan Simpton noted how strongly Catholic beliefs and
practices survived amongst Protestants. "A major intellectual transformation may alter the climate of opinion but old ideas have a habit of
persisting. 'Superstitions' were condemned with such vehemence by
Protestant reformers, that it is easy to forget how, even in Protestant
societies, pilgrimages and shrines, relics and miracles, survived the Reformation by more than a century."[104] "Erasmus," a religious reformer
himself, Simpton further wrote, "looked forward to the rapid demise
of the pilgrimage to Santiago. Yet the great Galician sanctuary was
probably more prosperous in the seventeenth century than it had ever
been in the Middle Ages. . . . In Catholic Europe of the eighteenth
century, obscure shrines rose to fame with the same facility as their
ancestors."[105]

The Protestants failed to thoroughly remove the Catholic ideas and practices from their community for roughly the same reason that the Catholic church of the high Middle Ages or the centralizing, Counter-Reformation Council of Trent (1545–63) was not successful in removing paganism and superstition from its members. European men and women, especially from the lower classes and, above all else, the peasantry, had to cope—as the peasantry still does throughout the rest of the world—with great amounts of suffering. Remove it, temper it, sublimate it, give it a purpose—they would use what means were at their disposal not to be overwhelmed by suffering. If this meant magic, superstition, and traditional sacrifices, or vows, deeds, sacraments, faith, or any mixture thereof, so be it. Peasants' commitment to orthodoxy and fear of logical contradiction ranked well below their desire to diminish their pain and give meaning to their suffering. In a world in which education and technological control were scarce and hunger, sickness, and death abundant, Christian faith for the great majority must have been in large part "first and foremost a system of rituals designed to wrench abundant harvests from heaven and persuade the Divinity to avert calamity, to ward off sickness and postpone the dreadful hour of death."[106]

NOTES

1. R. J. Zui Werblowsky, "Anthropomorphism," in *Encyclopedia Judaica*, 16 vols., ed. Cecil Roth (New York: Macmillan, 1972), vol. 3, 433. Werblowsky cites Moses Maimonides as an example of a Jewish thinker who sought to purge Judaism of all anthropomorphism.

2. For a discussion of Christ's relation to suffering, see Herbert Butterfield, *Christianity and History* (London: G. Bell and Sons, 1950), 87.

3. Isaiah 53:7.

4. Revelation 5:6–10.

5. V. M. Oberhauser, "The Lamb of God," *New Catholic Encyclopedia*, 16 vols. ed. William J. McDonald (New York: McGraw Hill, 1967), vol. 8, 339–42.

6. Theologians argue whether or not there would have been the Incarnation at all without sin. Aquinas took the negative position, "Precious Blood," in *New Catholic Encyclopedia*, vol. 11, 706. For a discussion of *Wergild*, see William Chaney, *The Cult of Kingship in Anglo-Saxon England* (Manchester: Manchester University Press, 1970), 222–28. Also expressing the dominance of the sacrificial consciousness in Christianity is the attention paid to Christ's blood. Christ's blood, like his heart, became an object of early Christian theology and popular devotions and came to symbolize the purity of Christ's passion and suffering. At communion, Christians were commanded to drink Christ's blood and eat his body, and thus made themselves part of his sacrifice. The Gospel writers focused on Christ's blood. In Gethsemane he sweated blood. Before Pilate he was flogged and scourged. And along the way to Calvary, he was crowned with thorns. After he died on the cross, out of his pierced side flowed water and

blood, which for the church fathers was the source of the church. In Romans, Paul argued that Christ's expiating blood spared us from God's wrath, Romans 3:21–26; 5:9. In Hebrews it is stated that "sprinkled blood [of Christ] speaks more graciously than the blood of Abel," Hebrews 12:24. In Ephesians it is declared, "In him we have redemption through his blood, the forgiveness of our trespasses, according to the riches of his graces," Ephesians 1:7–10.

7. Oscar Cullmann is quoted here by Karl Löwith, *Meaning in History* (Chicago: University of Chicago Press, 1964), 183.

8. Jaroslav Pelikan, *Jesus through the Centuries* (New Haven: Yale University Press, 1985), 95–108.

9. Ibid., 97.

10. Edward Westermarck, *The Origin and Development of the Moral Ideas*, 2 vols. (London: Macmillan, 1912), vol. 1, 353. Westermarck further remarked here that the sword was often understood to resemble the cross and frequently the name "Jesus" was engraved on its hilt.

11. Pelikan, *Jesus*, 99.

12. Roland Bainton, *Behold the Christ* (New York: Harper & Row, 1974), 144.

13. Cited in A. A. Schacher, "Crucifixion (In Art)," in *New Catholic Encyclopedia*, vol. 4, 494.

14. John 15:12–13.

15. Romans 12:1.

16. For a short discussion of Nietzsche as anti-Christian and seeker of a new conscience, see my chapter, "Friedrich Nietzsche: Beyond Good and Evil," in *Ethics, Living or Dead?* (Tuscaloosa, Ala: Portals Press, 1982, and Marshall, Minn: Venti Amati, 1982), 53–70.

17. F. X. Murphy, "Martyr," in *New Catholic Encyclopedia*, vol. 9, 313.

18. F. X. Murphy, "Martyrium," in *New Catholic Encyclopedia*, vol. 9, 315. Church fathers quarreled over what exactly made a martyr. They especially debated the question of how consciously and voluntarily one's faith had to lead to death in order to be a martyr. However, there was general consensus among the fathers that martyrs' suffering testified to God's special grace and, in some instances, to the presence of Christ himself.

19. For a discussion of the burial places of martyrs as regional centers of healing and miracles, see Aline Rouselle, "From Sanctuary to Miracle Worker: Healing in Fourth Century Gaul," *Ritual, Religion, and the Sacred*, vol. 7 of *Selections From the Annales*, ed. Robert Forester and Orest Ranum (Baltimore: Johns Hopkins University Press, 1982), 95–127, and Peter Brown, *The Cult of the Saints: Its Rise and Function in Latin Christianity* (Chicago: University of Chicago Press, 1981), esp., 113–20. Also, of general interest on what motivated early Christian pilgrims is Ronald Finucane, *Miracles and Pilgrims: Popular Beliefs in Medieval England* (London: J. M. Dent & Sons, 1977), esp. 59–82.

20. Murphy, "Martyrium," vol. 9, 315.

21. J. LeBrun, "Martyrologies," *New Catholic Encyclopedia*, vol. 9, 318. One of the ends of Eusebius during the fourth century of the church was to provide the Christians with a history of their martyrs. The mass itself, as well as the liturgical season, made reference to martyrs. To the horror of the Romans, the Christians not only venerated their martyrs, but they sought help and intervention from these fallen Christians. Apostle-martyrs, like Peter and Paul, John

and James, virgin-martyrs, like St. Lucy and St. Agnes, bishop-martyrs, individual martyrs, and groups of martyrs—all became the honored subject of special daily masses. One mass, for example, on March 10 celebrated the Forty Holy Martyrs. It commemorated the forty soldiers garrisoned in Armenia who, in 320, under the Emperor Licinius, were martyred for refusing to sacrifice to idols. (According to tradition, the forty were thrown naked upon a frozen pond, with a warm bath promised for any individual's recantation. "They prayed as forty had entered the fray, forty might attain the glory. One of them lost courage and plunged into a warm bath prepared nearby, where he died; but one of the guards, touched by divine grace, took his place, and so there were forty martyrs.") Dom Gaspar Lefebvre, ed., *Saint Andrew Daily Missal* (St. Paul: E. M. Lohmann, 1954), 1263.

22. Cited in Murphy, "Martyrs," 313.

23. Ibid.

24. Ibid.

25. Their self-mortification, however, did not exclude many of these ascetics from fulfilling the enormously important social function of inspiring flocks of Christians as well as being consulted by authorities during the fourth to the sixth centuries as civil authority itself entered a period of severe decline. See, Peter Brown, *Society and the Holy in Late Antiquity* (Berkeley: University of California Press, 1982).

26. Chaney, *The Cult of Kingship*, 80.

27. G. P. Fedotov, *The Russian Religious Mind* (New York: Harper and Row, 1960), 102.

28. Ibid., 109.

29. Brown, *Society and the Holy*, 15.

30. Brown, *The Cult of the Saints*, esp., 126–27, and his *Society and the Holy in Late Antiquity*, esp., 14–17.

31. Harold Grimm, *The Reformation Era*, 2nd ed. (New York: Macmillan, 1973), 44–45. Also see for a survey of the variety of lives of the saints and their place in the church, Butler's, *Lives of the Saints*, 4 vols., rev. ed. (New York: P. J. Kenedy and Sons, 1962); Maisy Ward, *Saints Who Made History* (New York: Sheed and Ward, 1959), and Lefebvre, *The Saint Andrew Daily Missal*. For a recent volume on saints that shows the limits of social science methodology to establish a significant typology or comparative scheme, see Donald Weinstein and Rudolph Bell, *Saints and Society: Christendom, 1000–1700* (Chicago: University of Chicago Press, 1982).

32. Cited in Jacques Le Goff, *The Birth of Purgatory* (Chicago: University of Chicago Press, 1984), 45.

33. J. Mahoney, "Intercession," in *New Catholic Encyclopedia*, vol. 7, 567.

34. See P. Molinar, "Saints, Intercession of," in *New Catholic Encyclopedia*, vol. 12, 971–74.

35. F. X. Lawlor, "Communion of Saints," in *New Catholic Encyclopedia*, vol. 4, 41.

36. Colossians 1:24.

37. Löwith, *Meaning in History*, 190.

38. Steven Ozment, *The Age of Reform, 1250–1550* (New Haven: Yale University Press, 1980), 242.

39. For a short but useful historical survey of the Catholic sacraments, see Joseph Martos, *Doors to the Sacred* (Garden City, N.Y.: Doubleday, 1981).

40. Eugenius III, cited in Donald Kagan, et al., *Western Heritage*, vol. A, 3rd ed. (New York: Macmillan, 1983), 249.

41. For a brief discussion of indulgences, see P. F. Palmer, "Indulgences," in *New Catholic Encyclopedia*, vol. 7, 482–84 and A. Boudinhon, "Indulgences," in *Encyclopedia of Religion and Ethics*, 12 vols., ed. James Hasting (New York: Charles Scribner and Sons, 1908–27), vol. 7, 252–55.

42. Urban II cited ibid., 253.

43. In his work *The Pursuit of the Millennium* (New York: Harper and Row, 1961), Norman Cohn remarked that in dramatic situations apocalyptic hopes gave rise to uncontrolled feelings, hatreds, and actions. He offers as an example how the hope of retaking Jerusalem during the First Crusade led the crusaders to "demand human sacrifice on a vast scale—not just the self-immolation of the crusaders but also the massacre of the infidel," 48.

44. For a recent study of purgatory, see Le Goff, *The Birth of Purgatory*.

45. Ibid., 357.

46. Ibid. Also, see J. Y. Ryan, "Purgatory," in *New Catholic Encyclopedia*, vol. 11, 1039.

47. Except for its transitoriness and hopefulness, purgatory was modeled on Hell. At the outset of his *Purgatory* (the second book of the *Divine Comedy*), Dante, who was purgatory's most vivid geographer, wrote, "I will sing of that second realm, where the human spirit is purged and becomes worthy of rising to Heaven." Although in Dante's *Purgatory*, suffering exceeds the earth's worst suffering, individuals consigned there are filled with hope. They know that their suffering is just and that they will eventually reach paradise. They only ask that their name be remembered "where the innocent are heard," Dante, *Purgatory*, 8.72.

48. Jacques Le Goff, *La Naissance du Purgatoire* (Paris: Gallimard, 1981), 179.

49. Etienne Gilson argues that in Dante's purgatory the sinful realize the true fullness of their human nature and complete the notion of their own individuality, cited in Erich Auerbach's *Mimesis: Representation of Reality in Western Literature* (Garden City, N.Y.: 1953), 171.

50. Ibid., 176.

51. Le Goff, *Purgatory*, 232–53.

52. On the emerging lay spirituality in the late twelfth and thirteenth centuries, see Michael Goodich, "Childhood and Rebellion of Thirteenth Century Saints," *History of Childhood Quarterly* 1, no. 2 (Fall 1973): 285–309.

53. Marvin Becker, *Medieval Italy: Constraints and Creativity* (Bloomington, Ind.: University of Indiana Press, 1981), 132.

54. Ibid.

55. Ibid., 108. For a general discussion of lay devotion in the twelfth and thirteenth centuries, see Jean LeClerq, et al., *The Spirituality of the Middle Ages*, vol. 2 of *A History of Christian Spirituality*, eds. J. Leclerq, F. Vandenbroucke, and L. Bauyer (New York: Harper and Row, 1982).

56. W. Ulmann, *The Individual and Society in the Middle Ages* (Baltimore: Johns Hopkins University Press, 1966), 69.

57. Le Goff, *Purgatoire*, 315.

58. Ibid., 316.

59. Fasting became, especially for women, a spiritual way to shape their own lives and sacrifices, while preparing themselves for the final banquet with the Lord himself. For a brilliant discussion of the function of food in general and fasting in specific in the lives of women saints in the thirteenth and fourteenth centuries, see Caroline Walker Bynum, *Holy Feast and Holy Fast: The Religious Significance of Food to Medieval Women* (Berkeley: University of California Press, 1987).

60. For a discussion of medieval concepts of the three orders and their power in defining authority, see Georges Duby, *Three Orders: Feudal Society Imagined* (Chicago: University of Chicago Press, 1980). Also of interest on the respective value of the orders is Robert Neville, *Soldier, Saint, and Sage* (New York: Fordham University Press, 1978).

61. For a penetrating discussion of the development of the medieval church's judgment on the value of the work of classes, "from the penitential labor of the Bible . . . toward a rehabilitation of labor which became a means of salvation," see Jacques Le Goff, *Time, Work, and Culture in the Middle Ages* (Chicago: University of Chicago Press, 1982), esp., xii, 53–70.

62. Cited in J. Mead, "Passion of Christ," in *New Catholic Encyclopedia*, vol. 10, 1060.

63. Ibid.

64. Ibid., 1061.

65. For discussions of St. Francis amongst thirteenth-century saints and religious movements, see Goodich, "Childhood," Weinstein and Bell, *Saints and Society*, esp., 48–51, and Friedrich Herr, *From the Beginnings of Western Thought to Luther*, vol. 1 of *The Intellectual History of Europe* (New York: Doubleday, 1968), 130–96.

66. Friedrich Herr, *The Medieval World* (New York: Mentor, 1962), 223.

67. John Moorman, *A History of the Franciscan Order: From Its Origins to the Year 1517* (Oxford: Oxford University Press, 1968), 26.

68. Herr, *The Medieval World*, 230.

69. Christopher Dawson, *Medieval Essays* (Garden City, N.Y.: Doubleday, 1954), 163–64.

70. Some scholars argue that of all the doctrines that sharply define Protestantism—the centrality of faith, the authority of scripture, the sovereignty of God, the calling of the believer, and the priesthood of all believers—only the last did not already have a place in the diverse and differentiating theological movement of the thirteenth-, fourteenth-, and fifteenth-century church. Clearly, in the period preceding the Reformation, theological diversity and a whole horizon of reform movements sharply questioned and openly contradicted every phase of the church authority and practice. This argument against the unprecedented revolutionary character of the Reformation is given additional support by the mounting agreement that the origins of modern secularity are not to be sought in the fundamental beliefs of Protestant faith, but in more recent movements we identify with the centralization of the state and the articulation of the capitalist market system, as well as the spread of literacy, rationalism, nationalism, and democracy. For connections between late medieval thought and the Reformation see Francis Oakley, *The Western Church in the Later Middle Ages*

(Ithaca: Cornell University Press, 1979), esp., 15–25, 313–18; Jaroslav Pelikan, *Reformation of Church and Dogma (1300–1700)*, vol. 4 of *The Christian Tradition* (Chicago: University of Chicago Press, 1984); John Bossy, *Christianity and the West* (Oxford: Oxford University Press, 1985); Heiko Oberman, *Forerunners of the Reformation* (New York: Holt, Rhinehart and Winston, 1966); Steven Ozment, "Homo Viator: Luther and Late Medieval Theology," *The Reformation in Medieval Perspective*, ed. Steven Ozment (Chicago: Quadrangle Books, 1971), 142–54; Ozment, *Age of Reform*.

71. Ozment, *Age of Reform*, 435–36.

72. This formulation of the saving Christ of the cross, was taken from Louis Bouyer, *Orthodox Spirituality and Protestant and Anglican Spirituality*, vol. 3 of *A History of Christian Spirituality* (New York: Harper and Row, 1965), 70.

73. Ibid., 33.

74. Ibid., 34.

75. Ibid., 39.

76. For a discussion of Luther's counsel, see John McNeill, *A History of the Cure of Souls* (New York: Harper and Row, 1951), 163–91.

77. Luther, *Letters of Spiritual Counsel*, ed. Theodore G. Toppert (Philadelphia: Westminster Press, 1955), 93.

78. Ibid., 134.

79. For a discussion of late medieval and Lutheran doctrine of satisfaction and will, see Pelikan, *Reformation*, esp., 22–36, 183–244. In *Christianity and the West*, Bossy contends that Luther did not mean what Anselm did by satisfaction.

What in Anselm had been an offer of compensation adequate to turn away due vengeance and restore amicable relations between offended God and offending man was taken by Luther as a submission to the punishment required by a criminal offence of public character. In Luther's penal or criminal theory of the Atonement, there was no transaction; the parties were not reconciled in the sense entailed by the English word, that two should become one, since the act was purely one-sided. There was no natural or social axiom to explain God's accepting Christ as a substitute for man in general, which in Anselm's theory was explained by kinship; it remained an impenetrable decision.

Bossy added, "Concealed in the Lutheran preaching of justification by faith alone, or later in the Calvinist message that the business of the Christian life was not reconciliation with God but obedience to his sovereign will, it carried instantaneous conviction. By collapsing their foundations it demolished at a stroke whole wings of the edifice of contemporary piety." 93–94.

80. Ozment, *Age of Reform*, 242.

81. Ibid.

82. Ibid., 243. For a further discussion of Ozment's interpretation, see his *"Homo Viator,"* where he apologetically agrees "Luther's *sola fides* is a *viva fides;* it embraces and places the whole man in Christ and frees him to serve his neighbor unmeritoriously," 151.

83. Source found in Roland Bainton, ed., *The Age of the Reformation* (New York: D. Van Nostrand, 1956), 109.

84. Luther, *Three Treatises* (Philadelphia: Fortress Press, 1970), 77.

85. Louis Bouyer, *The Spirit and Forms of Protestantism* (New York: Meridian Books, 1964), 60–61.

86. John Calvin, *Calvin: The Institutes of the Christian Religion*, 2 vols. (Philadelphia: Westminister Press, 1960), vol. 2, 1254.

87. Ibid., vol. 1, 672.

88. Ibid., vol. 1, 670.

89. Ibid., vol. 1, 706.

90. Ibid., vol. 1, 702–10.

91. Ibid., vol. 1, 702.

92. Calvin, "On the Providence of God," cited in Bainton, *The Age of Reformation*, 127.

93. Ibid.

94. Evelyn Underhill, *Worship* (New York: Harper and Row, 1957), 287.

95. Ibid., 288.

96. Ibid.

97. Ibid.

98. For a useful study of the range of interpretations of Calvin, see Basil Hall's "Calvin Against Calvinists," *Huguenot's Society Proceedings* 20, no. 3 (1962), 284–301.

99. For a study of Calvin's Geneva, see William Monter, "Crime and Punishment in Calvin's Geneva, 1562," *Archiv für Reformation* 64 (1973), 281–86. Also useful to understanding Protestant political order is Hans Hilldebrand, ed., *The Reformation: A Narrative History Related by Contemporary Observers and Participants* (Grand Rapids, Mich.: Baker Books, 1964).

100. Cited in Jean Delumeau, *Catholicism between Luther and Voltaire: A New View of the Counter-Reformation* (Philadelphia: Westminister Press, 1977), 15.

101. For a study on the limits of the Lutheran message, see Gerald Strauss, *Luther's House of Learning: Indoctrination of the Young in the German Reformation* (Baltimore: John's Hopkins University Press, 1978), esp., 300–308.

102. For more examples of Lutherans continuing medieval practices of faith, see William Monter, *Ritual, Myth and Magic in Early Modern Europe* (Athens, Ohio: Ohio University Press, 1983), 26–27.

103. Ibid., 46.

104. Jonathan Sumption, *Pilgrimage, An Image of Medieval Religion* (Totowa, N.J.: Rowman and Littlefield, 1975), 302–7.

105. Ibid.

106. Delmeau, *Catholicism Between Luther and Voltaire*, esp., 168–69.

4

Death to Sacrifice: The Eighteenth-Century Revolution Against Transcendence

The dead have no rights. They are nothing. . . . Our creator made the earth for the use of the living and not of the dead.

Thomas Jefferson

Francis Hutcheson launched the Scottish Enlightenment with his 1725 *Inquiry into the Origins of our Ideas of Beauty and Virtue.* . . . But there was one aspect of the book which became the butt of jokes, even among those who admired the general argument of Hutcheson. This was his attempt to measure morality by algebraic formulae. These had, by his second edition in 1726, become fairly elaborate. Thus, where B = Benevolence, A = Ability, S = Self-love, and I = Interest, we get these equations: "M = (B + S) × A = BA + SA; and therefore BA = M − SA = M − I, and B = M − I / A. In the latter case, M = (B − S) × A = BA − SA; therefore BA = M + SA = M + I, and B = M + I / A.

Cited in Garry Wills, *Inventing America*

By the end of the eighteenth century some of the audience could feel the pain of delinquents on the scaffold. The implication, paradoxically, is that inter-human identification had increased.

Pieter Spierenburg, *The Spectacle of Suffering*

As much as any eighteenth-century thinker, Jeremy Bentham (1748–1832) voiced the aspirations of a new humanity. These aspirations, as we will see, contradicted Greek and Christian thinking alike in assuming that man could live without sacrifices and victims and that a rational understanding and an ethical calculus of earthly pleasure and pain were not only possible but alone desirable. These aspirations entirely disregarded the noble's all-important measure of honor and on all counts defied the mentality of Europe's dominant type, the peasant. This new morality affirmed that our fates could be altered for the better by human effort; that we could measure and divide our misery and happiness into calculable pleasures and pains; and finally (defying everything, even what could be imagined) that we need not suffer on this earth. These aspirations contradicted the belief of all people, particularly the peasant, that men and women were born for pain.

The idea that "man was born for pain" was alien to Bentham's life and thought. Bentham himself lived a long life with little pain. The dark and irrational side of life was foreign to him. According to Leslie Stephens, Bentham remained a "child throughout his life."[1] His health was unbroken. He knew no great sorrow. He was by the account of John Stuart Mill a passionless man. No amorous adventure marked his life, and no woman, other than his cook and housemaid, ever entered his life. He was not married and had no children. He was scrupulously neat. His chief luxuries at the table were fruit, bread, and tea. He never drank to excess. Occasionally when he was old he took a half glass of Madiera. He nicknamed his "sacred teapot" "Dick," and he called his faithful walking stick "Dapple." He loved pets, owning a series of cats. Bentham once said, "I love everything which has four legs."[2] "His own lot," J. S. Mill noted, "was cast in a generation of the leanest and barrenest men whom England had yet produced."[3]

Bentham, who liked music, was without any appreciation of poetry in an age of great poetry. Imagination, inspiration, and intuition were missing from Bentham's spirit. The dark side of life eluded his understanding. Religion for him was a matter of self-regarding feelings, which at most might be motivated by concern for reward or punishment or sympathy with God.[4] "Matters of conscience and principles of rectitude he associated with reputation and honor; beauty, order, power and action he didn't even consider as 'springs to action.' "[5] The whole intimate side of human life escaped him and he was oblivious to matters of character.[6]

The primary means of human expression for Bentham were thought and work—and he considered their only positive goal was the improvement of things. He was free of any trace of pessimism. Bentham did not speculate on the limits of human nature. He had no notion that the practice of power often meant tragedy, or that evil itself accumulated in history. Prayer was foreign to Bentham's spirit. He considered faith and sacrifice to be psychological vestiges of a less enlightened age than his own.

Bentham's lifetime preoccupation was the happiness of mankind. For Bentham the world was something to be reformed. He saw it as his duty to chase away what he took to be the cobwebs of centuries.[7] He dedicated his life to the improvement of humanity by the reform of human laws, prisons, politics, and ethics.

Bentham saw those who argued for anything other than pleasure as the end of proper human action as obscurantists; "They were partisans of the principle of asceticism."[8] The ascetics, in Bentham's opinion, were divided into two schools, the moralists and the religionists. The former were motivated by hope for future reputation; the latter were driven by a fear born of "superstitious fancy, . . . punishment at the hands of a splenetic and revengeful Deity."[9] Judging them more extreme than the moralists, Bentham claimed that the religious "have frequently gone so far as to make it a matter of merit and duty to court pain."[10] Bentham considered among the most bizarre aberrations that religious breed of ascetic saints who for the sake of their souls have voluntarily yielded themselves as prey to vermin. Bentham further remarked that none of them, however, when wielding the reins of government ever allowed their preference for pain to pass laws to stock the body politic with highwaymen, housebreakers, and incendiaries, or purposefully turned the nation over to swarms of do-nothings and parasites.[11] Even the ascetics, Bentham held, ultimately took counsel, however distortedly, from the court of pleasure and pain.[12]

In reference to what Bentham took to be a natural attraction for pleasure and aversion to pain, he sought to destroy prevailing religious and legal notions of right and wrong. Bentham sought to reduce society and the moral principles upon which it was based to the most simple human impulses. In the spirit of Bacon, Hobbes, Locke, and Newton, Bentham sought to understand and guide the world in reference to two principles: first, in conformity with Epicurus's philosophy, Bentham argued that humans sought pleasure and avoided pain. Like Epicurus, Bentham sought to disassociate their pleasures and pains from the afterlife and fear of punishment. Second, articulating what is taken to be the essence of his utilitarianism, Bentham contended that the proper social criterion for all human action is: the good magnifies pleasure and minimizes pain for the greatest number of individuals involved.

It was this second principle that accounted for Bentham's commitment to an ethics of consequences rather than an ethics of intentions. Also, this second principle, distinguishing Bentham from Epicurus and the classical aristocracy, led him to pursue happiness by seeking the collective transformation of the world rather than by individually fleeing it.

At times Bentham made arguments on behalf of the fundamental principles of his utilitarianism. More commonly, however, Bentham simply assumed, as did Hobbes, that the entire spectrum of human experience could be reduced to pleasure and pain. Human life is arranged in such a way, according to Bentham, that a person always exchanges a pleasure for a pleasure, or must sacrifice a pleasure or impose upon himself pain for the sake of another pleasure. This is for Bentham the essence of all human action and labor.[13]

Even though Bentham distinguished as many as fifty-eight synonyms for pleasure alone and differentiated seven forms of pleasure and pain (in reference to their intensity, duration, certainty, propinquity, fecundity, purity, and extent), he still theorized as if happiness, enjoyment, and pleasure all characterized the same sensation and as if the two sovereign masters, pleasure and pain, comprehended happiness and suffering.[14] These assumptions allowed him to treat all human experience and values as homogeneous and quantifiable.[15] While Bentham did not reach the arithmetic excesses of his predecessors, like early eighteenth-century moralist, Francis Hutcheson, who offered algebraic formulae for benevolence's relation to morality and self-interest, Bentham was not least among the enthusiasts for stating laws in an age that believed mathematics and reason could measure all. (Hutcheson reached a laughable extreme when he calculated his formula of the good, that was benevolence (B) equals morality (M) plus Interest (I), divided by Ability (A).[16]

Beyond assuming the quantifiable character of human experience and morality, Bentham did not conceive that there were irreducible conflicts between the private and public realms. There were no heroes or saints in his world. Such abiding and pervasive moral dichotomies that characterize matters of honor, faith, and loyalty do not exist in the world of Bentham. Bentham was deaf to such ancient litigants of conscience as the dead and the gods; reason need only calculate for men and women to do the good.

Describing the reductionist character of Bentham's system, Elie Halévy perceptively wrote of the first postulates of the system:

First postulate: pleasure and pain are susceptible of becoming objects of a calculus, and a rational and mathematical science of pleasure is possible. This is what we call the rationalistic postulate of the Utilitarian doctrine. Second postulate: All the individuals who together make up society have an approximately equal capacity for happiness, and are aware that they possess an equal capacity for happiness. This is what we call the individualistic postulate of the Utilitarian doctrine. The value of Bentham's system is the value of these two postulates.[17]

Bentham sought to make himself the Newton of societal reform. Utilitarianism would, he intended, define the highest good, the social good. This reformist impulse, which controlled Bentham's whole adult intellectual life, came in the late 1760s with his conversion to the principle of utility, which Bentham himself later defined: "By utility is meant that property in any object, whereby it tends to produce benefit, advantage, pleasure, good, or happiness . . . or (what comes again to the same thing) to prevent happening of mischief, pain, evil, or unhappiness to the party whose interest is considered: if that party be the community in general, then the happiness of the community: if a particular individual, then the happiness of that individual."[18] Influenced by the Italian theorist of punishment, Beccaria, and the French *philosophe*, Helvétius, Bentham took this principle of utility as the founding principle (the DNA) of a new human moral community.

Bentham used the principle of utility in his first anonymous writing on government to criticize eminent jurist Sir William Blackstone's *Commentaries on the Laws of England*.[19] Bentham argued that Blackstone mistakenly sought justification of the law in tradition and authority on the one hand, and the idealized principles of rights and duties on the other, rather than in the rational study of the most natural and elemental principles of human action and morality that the principle of utility provided.

Bentham, too, sought to apply the principle of utility. In one instance he did this in seeking to design an ideal prison system, which, in large part, he did at his own expense in the 1790s. This project carries the name of Panopticon. In his immense attempt to reform the law of all nations (found in his unfinished Constitutional Code), Bentham attacked all sanctions of religion and law, conscience, and abstract right. He did so in the name of humane utility, which he believed, in contradiction to the French and American Revolutions, provided the real road to human happiness.

Bentham's felicific calculus aimed at the removal of all unnecessary pain and suffering. Underpinning all of Bentham's theorizing was the assumption that all human experience could be broken into its parts: every abstraction could be reduced to things, and every question could be resolved into basic units. Natural rights and duties, such as those put forward by the American and French Revolutions, had no substantive place in Bentham's moral system. The good was simply the proper calculation of the pleasure of social actions. Outdoing the most optimistic medieval thinkers, who saw the bad and evil as only the deprivation of the good, Bentham considered them not as having their source in human will and perversity, but as miscalculations of pleasure. "Vice," Bentham wrote, "may be defined to be miscalculation of chances: a mistake in estimating the values of pleasures and pains. It is a false moral arithmetic."[20]

For Bentham, suffering had no value in itself. It was not a necessary price people must pay for their own integrity or service to their gods. Suffering, like mischief, unhappiness, and misery, was a only a type of pain. The misery that the peasants took to be their whole destiny Bentham took to be a divisible, calculable, and reformable set of pieces. The only place pain and suffering had in Bentham's world was that which nature insisted on having or which society's improvement required. While knowing that punishment was needed socially inflicted pain, Bentham never conceded any intrinsic or enduring place to pain and suffering in human ethical transaction with the self, the other, or the divine.

Sacrifice, the quintessence of consciously chosen and valued suffering, had no value for Bentham. It did not constitute an unrepayable gift or the source of a venerable heroism, nor was it part of humanity's individual and communal transaction with God. The sacrificial requirements of love, friendship, or the duty of Kant's man of goodwill had no place in Bentham's moral universe.

For Bentham, utility replaced sacrifice as the first principle of value. Suffering should give way to happiness. And if for no other reason than this, Bentham was terribly modern, truly revolutionary. This becomes especially true when his rational optimism is set against the realities of his own era.

THE SEARCH FOR AN EARTHLY CALCULUS

In the eighteenth century, sickness, disease, cruelty, and violence were still among the greatest kingdoms holding sway over humankind. Prisoners were still locked in fetters, from which death alone promised escape. Punishments were still cumulative; whole families were banished for the crime of one of its members and the family home was razed. The death penalty abounded for an array of crimes, not the least of which included duelling, forgery, and theft. "In 1787 a parricide had his hand cut off, was broken on the wheel, then consigned to the flames."[21] Torture was frequently used as a preliminary to execution, and there were prisons and workhouses galore in France. Underground dungeons in which men were ankle deep in water were common in the ancien régime. And there were iron cages, like those of the Parliament of France, in which "a man could not stand upright and could stay for years without seeing sunshine, a fire, or a confessor."[22]

Medicine, which by our standards was not yet a science, offered no hope for the majority to escape a short and painful life. Pregnancy and birth were perilous for mother and infant alike. Fevers and infections collected and abounded in hospitals, which, lacking sanitation, were as likely to kill their patients as cure them. And surgery, even if not conducted by a quack or some sort of self-promoting barber, was still lacking quick means to anesthetize patients, to enter their bodies, to quench the bleeding, and to heal the very wounds purported cures inflicted. To surrender yourself to hospital or doctor was to court death.

Speaking of eighteenth-century France in *Death and the Enlightenment*, John McManners commented that of every one thousand infants, only two hundred would go on to live to the age of fifty, and only one hundred to the age of seventy.[23] In the worst case, that of orphans, "Only one foundling in ten lived to reach the age of ten."[24] In the eighteenth century, cold, hunger, starvation, and violence—not particular diseases with specific causes—killed the great majority. Misery still abounded for most. The first physician of Strasbourg reported in the late eighteenth century that misery and despair were common and cited cases of twelve and even fifteen people occupying as little as 120 square feet; people "eaten away with their own excrement, and crawling with maggots"; and a woman who "admitted without emotion that in her extreme want she had killed her child with a meat cleaver, cut off one thigh, and boiled it. Interrogated as to the reasons that made her commit such an act, she indicated that it was poverty, and God had forsaken her."[25]

With the absence of hygiene and sanitary conditions, which was the case for most people other than the prospering middle class, little help could be expected from medicine, which was still a hundred years from being a full-fledged scientific discipline.[26] Diseases were not yet successfully identified. Such names as "putrid angina, complications of humors, looseness, chest pains, itch, catarrhal flux, and shivering fit" suggest the limits of eighteenth-century medical taxonomy. Moreover, explanations of a person's illness in terms of the seasons ("summer boils a man") or the internal movement of his humors suggests the absence of any clear etiology of disease.[27] Cures for the insane were still commonly sought in public beatings, repeated dunkings, and prayer services for their cure. Such vivid examples as wrapping a man's penis in a fowl to cure the pox or having him eat snakes to live forever testify to the abundance of old wives cures and to the superstitions that abounded. Of the bountiful number of quacks, none gained as much notoriety as Franz Mesmer, who, once in the limelight of Paris, joined his theories of animal magnetism to notions of bodily fluids, astrology, and self-help.

The desire to relieve pain drove people to consider all possible remedies. Doctors, seeking to combat the quackery of the abundant painless cures, contended that pain was still a wise provision of nature. Pain, they argued, was even required in order to have a successful operation and cure. It was well into the middle of the nineteenth century before nitrous oxide—laughing gas—and its successor, ether, moved from the fad of smelling intoxicating gases and to become an established element in painless surgery and anesthesia—and it was well into the century before painlessness was not equated with quackery.[28]

The kingdom of pain and misery, which Bentham attacked, still un-differentiatedly ruled the world in the eighteenth century. Suffering made the great majority of society far more irrational than rational, far more desperate than trusting, far more willing to resign themselves to misery than to expect happiness. The majority considered that each man and woman had sufficient pain onto themselves. The loves and hates of one's own family and village sufficed for a lifetime. If one were to survive, one dare not cry the tears of others. Heaven was, if at all, for a time and place beyond this earth.

Bentham disagreed. Bentham denied the assumption that humanity had to live amidst suffering and trade in it to keep the affections of the gods. He dissented from the near universal proposition that as long as there was parent and child, old and young, man and woman, human exchanges of pleasures and pains would be radically asymmetrical and, thus, never fair. Bentham gave no place to irreversible and tragic suf-fering. He resisted any notion that inferred that pain and misery will forever exceed human calculation. Except for sharing the belief that it is better to be pleased than pained and its corollary that some pleasure must be purchased at the cost of some pain, Bentham challenged the old order's first beliefs about pleasure and pain at every point. He de-fied its entire collective imagination with his utopian preachments about a new public order, in which all people would learn to compromise their pains and pleasures for the happiness of the majority and human-ity as a whole.

Bentham, however, was more than a utopian prophet. He was also one of many heirs of a great process of secularization that had been underway since the high Middle Ages. At the heart of this transfor-mation—which both demystified and dechristianized thought and ac-tion—was a radical reevaluation of humanity's place in being. Suffering was no longer conceded to be an integral part of the cosmic order and, accordingly, sacrifice was considered not only gratuitous, but superflu-ous. It was no longer considered to be a fundamental means to authen-ticate self, maintain society, and correspond with God. It was repu-diated as a multidimensional language of human value. Increasingly understood as pertaining to the practices of primitives, restricted to the ceremonies of high churches and their abstract Christian theologies, and, finally, abandoned to the interior processes of individuals, sacrifice no longer commanded cultures and human transactions.

Joined to the reduction of sacrifice's place in human life was the weakening of the hold of the dead and the gods upon the living. As Western men and women enjoyed an improved life, they correspond-ingly took the most important exchanges to be with the living in the here and now. Happiness, less and less, was something remote; more and more it was measurable, tangible, and immediate.[29]

This general process of secularization was associated with profound movements of *laicization* (the end of priestly power), dechristianization, demystification, and desacralization. It marked the displacement of supernaturalist preconceptions with nature as well as attributing autonomous values to the human worlds of personality, work, decision making, social relationships, juridical procedures, socialization, healing, and life transitions.[30]

In the most abstract terms, secularism involved the struggle of reason over faith, science over theology, reform over resignation, progress over tradition, society over nature, city over countryside, state over old order, middle class over aristocracy. Historically, it can be identified with the spread of the rationalizing forces of Catholicism, central monarchies, and urbanism from the Middle Ages onward, insofar as each of these forces, as different as they were, attacked folk and popular understanding of the world.[31] Additionally, secularism is directly associated with a range of movements from the Renaissance and Reformation onward, which seek to purge religion of cultural, traditional, folk, magical, and superstitious accretions. Beyond this, secularism was associated with such cultural and, at points, anti-Christian movements, as civic humanism, classical humanism, skepticism, and relativism, which had profoundly influenced Western intellectual life from the Renaissance onward. Christian reform movements themselves, such as Lutheranism, Calvinism, Deism, and Unitarianism aided, even dovetailed with, secularizing forces. They purged faith and practice of immanentist conceptions of deity, progressively applied the canons of reason to doctrine, and reduced mystical, miraculous, sacramental, and sacerdotal claims. In the eighteenth and nineteenth centuries, such revivalisms as Methodism and Pentecostalism, with their preoccupations with emotional sincerity, also had the effect of denying ritual and sacrifice their traditional places in human life and value.[32] As much as any other thinker, Bentham's work voiced the vast, multifaceted process of demystification, which separated traditional Western attitudes toward suffering and sacrifice from modern attitudes toward them. Bentham served the Enlightenment.

THE DEMYSTIFICATION OF THE WORLD

The Enlightenment can be understood as primarily a Western movement of eighteenth-century thinkers, philosophes, among whom Bentham numbered. The philosophers had among their most important goals the removal of suffering from human life and the mysterious from human consciousness.[33] As they did throughout the great Diderot *Encyclopedie,* they attacked suffering as superfluous in all its forms. They found the notion of the eternal pains of hell incompatible with the idea of the goodness of God. They judged sickness as being solely mechanically determined and worthy only of rapid cure.

They intended to replace ignorance and superstition with reason and light. Their natural enemies were the witch, the magician, the superstitious, the peasant, and the priest. They were antithetical to the medieval, the Gothic, the Roman Catholic—and anything else that they identified as thwarting their hopes for a rational order. The philosophes, who by class origin might be from either the aristocracy or the middle class, were defined by their enthusiasm for rational reform. While the philosophes in majority claimed to find harmony between what they defined as Christianity's essential claims and their own benign rational deism, however, in places, particularly in France, the philosophes moved into direct and open confrontation with Christianity.[34] Their rationalism, modeled on scientific thought, predicated a questioning skepticism that could not but prove antithetical to the doctrinal mysteries of Christianity. In some instances, the most radical philosophes, like Thomas Paine, Baron von Holbach, and others, boldly challenged Christianity, denying its mysteries, miracles, and prophecies as "the three frauds."[35]

Voltaire (1694–1778), exemplary of Enlightened thinkers, attacked Christianity both obliquely and directly. In contradiction to Leibniz, who insisted all that is is good and whom Voltaire made the butt of his satirical *Candide,* Voltaire found no sign of God's providence in the Lisbon Earthquake of 1755, which took between thirty thousand and forty thousand lives. Voltaire responds in verse, asking in a critique of Pope's "Essay on Man," "Ask if pride cries, 'Good Heaven, thy creatures save.' If 'tis presumption that makes mortals cry, 'Heav'n, on our sufferings cast a pitying eye.' All's right, you answer, the eternal cause rules not by partial, but by general laws. Say what advantage can result to all, from wretched Lisbon's lamentable fall?"[36]

For Voltaire man found no hope for his misery in providence, nor did he believe that our prayers would deflect nature upon its course. In an article on "providence" in the *Philosophical Dictionary,* Voltaire taunted the old believers by asserting "I believe in a general Providence, my dear sister, from which has emanated through all eternity the law that governs everything . . . ; but I do not believe that a particular Providence changes the economy of the world for your sparrow or your cat."[37]

Voltaire consistently aimed his most severe attacks against what he took to be ignorant priests and an arrogant church. "The most absurd of despotisms, the most humiliating to human nature, the most contradictory, the most deadly," Voltaire wrote, "is that of priests."[38] "Of all priestly dominations, that of the priests of Christianity is beyond question," he added, "the most criminal."[39] In his *Philosophical Dictionary*

(1764), Voltaire chose, with the use of irony, mockery, and exaggeration, to cast doubt on every essential Christian mystery: the Trinity, providence, the incarnation, miracles, and grace.

Voltaire sought to reduce belief to a rational credo. His faith amounted to God, the rational nature God created, and a humanity that could learn the laws of nature and its maker. Everything else was superstition, according to Voltaire. "Strictly speaking there is no heaven: there is a prodigious quantity of globes which revolve in empty space, and our globe revolves like the others."[40] A real miracle, Voltaire argued, is not a dead man walking two leagues carrying his head in his hands, but it is the admirable order of nature itself: "the rotation of 100 million globes around a million suns, the activity of light."[41]

The empty spaces of infinity, which had so terrified and driven Pascal to belief a century before, had no such similar effect on Voltaire and his fellow philosophes. Considering themselves to be the heirs of Bacon, Descartes, Newton, and others, they spoke as if they were the representatives of a new science that would rationally explain heaven and earth. They viewed nature as autonomous from human needs and God's providence.[42] Nature no longer supported revelational discourse between God and humanity. Nature was no longer a medium for grace and miracle. Nature henceforth was indifferent to human sin and divine mercy. At most, nature was a place where a rational person could encounter the rational laws of his rational maker.[43]

According to Robert Lenoble, this concept of nature was much better armed to attack religion than that of Epicurus and Lucretius.[44] Having the advantages of a body of scientific discoveries, the philosophes stood ready to claim that nature in all facets operated by knowable and predictable laws, which were entirely rational and uncontravenable by God himself.

Some philosophes carried their offensive even further. Late in the eighteenth century (1770 in France and 1780 in England) avowed atheism emerged.[45] Radical philosophes made use of a deterministic view of nature to reduce the hostile forces in the world to knowable mechanisms and to presume that in human technology lay the promise of happiness. "Otherwise stated," Lenoble wrote, "the mastery of the physical world became the means to steal from the bad not only the empire of things but the faith and the soul of men. Moreover, thanks to psychological atomism and to new forms of utilitarianism, by extending laws of the mechanical cosmos to man, they sought to chase from the soul all mystery and every supernatural inquietude."[46] The more enlightened their rationalism was, Lenoble argued, the less it sought reconciliation with religion, seeking in its place a world of total immanence, in which there is "Nothing but earth, nothing but man!"[47] This rationalism was passionate—a mystique onto itself, whose secularized view of nature left man with no reason to pray but only the capacity to reflect upon his place in the order of things.[48]

The philosophes sought to engage in a giant housecleaning of human institutions. They undertook to dethrone the personal God, the linchpin of the Western supernatural world. Christ, Mary, the angels, the saints, and the dead—all with whom Christians bartered, bargained, and supplicated—were understood to stand in the way of rational, calculable, predictable order. Wanting a world in which human beings did and took measure of their own giving and taking, they sought to exorcise all that was irrational, uncontrollable, and incomprehensible. Their first moral program was that humanity first not be in any sense the victim of God and, then, it not be the victim of its own ignorance and power.

Illustrative of the philosophes' attempt to save humanity from being the victim of its own beliefs, Thomas Paine argued that at the corrupt center of supernatural religion was the demand that humanity bow down before "a supernatural tyrant of priestly imagination" who *punished the innocent for the guilty,* who lighted the fire of everlasting torment for the mass of mankind."[49] He considered the Old Testament to be a collection of obscene and debauched stories, filled with "cruel and tortuous executions," and "unrelenting vindictiveness," more worthy of "the word of a demon than the word of God."[50]

On a more theoretical plane, David Hume judged divine providence to be an anthropomorphic concept and monotheism, an attempt to flatter God. He declared the Old Testament's representation of the Almighty as avenging the sins of the guilty upon the innocent to be "indecent if not blasphemous."[51]

Baron von Holbach, one of the most militantly antireligious philosophers, attacked sacrifice itself as the evil essence of all priestly religion: "We find, in all religions of the earth, *a God of armies, a jealous God, an avenging God, a destroying God, a God who is pleased with carnage,* and whom his worshippers, as a duty, serve to his taste. Lambs, bulls, children, men, heretics, infidels, kings, whole nations are sacrificed to him."[52]

The philosophes' desire to spare man useless suffering explains their revulsion to war, violence, ignorance, prejudice, superstition, and sacrifice. For humanity to have its own worth, it must define its own exchanges, be the source of its own gifts, promises, and responsibilities. The philosophes conceded religion an existence only insofar as it was in the service of a fraternal, tolerant, and rational deism. Voltaire, who told his readers in a staggering array of metaphors, "Judaic-Christian religion is a virulent infection, a terrifying madness, *a bloodthirsty monster,*" proposed to reduce religion to merely a matter of public thanksgiving. He wrote Boswell, "Let us meet four times a year in a grand temple with music, and thank God for all his gifts. There is one sun. There is one God. Let us have one religion. Then all mankind will be brethren."[53]

Purposeless suffering confronted the philosophes with a disordered and irrational world, a world that not only heaped boundless pain on humanity but defied the order they now found in the universe and willed in human earthly affairs. Some philosophes, as well as a segment of the urban middle class (who did not live and work daily with animals) were even disturbed by senseless, innocent suffering by animals. Bentham wrote in 1789, "The day may come when the rest of animal creation may acquire those rights which only human tyranny has withheld from them."[54] (While the dog had already established himself in the upper class mind as humanity's true and tested friend, the cat was to wait a century for similar but never equal veneration). Philosophe Karl Linnaeus went so far as to speak of plants as being endowed with a capacity for pleasure and pain.[55] Poet William Wordsworth a few generations later wrote, "Tis my faith that every flower enjoys the air it breathes. I would not strike a flower as many a man would strike a horse."[56]

The philosophes were modernity's intellectual priesthood. Their intention and glory was to remove suffering from the world. Reform in all its forms—the removal of war, relaxation of censorship, religious toleration, abolition of torture, amelioration of serfdom, legal and prison reform, improvement of public health and hospitals—was joined to a broad humanitarian movement whose end was to save humanity from needless pain and suffering.[57]

As much as any other Italian thinker, Cesare Beccaria (1738–94) expressed and shaped the new ethics. In his small volume *On Crimes and Punishment* (1764), Beccaria—whose influence on Bentham was great—technically sought to define a rational punishment that would educate and whose pain would be justified by its proportional pleasurable results. What defined his moral stance and provided him with such a large readership was his passion to end the innocent suffering of his fellow humans, even if they were prisoners. His victims—the victims he would serve—were not living creatures who were offered to supernatural deities but those who suffered torture in the hands of others and under the power of destructive human agencies.[58] Beccaria declared it his purpose

to demolish the accumulated errors of centuries by rising to general principles, curbing at least, with the sole force that acknowledged truths possess, the unbounded course of ill-directed power which has continually produced a long and authorized example of the most cold-blooded barbarity. And yet the groans of the weak, sacrificed to cruel ignorance and opulent indolence; the barbarous torments, multiplied with lavish and useless severity, for crimes either not proved or wholly imaginary; the filth and horrors of a prison, intensified by that cruelest tormentor of the miserable uncertainty.[59]

Beccaria claimed that his life would be consoled "if by defending the rights of man and of unconquerable truth, I should help to save from the spasm and agonies of death some wretched victim of tyranny or of no less fatal ignorance, the thanks and tears of one innocent mortal in his transports of joy would console me for the contempt of all mankind."[60]

In his utopian *Memoirs of the Year Two Thousand Five Hundred* (1771), philosophe Louis Sebastien foresaw a kingdom in which suffering would be eliminated and humanity would not victimize humanity. He foresaw an era when there would be no rack, wheel, dungeon, or galley; when the laws of the land would be so internalized that the guilty man would seek his own death. Humans, in this utopia, would not intentionally cause other humans pain. Occasional *cahiers* on the eve of the French Revolution demanded nothing less than the end of cruel and unusual punishment. The revolutionary Code of 1791 went further. It prescribed for all classes mechanical beheading, claiming that it was the least cruel method according to science. (Dr. Guillotine himself did not design the beheading machine, but he conducted experiments that sought "to prove that severed heads feel no pain."[61])

The philosophes exemplified an age in which the entire elite was less and less resigned to the kingdoms of suffering and death.[62] While death was still familiar to eighteenth-century men and women of all classes, the upper classes no longer fatalistically accepted disease and presumed that early death was a likely eventuality. In the second half of the century, the young abandoned a fatalism about growing old and dying.[63] If not with successful practice at least by presumption, medicine extended its concern to hygiene and the treatment of the handicapped and birth defects. Concern for the condition of the insane increased, and proposals for the reform of asylums multiplied.[64] In the spirit of the era, even the church softened its view of the afterlife. The damned in hell were thought to experience less pain and despair.[65] Hell survived like the Hapsburg and Ottoman empires—and whole kingdoms of Satan, suffering, and religion came apart as the upper classes of the age insisted on earthly pleasure and more and more found the solace of their mortality, not in an eternal afterlife that God provided, but in a posterity of elevated human memory.[66]

THE AUTONOMY OF MAN

The assertion of the autonomy of the human order was not just the consequence of a set of intellectual revolutions from the Renaissance onward. It was also a result of a series of material and social revolutions that since the high Middle Ages had made the upper classes ever more willing to consider this earth their home.

All fields of human activity—from agriculture and navigation to bridge building and mining—displayed new technologies and increases in applied intelligence. Also enhancing the sense of human power was the growing power of the state. Under the guidance of Enlightened despots in the second half of the eighteenth century, European governments from Spain to Russia sought to reform society. They increasingly intervened into matters of commerce, manufacture, defense, and other arenas. Like some new form of providence itself, the state took an interest in all human activity. In the form of the state and its activities, humanity increasingly became its own guardian.[67]

Also, expanding capitalism increasingly suggested a world in which humans were in control and responsible for their own affairs.[68] "To explain humanitarianism, then," Thomas Haskell argued, "what matters in the capitalist substructure is not a new class so much as the market, and what links the capitalist market to the new sensibility is not class interest so much as the power of market discipline to inculcate altered perceptions of causation in human affairs."[69] He further elucidated his point on the origins of eighteenth-century humanitarianism:

What happened was that the conventional limits of moral responsibility observed by an influential minority in society expanded to encompass evils that previously had fallen outside anyone's operative sphere of responsibility. The evils in question are of course the miseries of the slave, which had always been recognized but which before the eighteenth century had possessed the same cognitive and moral status that the misery of a starving stranger in Ethiopia has for us today.[70]

The new definition of contract, conceived as promise between two capable, rational, and responsible individuals, came to rule a civilization. The new ethic of the contract was that men and women could and should carry out their promises.[71] It revealed the new confidence of representatives of business, who now held one another to be in control of and, therefore, responsible for themselves and their actions. If Haskell's thesis is correct, Western humanity's sense of responsibility followed the powers of its commerce.

Although the philosophes themselves were not, in a majority, from the middle class, their preachment about human autonomy coincided with and had the middle class's support. Like the bourgeoisie, the philosophes' notion of the happy life was not the religious contemplative life, nor the aristocrats' refined order. Sacrifices to God and on the battlefield did not win their praise. Rather, the philosophes valued a life dedicated to productive work and reform. Their goods were earthly; most simply defined, they satisfied what they took to be immediate and natural human needs. The philosophes conceived of man, be he economic, political, or in any other field, as meriting what he earned. The person they idealized no longer felt the need to sacrifice himself for the church. He did not make his will an instrument of repentance and amends. Instead, at least as idealized, he dies content, knowing he has lived his life fully. Death—the consummation of human pain, suffering, and helplessness—no longer drove the dying man into the hands of God. As best they could, they sought to die their own death on their own terms.[72]

The philosophes and the bourgeoisie were fellow conspirators in creating an autonomous world. What the philosophes taught with words, the bourgeoisie instructed by action. Elinor Barber wrote:

As social values in other areas of life became more and more secular, as politics, art, and learning, for example, became secularized, and as, furthermore, the commercial and industrial bourgeoisie became an ever larger minority of the population, so it became more difficult for this bourgeois class not to assert, to some extent, the this-worldly and rational assumptions underlying its work and its life. A more general secular morality was now conceivable, and for the bourgeoisie, which had no place in traditional religious and aristocratic conceptions of man and society, it provided a meaningful definition of its human condition.[73]

The pursuit of earthly happiness, as taught by the philosophes and practiced by the bourgeoisie, was inseparable from the amelioration that occurred in the life of Western propertied classes in the course of the eighteenth century. The lofty philosophical doctrine of the natural human pursuit of happiness was anchored in the realm of material fact. Greater numbers of Europeans and Americans than ever before were better fed, housed, and clothed. The doctrine of happiness could be boiled down to more food and drink, better houses, with more comfortable beds and more furniture.[74] Benjamin Franklin considered "a warm house in a country town, an easy horse, some good old authors, cheerful companions, stout ale, a bottle of burgundy, and governing one's passions [as] the *summun bonum* of age."[75]

In some sense, abundance had already started to make and was continuing to make a new European mind and sensibility. Abundance caused a civilization to recalculate its pains and pleasures. Already in the 1690s, according to Joyce Appleby, observations of Englands' growing abundance sparked a "new impulse animating the lively round of goods that encompassed Europe and its colonies in a new trade system."[76] One observer tellingly described society's growing desire for pleasure in these terms, "The wants of the mind are infinite, man naturally aspires, and as his mind is elevated, his senses grow more refined, and more capable of delight; his desires are inlarged, and his wants increase with his wishes, which is for everything that is rare, can gratify his senses, adorn his body and promise the ease, pleasure and pomp of life."[77] Improvements of material life of the eighteenth century supported a spreading hedonism and Epicureanism and, in addition, fueled the age's increasing belief that humanity could take upon itself the ordering of its pleasures and the making of its happiness. The vast convergence of this age's increasing prosperity and utilitarianism was well revealed when John Adams wrote:

Upon this point all speculative politicians will agree, that the happiness of society is the end of government, as all divines and moral philosophers will agree that the happiness of the individual is the end of man. From this principle it will follow that the form of government which communicates ease, comfort, and security, or in one word, happiness, to the greatest degree, is the best.[78]

A NEW EYE OF CONSCIENCE

Eighteenth-century theater, with its *comédie larmoyante* (tearful theater), and early novels expressed this new sensibility. The theater invited the middle class spectator to empathize with the plight of the peasant, the down trodden, and the native.[79] Pity was not new. It was felt by Greek and Roman, Jew and Christian. But the sensibility of this new humanitarianism, Crane Brinton wrote, "differs from the pity or charity of earlier times in many ways. It was based . . . on the very different world view that sees suffering not as part of the order of nature and human nature, above all, not as ordained by God, but as unnatural, as the product of accumulated human errors happily remediable now that we know what the errors were."[80]

The Enlightenment, indeed, provided significant sections of Western upper class populations with a new conscience: a conscience that not only recoiled from pain and suffering as unnecessary and ugly, but a crusading conscience that attacked ignorance and cruelty in whatever forms they appeared, and that made the defense of victims (those who suffered innocently and purposely) its first moral passion. In the following century, it was that conscience (often fired by romantic and revolutionary passions) that formed societies for the prevention of cruelty to animals and children, established laws for the improvement of the life and conditions of the poor, abolished slavery, and gave birth to whole political movements, parties, and radical parties committed to the alleviation of human suffering.

This new conscience asserted a universal duty to establish a new human order. No impediment to this order—be it the vagaries of nature, the unpredictability of God, or the long-standing claims of the dead—was countenanced. Humanity, perhaps the most ethereal abstraction of all, became the new God. Here, in some sense, humanity fell in love with itself. Even such a cynic as Voltaire professed a "love of the human race."[81] Posterity, humanity idealized and perfected, came in the words of Carl Becker "to exorcise the double illusion of the Christian paradise and the golden age of antiquity." "For *the love of god*," Becker continued, "they substituted *love of humanity*, for the vicarious atonement, the perfectibility of man through his own efforts; and for the hope of immortality in another world the hope of living in the memory of future generations."[82]

A new eye was substituted for the omniscient eye of God. Peering into the depths of human conscience was now the eye of humanity reformed, idealized, perfected.[83] This eye has become the first religion and the new conscience of the secular person.

THE STATE AND NEW AND USEFUL SPECTACLES OF SUFFERING

The philosophes had a great ally in the state in their efforts to rationalize and secularize the world. Since the high Middle Ages, the state had warred to make itself the uncontested and legitimate sovereign within the kingdoms of Europe. As De Tocqueville pointed out regarding the ancien regime, the rationalism of the early modern state made it a fierce and constant enemy of the diverse hierarchical, privileged, and exception-filled world of medieval society.

At the heart of the state's quest for power was the attempt to monopolize violence. Historically this meant for the state the need to substitute public punishment for private vengeance. In *The Spectacle of Suffering*, Pieter Spierenburg convincingly argued that starting in the high Middle Ages—the twelfth century to be exact—the state began to attack private vengeance.[84] It not only imposed its law and punishment in matters that once were exclusively understood to belong to the realm of private honor and vengeance, but it elevated its processes of justice and punishment into public advertisements for its dominance. "The emergence and stabilization of criminal justice, a process going on from the late twelfth until the early sixteenth centuries, meant . . . ," Spierenberg wrote, "ultimately, vengeance was transferred from the victims and their relatives to the state."[85]

To illustrate its power to punish, the state established permanent visible sights for executions, erected large and impressive gallows, and appointed executioners. The increasing inviolability of the executioner (the hated hangman who stole the rights of private vengeance and carried out the new state's repression) showed the increasing preponderance of the state and its ability to monopolize and stage-manage the application of public violence. By the eighteenth century, the state with its armies of soldiers, police, officials, and tax collectors could afflict and forgive pain as no other earthly agent. As there were victims of nature, so now clearly there were victims of the state, as Voltaire and other philosophes dangerously pointed out.

As the state became more confident of its power in the course of the seventeenth and eighteenth centuries, it more uniformly and dispassionately inflicted its punishment. No king, no high official need be present any longer at the state's punishment and executions. The state could carry out its business as a matter of certain and regular fate. The state increasingly resembled a machine of punishment that could efficiently and unerringly administer pain.

In the period after 1750, Spierenburg contends, a major revolution in sensibility occurred: the gallows became offensive.[86] The most brutal punishments and terrible deaths, as well as the exposure of the mutilated bodies of the executed, were considered barbaric to the new upper and middle class definers of Western sensibility. This shift in sensibility was, according to Spierenburg, far more important in altering punishment than rationalism and humanitarianism, whose proponents (including Beccaria) used arguments formulated two centuries earlier. Equally important, the more secure states and authorities of Europe no longer found it necessary to punish brutally and publically. Confident of its power to dominate society and increasingly able to avail itself of new opportunities for confinement for enemies, the state curtailed its most ignominious brutalities and removed its punishments from the eyes of the public, placing them in the confines of prisons and penitentiaries.

By the end of the nineteenth century, many of Europe's states had abandoned the need for capital punishment itself. The state no longer needed to sacrifice lives on the altars of its authority, it no longer needed victims for its spectacles of suffering. It was now safe to let the gallows and the hangman become shadowy memories in a forgotten past of pain and horror. The new state's power and legitimacy could be found in its predictable and machine-like efficiency. It could return its punishment to private spaces of prisons and penitentiaries, while it carried on its bid for legitimacy on higher and more noble grounds. It could claim, as we will see in following chapters, that it ruled not by its threats to cause suffering but by its promise of happiness. This was a great revolution. In place of the state, which had won legitimacy by the monopoly of pain, was a new state pledging itself to human happiness.

More and more during the next two centuries people came to expect the state to secure them a happy world. The assumption was—and remains—that the state itself can be tamed.

The guillotine, the instrument of the French Revolution, well illustrated that convergence of the new sensibility and the growing power of the state. Ironically, as Daniel Arasse showed in his recent *The Guillotine and the Terror,* the guillotine was first adopted by the French revolutionists as a benign and scientific instrument.[87] Several arguments underpinned its advocates' thought. First, the guillotine would not botch the job of execution, which many of the executioners did with a misswung axe or an improperly strung rope. Second, it would provide a swift death, ending the prolonged agony associated with torture and executions. Third, in contrast to the old order where aristocrats alone died by being beheaded by sword, the guillotine would serve universal democracy by granting all the same ennobling death by the sharp blade. Furthermore, advocates of the guillotine argued that criminals' bodies would not be subjected to medical experimentation in exchange for release from punishment as Diderot (editor of the *Encyclopedie*) and other philosophes proposed, illustrating how close humanitarianism and utilitarianism could come. No longer would the hangman seek right up to the end additional suffering to compensate wrong or lead the victim to call upon God's mercy. Finally, the maimed body of the executed would not be put on display to demonstrate the wrongness of the crime and the power of the state to punish. The guillotine, proponents argued, would prove to be a painless and efficient machine of justice.

The makers of the revolution, of course, quickly found other uses for the guillotine. Its terror served well the new and nervous state's tenuous authority. The guillotine took the heads of king and queen as quickly as the heads of thiefs, murderers, hoarders, and price gougers. The guillotine's terror was more remote, thus more sublime than the executioner's. It also provided the state with immensely good theatre. Announcing the day's list of the condemned, transporting them to the place of execution, observing their comportment on the way to their death and under the blade, were elements of the live drama of the guillotine. There was also an attractive gore to the spectacle. There was a great spurting of blood from the body. The decapitated head was lifted by its hair and displayed to the crowd, giving everyone a final glimpse of a life before it found its way into the hideous basket that gathered decapitated heads.[88] The decapitated head became the enduring icon of the person; death itself was secularized. And then too, there was the fascinating but imponderable terror that went with the possibility that the severed head of the victim continued to think of his own death after its decapitation. The living head produced a river of gossip and an extensive literature of *les anecdotes sur les decapités.*

The guillotine provided the founding sacrifice of a new order of society. Executing Louis XVI was the sacrifice that gave birth to the new order. Out of his decapitated head a new social body, according to Arasse, was born.[89] The crowd dipped its hands and clothing in the king's blood and shouted out, *"Vive la République!"* The most fervent of the revolutionaires referred to the guillotine as the *sacram sanctam Guillotinam* and a popular litany ran:

> Saint Guillotine, protectress of patriots, pray for us;
> Saint Guillotine, terror of the aristocrats, protect us;
> Kindly machine, have pity on us;
> Admirable machine, have pity on us;
> Saint Guillotine, deliver us from our enemies.[90]

The revolutionary government had anticipated where Western states had been in the preceding two centuries and anticipated where they were to go in the succeeding two centuries. The state had been the primary agent of rationalization and secularization. It would not punish to carry out revenge for private wrongs or to secure each victim his final sacred moment, the sacred *hora mortis* when he might win his salvation.[91] Instead, it controlled punishment and executed victims in accord with its interests in monopolizing violence. As the state's power grew in conjunction with the secularizing growth of capitalism and a rising urban order and middle class, it increasingly tempted ever greater numbers of its citizenry to believe that the state could serve as an agent of its hope. The state, as nationalists, liberals, socialists, and communists came to hope in the nineteenth and twentieth centuries, would diminish humanity's pain and suffering, and secure its pleasure and happiness. Like the guillotine itself, the state—reformers like Bentham and revolutionists like Robespierre believed—would prove a reasonable and just instrument for the progress of humanity. Such optimism itself was a strange spectacle and a dangerous belief.

LAST EFFORTS AT BANISHING MYSTERY

When Bentham was eighty-two he wrote a friend that he was "still in good health and codifying like any dragon."[92] Two years later in 1832, Bentham calmly awaited his death, and as his end drew near, he said to his friend at his bedside, "I now feel that I am dying; our care must be to minimize pain. Do not let the servants come into the room, and keep away the youths; it will be distressing to them, and they can be of no service."[93]

Consistent with his rational pragmatism, Bentham chose to make his body of use to science. Bentham had meditated much on the uses of the dead to the living and the dead, and he saw the dissection of his body as being to the benefit of the rest of humanity.[94] Of less explainable practical motivation, Bentham had his skeleton, "covered with the clothes he commonly wore, and supporting a waxen effigy of his head, carefully preserved in the Anatomical Museum of the University College, London."[95] "Across one knee," biographer Charles Atkinson wrote, "rests his favourite stick, 'Dapple,' and at the foot of the figure lies the skull, with the white hairs of the old man still clinging to its surface."[96] Tradition brings Bentham annually out of his closet to preside over a lecture given in his honor.

Demonstrating just how far Bentham carried his practicality toward death, he wrote in the last years of his life a manuscript titled *Auto-Icon, or the Uses of the Dead to the Living.* In this unpublished work he suggested "how every embalmed man might be his own statue."[97] One of the picturesque suggestions Bentham offered his fellow country dwellers was to alternate trees and auto-icons of their family members along the approach to one's house. He specifically noted that faces of the auto-icons could be varnished and the clothing rubberized to protect them from the elements. Secularism here wore an interesting face.

Bentham had succeeded in his life plan of squeezing every last bit of mystery out of life. Even the dead were converted into the service of humanity.

While Bentham's notions of medically and aesthetically utilizing the dead found no following, his utilitarianism, more than any other single doctrine, voiced the growing commitment of a civilization to secular reform. He offered a vision of human happiness devoid of every speck of the transcendent. The world for him was a matter of pains and problems, of solutions and happiness, and nothing else. Language was "dedivinized"; myth and symbols, however abstract and utopian, were corralled within the physical and the secular.[98]

Bentham and the philosophes set the final imaginative and moral boundaries of socialism and communism, as well as positivism, pragmatism, and technocratism. The ideology of every nineteenth-century reform movement started with the assumption that the world was filled with unnecessary pain and new institutions and technologies could remove it.

Bentham and his followers did not assume that modern people would forever cling to the dead and their own sufferings. Nor did they attribute permanence to human hate, which out of resentment, grudge, or even a sense of fairness insist that one portion of humanity be made to suffer for the suffering caused another. They did not believe that suffering was inevitable, nor did they ever imagine that out of the defeat of undifferentiated suffering—misery—would spring a new world of smaller but infinite particular pains. They left unthought the possibility of a kind of new spiritual Malthusian law of modern civilization that contended: as the lot of humanity was improved, as men and women were given more time and energy to cultivate their pleasures and potentials, their new wants would convert themselves into everexpanding pains and problems, thus outstripping all supplied pleasures and happiness.

The philosophers did not believe what all preceding history seemed to teach: people would insist upon their suffering as a matter of human honor, dignity, and loyalty. They did not see sacrifice, self-imposed pain, and suffering as having an abiding place in all human moral discourse. Nor did they consider suffering as something humans will always insist on inflicting upon one another. In their great optimism, they saw suffering at most, like Bentham's body, as something to be dissected for the good of humanity. It was never more than a currency required for the purchase of happiness.

Bentham and his disciples did not convince everyone. Their dreams were still remote to the new urban masses and the traditional peasants in their fields than Christianity. Indeed, in the course of the nineteenth century, they were the popular target of fellow intellectuals who believed that human existence required suffering, that the suffering of the living was not calculable, that certain kinds of suffering were willed, and that other kinds of suffering not only ennobled the individual but gave special status and redemptive worth to its victims.

Here we encounter that great division of modern conscience, which traditionally is understood to separate the philosophes and the romantics. As Bentham and the philosophes strove to cure humanity with the utility of the greatest happiness for the greatest number, so the romantics sought redemption in suffering and sacrifice. The pain and suffering, which the philosophes dissected and buried, was exhumed, resurrected, and, like Bentham's own body, put on display by the romantics. They made suffering a value.

NOTES

1. Leslie Stephens, *The English Utilitarians,* 3 vols. (New York: 1968), vol. 1, 230.

2. Ibid., 230–31.

3. John Stuart Mill, *On Bentham and Coleridge* (New York: Harper & Row, 1950), 62.

4. Ibid., 66.

5. Ibid., 67.

6. Ibid., 70–71.

7. Ibid., 73–75.

8. John Stuart Mill, *Utilitarianism, on Liberty, Essay on Bentham,* ed. Mary Warnock (Cleveland: Meridian, 1962), 41.

9. Ibid.

10. Ibid., 42.

11. Ibid., 43.

12. For a discussion of Bentham and religion, see David Baumgardt, *Bentham and the Ethics of Today* (Princeton: Princeton University Press, 1952), 98–105.

13. Elie Halevy, *The Growth of Philosophic Radicalism* (Boston: Beacon Press, 1960), 260.

14. Mill, *Utilitarianism*, 69–77.

15. Alasdair MacIntyre, *A Short History of Ethics* (New York: Macmillan, 1966), 234.

16. Garry Wills, *Inventing America: Jefferson's Declaration of Independence* (New York: Doubleday, 1979), 149.

17. Halevy, *Philosophic Radicalism*, 492.

18. Christina Sommers, *Right and Wrong* (New York: Harcourt, Brace & Jovanovich, 1986), 73.

19. Jeremy Bentham, "Fragment on Government," 1776, in *A Bentham Reader,* ed. Mary Mack (New York: Pegasus, 1969), 45–72.

20. Bentham is cited in Ernest Albee, *A History of English Utilitarianism* (New York, 1962), 181.

21. John McManners, *Death and Enlightenment* (Oxford: Oxford University Press, 1985), 369.

22. Ibid., 407.

23. Ibid., cited in Richard Golden, *Social History of Western Civilization,* 2 vols. (New York: St. Martins Press, 1988), vol. 2, 100.

24. Ibid., 105.

25. Cited in Jean-Pierre Peter's, "Disease and the Sick at the End of the Eighteenth Century," in *Biology of Man in History: Selections of the Annales,* ed. Robert Forster and Orest Ranum (Baltimore: The Johns Hopkins University Press, 1975), 82.

26. For a brief study of the history of medicine and its adjoining fields, see Bernard Seeman, *Man Against Pain. 3000 Years of Effort to Understand and Relieve Physical Pain* (New York: Chilton, 1962), and "Medicine, History of," *Encyclopedia Britanica,* 201–4.

27. Seeman, *Man Against Pain,* 96–97.

28. Ibid., 110–17.

29. Wills, *Inventing America,* 164.

30. Brian Wilson, "Secularization," *Encyclopedia of Religion,* ed. Mircea Eliade, (New York: Scribner, 1961), vol. 13, 159–65.

31. For a variety of scholarly essays on the fate of popular culture in early modern European history, see Steven Kaplans, ed., *Understanding Popular Culture: Europe from the Middle Ages to the Nineteenth Century* (Amsterdam: Mouton, 1984).

32. Wilson, "Secularization," 162.

33. For a searching article critical of the notion that the Enlightenment was only a matter of lofty thinkers, see Robert Darnton, "In Search of the Enlightenment: Recent Attempts to Create a Social History of Ideas," *Journal of Modern History* 43, no. 1, (1971): 113–32.

34. For a discussion of the spread of secularism and even de-Christianization, see Michael Vovelle, "Le tournant des mentalités en France 1750–1789: la sensibilité pré-revolutionaire," *Social History* 5, (May 1977), 606–29.

35. See Thomas Paine, *Age of Reason* (New York, 1942), 238. For an exemplary tract of eighteenth-century anti-Christianity, which argues that theology is "a continuous insult to the human mind," see Jean Mesilier's *Superstition in All Ages* (New York: 1972). The work is an alleged abjuration of Christianity by a dying Roman Catholic priest.

36. Voltaire, "The Lisbon Earthquake," in *The Portable Voltaire,* ed. Ben Redman (New York: Viking Press, 1949), 561.

37. Cited in Franklin Baumer, *Religion and the Rise of Scepticism* (New York: 1960), 89.

38. Lucien Goldmann, *The Philosophy of the Enlightenment* (Cambridge, 1973), 68.

39. Ibid., 86.

40. Ibid., 143.

41. Ibid., 311.

42. For elements involved in the secularization of nature, see Philip Sherrard, "The Desanctification of Nature," in *Sanctity and Secularity: The Church and the World,* ed. Derek Baker (New York: Barnes and Noble, 1973), 1–20.

43. For a discussion of deism as an idea that emptied most religious content from God, see E. Graham Waring, ed., *Deism and Natural Religion* (New York: Ungar, 1967), v–xvii.

44. Robert Lenoble, *Histoire de l'idée de nature* (Paris: Editions Albin Michel, 1969), 366.

45. David Berman, "Enlightenment, UnBelief During the, " *The Encyclopedia of Unbelief,* ed. Gordon Stein (Buffalo: Prometheus, 1985), 164.

46. Ibid., 366.

47. Ibid., 368.

48. Ibid., 368–82.

49. Cited in Amato, *Guilt and Gratitude,* 61.

50. Thomas Paine, *Age of Reason,* 24.

51. Cited in Amato, *Guilt and Gratitude,* 61.

52. Ibid.

53. Ibid., 62.

54. Keith Thomas, *Man and the Natural World* (New York: Pantheon Books, 1983), 179–80.

55. Ibid., 108, 179.

56. Ibid., 179.

57. For the relation of love of humanity, reform, and humanitarianism as a new sensibility, see Shelby McCloy, *The Humanitarian Movement in Eighteenth-Century France* (Lexington: University of Kentucky Press, 1957), esp. 1–6.

58. For the etymology of the word *victim,* whose first definitions were exclusively religious and whose general currency dates only from the latter part of the eighteenth century, see *Oxford English Dictionary,* 2nd ed.

59. Cesare Beccaria, *On Crimes* (Indianapolis: Bobbs-Merrill, 1963), 9.

60. Ibid., 10.

61. John McManners, *Death and Enlightenment* (Oxford: Oxford University Press, 1985), 407.

62. For attitudes towards death in the eighteenth century, see McManners, *Death and the Enlightenment*, 85. Also of interest is Philippe Ariès, *The Hour of Death* (New York: Knopf, 1981). Also of interest on the Western attack on death is William Coleman's "Health and Hygiene in the Encyclopedia," *Journal of the History of Medicine and Allied Science* 29 (1974), 399–421.

63. McManners, *Death and the Enlightenment*, 55, 84.

64. Andrew Scull, "The Insane in Modern Society," in *The Other Side*, 3rd ed., 2 vols. ed., Peter Stearns (New York: Harcourt, Brace & Jovanovich, 1984), 145–54.

65. McManners, *Death and the Enlightenment*, 142.

66. Ibid., 148–90.

67. Amato, *Guilt and Gratitude*, 58.

68. Thomas Haskell, "Capitalism and the Origins of the Humanitarian Sensibility," *The American Historical Review* 90, Nos. 2 & 3 (April 1985, June 1985): 339–61 and 547–66.

69. Ibid., no. 2, 342.

70. Ibid., 359.

71. Ibid., no. 3, 560.

72. Ibid., 60.

73. Elinor Barber, *The Bourgeoisie in the Eighteenth Century* (Princeton: Princeton University Press, 1955).

74. Crane Brinton, ed., *The Portable Age of Reason* (New York: Penguin Books, 1977), 20. For a treatment of comfort in the eighteenth century, see Witold Rybczynski's, *Home: Short History of an Idea* (New York: Viking, 1986), esp. 51–121.

75. Howard Mumford Jones, *The Pursuit of Happiness* (Ithaca: Cornell University Press, 1966), 79.

76. Joyce Appleby, "The Birth of Consumer Society," "Consumption in Early Modern Social Thought (Paper delivered at the Clark Lecture Series, University of California, Los Angeles, Spring, 1989), 9.

77. Ibid.

78. Ibid., 97.

79. Crane Brinton, *A History of Western Morals* (New York: Harcourt, Brace & Jovanovich, 1959), 308–28.

80. Ibid., 309.

81. Voltaire's professed "love of the human race," cited in Brinton, *A History of Western Morals*, 310.

82. Carl Becker, *The Heavenly City of the Eighteenth-Century Philosophers* (New Haven: Yale University Press, 1932), 130; emphasis added.

83. Amato, *Guilt and Gratitude*, 57.

84. Pieter Spierenburg, *The Spectacle of Suffering: Executions and the Evolution of Repression: from a Preindustrial Metropolis to the European Experience* (Cambridge: Cambridge University Press, 1984).

85. Ibid., 10.

86. Ibid., 183–99.

87. Daniel Arasse, *The Guillotine and the Terror* (New York: Penguin, 1989), 7–25.

88. Ibid., 93–132.

89. Ibid., 48–72.

90. Ibid., 74.

91. Ibid., 30.

92. Jeremy Bentham, *Dictionary of National Biography,* ed. Sir Leslie Stephen and Sir Sidney Lee, 22 vols. (Oxford: Oxford University Press, 1964), vol. 2, 269–80.

93. Charles Atkinson, *Jeremy Bentham, His Life and Works* (New York: Augustus Kelly, 1969), 207–8.

94. Bentham, *National Biography,* 276.

95. Atkinson, *Jeremy Bentham,* 208.

96. Ibid.

97. Bentham, *National Biography,* 277.

98. Eric Voegelin, *From the Enlightenment to Revolution* (Durham: Duke University Press, 1975), 22–23.

5

An Expanded Heart: A Century of Reform, Feelings, and Empathy

She [France] has shed her blood for you. Oh how poor she is! For your sake she has given without counting.

Jules Michelet, *The People*

The motives, the processes, the mysteries that made man accept religion and expect God to accomplish what he was unable to do, lead him nowadays into politics and make him expect those things from the state.

Jacques Ellul, *The Political Illusion*

The *Titanic* reports do show one thing important to us: distancing of God from the detail of human disaster. . . . The trenches of 1914 to 1918 and the suffering in them insisted terribly on this notion of distance between God and human error.

Owen Chadwick, *The Secularization of the European Mind in the Nineteenth Century*

In 1900 it appeared that Bentham and the *philosophes* had triumphed. In nearly every way, human power had expanded itself. Collectively, humanity was ordering the world in accord with its desire for a better earthly life.

Tracks crossed continents. Canals linked oceans. No part of the globe, except the poles, was any longer considered remote. The nation-state and industrial capitalism were in the process of annexing the world to human power and interest. Almost everywhere in Europe, people had become both more nationalistic and international.

In the Western world, slavery and serfdom had been repealed. Standards of living were being improved almost everywhere in urban and rural Europe. Public health, sanitation, and hygiene all made great progress in their mounting assault against the contagious, diseased, putrid, and singly foul odored.[1] Edward Tannenbaum wrote, "people are better, wore better clothes, and had better health care, more schools, and cheaper entertainment than ever before."[2] The use of torture had been sharply diminished. Especially in Western Europe, children, women, the elderly, the injured, and the worker had become the objects of special concern and legislation. Awareness, responsibility, and guilt sprang up regarding Europe's underclass. *Les misérables* were no longer a pitiful but permanent and unchanging part of humanity. In countless ways, the peoples and institutions of Europe were cleaning themselves up, making themselves more responsible for a fuller and happier human life for all.

Democracy advanced. Europe was moved by a new spirit. Hierarchic and traditional communities were threatened and overturned almost everywhere, and even the most remote European regions and villages were for the first time irreversibly penetrated and influenced by new forces and ideals of market, government, and national life. The old and the traditional were swept aside. While class conflict was real, the notions that each individual was equal in pleasure and pain to every other and that the business of society was social improvement gained ground. Increasingly, governments were judged by the criterion of being rationally beneficent. By century's end, as industry and its calculations were manifestly conquering the world, Bentham's followers were vindicated: human happiness clearly was a fit object of social policy.[3]

"A Royal Commission of 1869 investigated the problems of public health and once again declared that among things 'necessary for civilised social life' were good water supplies and proper drainage, the removal of nuisances (including smoke), healthy houses, clean streets, the inspection of food, and the provision of adequate burial grounds."[4] By 1900, most of the commission's recommendations were on the verge of being accomplished in England. There was no question that the population of this leader of the new democratic industrial order was living longer and better than it ever had before.[5] Even workers, unlike their predecessors of the early stages of industrialization, were more likely in majority to drink to be sociable than to drown their sorrows.[6]

Social progress came by fits and starts. It began in the 1820s, in England, the leader of the industrial and commercial revolution, with Peel's reform of the penal code and prisons and the Catholic Emancipation Act of 1829 and culminated on the eve of the First World War with a river of liberal legislation by Lloyd George's government that covered trade unions, education, child welfare, old age pensions, and national insurance. England had become a happier place. Under the spur of religious, liberal, and socialist consciences, as well as the Benthamite measure of improved law and governmental efficiency, England had transformed itself into a modern society. By the century's end, it was nearly universally agreed that governmental obligation was the health, well-being, and development of its people.

In the nineteenth century, all Western societies had launched attacks against the roots of human misery. Universally, there had been improvements in quarantining procedures against contagious diseases. A greater separation between humans and animals had occurred; this lessened the transmission of diseases. Rising standards of public health required better housing. There was improved sewage disposal, purer water, environmental cleanliness, cleaner air. Also, there were better food standards, as well as higher standards of personal hygiene and nutrition, both of which raised people's resistance to infection.[7] Cholera, tuberculosis, diptheria, typhoid fever, and plague were in retreat throughout the West by the close of the century.

By 1900 a great revolution had occurred. There had been, to use a very apt phrase of Martin Pernick, a "medicalization of human suffering."[8] Disease, sickness, and pain were no longer accepted as a matter of fate. They were now understood to be problems to be broken down, analyzed, and solved. In analyzing typhoid, scarlet fever, and other diseases, scientists formulated the rudiments of epidemiology and public health. In unprecedented numbers, infirmaries and hospitals, armed with the new tools of anesthesia, antiseptics, and surgery, sprung up in the nineteenth century to meet the afflictions of growing urban populations. Qualified public health and administrative officials and professional medical associations of doctors and nurses and surgeons established themselves as society's experts on illness, disease, and pain. Supported by medical schools, a growing body of scientific materials, a new concern for medical records, and laws for certification, doctors and health officials launched a major offensive to take control of the kingdom of pain and suffering. Medicine differentiated itself into specialties to conform to new knowledge and to confront newly diagnosed pains and illnesses.

Medicine had already established a beachhead early in the century with the use of an effective innoculation and vaccine against smallpox.

Thanks especially to the pioneering work of Frenchman Louis Pasteur and German Robert Koch in the new science of bacteriology, which took form in the 1870s, by 1914 medicine had at its disposal a vast range of active and passive vaccines for prophylaxis and therapy.[9] Also, radiation, chemistry, and especially pharmacology offered doctors a new arsenal of means to attack pain.

Nothing taught the revolutionary doctrine of the noninevitability of pain so surely as did the advent of anesthesia. With the successful use of ether and chloroform in the 1840s for surgery, gynecology, and dentistry, the longstanding assumption that pain was the measure of a good operation was increasingly challenged in the following decades. Supplemented by antiseptics and a range of drugs, anesthesia not only opened the door to modern surgery, but it aided democracy by contradicting persistent older beliefs that held that different sexes, groups, and races were meant to bear different amounts and types of pain. Anesthesia's message ultimately was democracy's and Bentham's: individuals are equal in their pain and their potential happiness.[10] Anesthesia spread hope for a painless world.

By the end of the nineteenth century, commented Guy Williams, "Pain had become less inevitable. . . . Good health could be regarded as a normal state of being, to be expected and enjoyed by a vast majority of civilized people. In medicine the century was an Age of Miracles."[11]

By 1900 great numbers of the Western upper classes took the possibility of the elimination of suffering to be a moral imperative. What was once considered to be only a matter of the afterlife or the dream of the land that could never be, now was internalized and represented a new interior force. This imperative, whose headwaters are the teachings of the philosophes, grew in the course of the nineteenth century. Among the most important tributaries of this new conscience, were the West's ever increasing technological, economic, and political powers. Also adding to this new conscience were the mounting claims of liberals, socialists, union leaders, philanthropists, and others that man owed man freedom, justice, subsistence, education, and yet other things required for a full and happy life. By 1900 an awesome horizon of problems and victims, on the one hand, and possibilities, and dreams, on the other, had been assembled before the Western conscience for deliberation and action. God, his providence and miracles, were driven inward, retaining their vitality only in the hearts of believers and the confines of the churches.[12] The saints and shrines lost almost all their power to cure believers in the urban middle and upper classes—and even no longer ruled securely among the peasants and the villages of rural Europe.

In the course of a century, the human heart had been immensely expanded. People now felt responsible for more than they ever had before. This new sensibility exceeded any specific form of conscience, any particular claim to justice, any special cause, movement, or program. Dominating so much of the Western conscience, rhetoric, and politics, this sensibility determined the moral assumptions of a whole civilization. Though it could be vague, diffuse, and contradictory, this sensibility, nevertheless, clustered around the moral imperative that suffering was wrong and something should be done about it. Individuals, groups, parties, bureaucracies, and whole nations were taken hold of by the new sensibility as they "discovered" the horrible but now curable suffering of poverty, homelessness, prisons, child abuse, old age, malnutrition, and other evils. At times the horizon of problems and victims created by new powers and aspirations became in their numbers and myriad forms crushing and a matter of despair. Eugen Weber explained this paradox of "the discrepancy between material progress and spiritual dejection" in these terms: "Higher expectation at every level made deviance more depressing, better information more ominous, and traditional acceptance more difficult to maintain."[13] Weber additionally explained this paradox that was so exaggerated in turn of the century France and is so bitingly familiar to us in the contemporary United States in these terms,

So much was going right even in France, as the nineteenth century ended; so much was being said to make one think that all was going wrong. That need not be surprising. Public discourse turns mostly about public matters—especially politics; and the style of politics calls for catastrophic imagery. A great deal of political debate [which vies for the majority's sharply limited interest in it] either takes place on the brink of doom or envisions it looming on the horizon.[14]

In *The Idea of Poverty,* Gertrude Himmelfarb postulated the existence of "a new moral imagination in the nineteenth century." [It] could no longer take comfort in the ancient adage, 'For ye have the poor always with you.' "[15] "Whatever progress has been charted on the graph of 'progress and poverty,' " she further remarked, "it is poverty that still strikes the eye and strikes at the heart. It is as if the modern sensibility can only register failure, not success, as if modernity has bequeathed to us a social conscience that is unappeasable and inconsolable."[16]

This new moral imagination was predicated on an ever expanding sympathy to all who suffer or who may potentially suffer. In its most generalized form, this imagination (not dissimilar to Kant's categorical imperative) stood beyond any specific cause or desired consequence. It dictated that the good is to make oneself universally accountable for the alleviation of all suffering present and possible.

This sensibility—committed to a great clean up and affecting a great reversal in Western consciousness about the very personage of suffering and death—accounted for the formation of whole new armies of victims. First and foremost among the victims were the poor, who formed for writers, politicians, and social reformers alike, an alternate nation. Afflicted by this sensibility, the young novelist and future English prime minister, Benjamin Disraeli, wrote in *Sybil* (1845) of the poor and the rich: "Two nations; between them there is no intercourse and no sympathy; who are as ignorant of each other's habits, thoughts, and feelings as if they were dwellers in different zones, or inhabitants of different planets."[17] Throughout the century, streets were lighted up, roads made wider, and government reports filed, and the poor emerged with an ever stronger role in the moral imagination of emerging middle class civilization.

Workers, women, children, and the elderly, the sick, and the handicapped followed the poor onto the stage of moral conscience. Misery, so common to and so manifest in the old order, was not even allowed to be hidden in private dwellings, dark hovels, and blocks of concentrated slums. Revealing this moral surge of reform that moved the American progressive period, John Spargo wrote in *The Bitter Cry of the Children*,

For each evil, however, there was thought to be a remedy. Full of buoyant optimism, men and women banded together in countless charitable, rescue and humane societies to prevent and alleviate the social and economic malaise. Private philanthropy poured millions of dollars into the channels of reform. Inspired by the example of the Toynbee Hall in London, social workers rapidly established settlement houses in the slums of the nation's great cities, institutions that became elaborate social service agencies and "spearheads for reform." The churches adapted themselves to the demands of "socialized Christianity," and the state supplemented the work of private agencies through legislative regulations and appropriations.[18]

The ability, indeed the very compulsion, to conjure a world free of suffering showed itself at its extremes with an increasing interest in euthanasia and eugenics: if suffering could not be cured, its very source would be obliterated. In 1908 the Eugenics Education Society was formed; in 1912 the first international eugenics congress was held in London. A recent "Plea for Beneficent Euthanasia" revealed one part of the sensibility of its proponents: "We reject theories that imply suffering is inevitable or that little can be done to improve the human condition. We hold that the tolerance, acceptance, or enforcement of the unnecessary suffering of others is immoral."[19] The desire to avoid pain led some people to embrace systematic doctrines for either preventing or ending life and others to the more extreme position of arguing, better no life at all than one of suffering. It was as if suffering were a foul pollutant in whose very presence no dignified or decent person could live.

Members of humane societies in England and America, whose numbers sharply increased in the last decades of the nineteenth century, extended their sympathy to the animal kingdom. Their origin, according to James Turner, was utilitarianism and the French Revolution: the former stressed the importance of the pain the animal suffered and the latter suggested the rights that belong to every creature.[20] (Scot John Oswald, in 1791, "hailed the French Revolution as offering hope to animals as well."[21])

"In 1800," James Turner wrote, "sympathy was a tenuous, fitful, and often superficial response to the distress of others. By 1900 compassion for suffering was second nature. It is hard to overestimate the importance of this revolution. On it depends much of our literature, a great deal of our religion, and not a little of our politics."[22] He continued: "To ignore the critical role of love of animals in shaping and disseminating this modern sensibility would be blind. . . . By nurturing a compassion for animals, they had nourished as well a broader humane impulse, a hostility to pain and suffering in human being and animal alike."[23] One observer, Harriet Ritvo in *The Animal Estate,* saw the transformation of England in the early nineteenth century into a nation that came to love its pets. People had grown stronger and "animals became significant primarily as the objects of human manipulation. . . . Once nature ceased to be a constant antagonist, it could be viewed with affection and even, as the scales of power tipped to the human side, with nostalgia."[24]

In *Man and the Natural World: A History of Modern Sensibility,* Keith Thomas noted that by the late Victorian period, "Some humanitarians"—as if they were our contemporaries today—"would urge the right of animals to 'self realization.' "[25] While animal advocates (almost always from upper urban classes) could be selective and fickle with their empathy for suffering—for instance, they could care more about stray cats than abandoned children and be more outraged by the lower class's dog fights than the upper class's fox hunting—most often they established a linkage between animal and human suffering.[26] While "not all animal-lovers were either social reformers or lovers of humanity," very few openly confessed what antivivisectionist Anna Kingsford did: "I do not love men and women. . . . I cannot love both the animals and those who systematically mistreat them."[27]

In most cases, the sensibility that measured the good by a world without suffering, conceived of reform and democracy as serving humans and animals alike. Inspired by Darwin's theory of the origins of life, some people even drew a conclusion, not alien to the thought of Bentham, that animal and human pain were identical. At the end of the nineteenth century, "The Humanitarian League put forward a programme for the reform of prisons, punishments, wages, the poor law and the position of women as part of 'a comprehensive doctrine of humaneness, to be applied to all sentient beings.' "[28]

Going beyond those "whose heart was opened to their dog alone," serious animal advocates universalized their concern. They claimed to care about not just the suffering of a few select domestic animals like the dog, the cat, and the horse, but the suffering of all animals. To the chagrin of the members of the Royal Society for the Prevention of Cruelty to Animals, the antivivisectionists, who proved to be among the most dedicated in the cause to eliminate all animal suffering, split from the Royal Society and established their own society in the 1870s. They sought to move opinion and law against the right of experimental scientists to inflict any pain whatsoever on animals.[29] They were understood by their opponents to argue that no amount of human happiness, real or potential, merited any pain, however slight, to an animal. The antivivisectionists countered, arguing in effect that only "a hardened heart" and "a cruel civilization" would seek its own benefit and enlightenment by means of torture.[30]

This debate involved the definition of suffering and the establishment (if at all possible) of hierarchies and equivalences between types of human suffering and animal suffering. It was inseparable from a host of questions about the means and consequences of trying to secure a painless world for all sentient beings. But, above all else, it revealed a sensibility that was implacable in its conviction that things are not right with humanity, society, or God as long as sentient creatures suffered.

This was the conscience that the philosophes, Bentham, and the French and the Industrial Revolutions, had fathered, and romanticism had mothered. It belonged to men and women who believed they should be free, satisfied, and happy on this earth. This conscience contended that the comfortable and secure domestic order, which eighteenth- and nineteenth-century Western society had provided for the few, should now belong to all. It called for a world in which Bentham and his cat, and the rest of humanity, would be at home.

This sensibility seemed out of place in the expanding Western world of 1900, whose powers, sometimes ruthlessly, almost always totally, overwhelmed the societies, peoples, lands, waters, and animals of the world it encountered. Also, this sensibility stood in sharp antithesis to those pervasive biological, economic, cultural, and social *fin de siècle* doctrines that taught that the world belonged to the strong. It contradicted a century that was preoccupied with human suffering and whose romanticism found the values of individuality, heroism, martyrdom, and even redemption in suffering.

ROMANTICISM: THE CULTIVATION OF SUFFERING AND VICTIMS

There is no question that romanticism added feeling, passion, and compassion to the Enlightenment project of humanity saving humanity. For growing numbers of literate upper and upper middle class Europeans it meant a fuller heart and the greater likelihood that they would make their own suffering and the suffering of others a primary matter of identity.[31]

Romanticism marked a significant, in truth, a cataclysmic, shift of Western sensibility. Whether romanticism's genesis is understood in reference to its formal intellectual beginnings, with such thinkers as Rousseau and the representatives of the German *Sturm und Drang* movement of the 1770s (exemplified by the young Goethe and his early *The Sorrows of the Young Werther*), or is conceived to have its origin in a century-long mounting concern for emotions and sympathy, expressed by such phenomena as the birth of the novel, the new philanthropy of urban and religious thinkers, or the central place of sympathy (fellow feelings) in the ethical systems of such thinkers as David Hume and Adam Smith, romanticism was a true revolution in Western sensibility. Its heirs were nothing less than the two succeeding centuries and the greater place they allotted feelings, passions, empathy, and causes and victims in the Western conscience.

The role of romanticism in fashioning a new sensibility is not without parallel to the effect lay devotion exercised over urban Catholic Europe's spirituality and conscience in the twelfth and thirteenth centuries. Perhaps romanticism and lay devotion both were the consequence of same essential force: as civilization succeeded in expanding its control over diverse facets of life, so too, correspondingly, were ever greater numbers of children of its prospering classes drawn to the cultivation of themselves and their hearts. (There is a kernel of truth in the notion that St. Francis was among the first romantics.)

Secure in some measure in their own environment and freed of the ever-present pain and misery of the traditional rural order, the romantics—the literate youth of a new and prospering order—came to enjoy the privileged position of having choices to make about life and identity. They had a surplus of time, consciousness, and imagination to cultivate themselves. Love and happiness as well as sorrow and melancholy could be considered emotions of choice. Arts and literature themselves served as elaborate devices for making oneself interesting and unique.

Romanticism was about emotions and identities of choice. In comparison to most of the human past, romantics had greater freedom to explore themselves and the world, and to take their explorations seriously. They traveled—from country to city, from land to land, and nation to nation. Their trips were real and imagined, idealized and fantasized. In mind or body, they went to Italy or Greece, Niagara Falls or the Near East. The world was a smaller, safer, and more accessible place. Where one went defined one's identity. The point of romantic traveling, which like medieval pilgrimages served to satisfy curiosity, overcome boredom, and display wealth, was not however to seek physical cures or secure salvation, but to find or declare one's true inner self. Romantics traveled not just across space but also across time. Like Walter Scott, many were infatuated with the Middle Ages. Others, like the Brothers Grimm, hunted down the real German as revealed in distant folktales. Yet others carried out equivalent searches, with the use of other disciplines, to discover the origin of their cherished folk. As Eric Hobsbawm pointed out in his preface to *The Invention of Tradition*, many used history to invent peoples and traditions.[32] In literature, painting, and music, as well as the newer fields of comparative religion and ethnography, romantics defined themselves and their world. Romanticism was a veritable explosion of restless energy, imagination, and empathy.

If psychic mobility was one characteristic of romantics, freedom of choice was another. Revealing a world of greater social change, romantics chose who they were and what they were to be associated with. Romantics made the return to religion fashionable. Many reclaimed their Catholic inheritance, declaring the world of rationalism sterile. Others like Blake (1757–1827) fashioned their own mystical and eclectic religion. Others assented to a range of occult things.

Serving causes and victims went, as the examples of Voltaire and Beccaria make evident, to the heart of the philosophes' passions and identities. However, as a result of the French Revolution and the Napoleonic Revolution on the one hand and a profoundly expanded social imagination and empathy on the other, victims and causes multiplied at geometric rates. Every group that was not at the imagined center and top of society could be, and often was considered to be a victim, a sufferer. There were those denied liberty, rights, and freedom; there were those denied autonomy, tradition, and culture. (Even the peasant, whom the philosophes despised and who by most measures stood for commonplace and unalterable human suffering, began to win sympathy in some circles by the early decades of the nineteenth century. The peasant was usually idealized either as good national stock, basic decent humanity, or the enduring Christian.)

Increasingly in the West, it became contagious, fashionable, and even politically necessary to choose sides among victims. Already by the first

half of the century, there were in existence competing markets of victims: slave (black or Christian), serf, peasant, or worker, or Jew, Pole,
Italian, German, or Greek. Keats and Shelley joined the Greek struggle
for independence; Michelet dedicated himself to the French people and
their revolution for all humanity; Mickiewicz identified Poland, which
did not then exist on the map, as the Christ of nations; and Mazzini
merged the struggle for an Italian republic to all European people's
quest for nationality and freedom. Causes became identities.

Suffering itself became a vehicle for self-identity and expression. One
announced oneself to the world by one's suffering. It became a multifaceted rhetoric. To affirm the intractable presence of suffering in the
human world was a means to contradict the rational world of the reformers. To embrace suffering could be the way to leave the world of
words and books and enter life. Wordsworth, for example, wrote in his
Lyrical Ballads:

> Enough of Science and of Art
> Close up those barren leaves;
> Come forth, and bring with you a heart
> That watches and receives.

Likewise, some thinkers used suffering to argue for religion. Suffering, apologists contended, demanded what reason, science, and reform
could not supply. German and Russian intellectuals used what they took
to be their people's acknowledgment of suffering as proof of the superiority of their souls over the superficial French "spirit" or English
"mind."

Suffering too served the romantics' personal needs. Sorrow, misery,
and suffering provided fertile material for self-dramatization. Identifying oneself with suffering was a way to assert one's own sincerity and
profundity. It served many as a shortcut to "originality." To suffer, as
Jean Jacques Rousseau, founder and master of that art of self-cultiva-
tion, taught, made one sensitive, serious, interesting, something other
than a superficial, materialistic, and vulgar member of the middle class,
whom artists and bohemians, from Baudelaire's time on, condemned
with such righteousness and spleen.[33]

Romanticism established a rhetorical affinity for the suffering of others. Under its influence, nineteenth-century intellectuals enrolled
themselves in the causes of victims. Repeatedly in the course of the
century radical intellectuals tragically martyred themselves for the highest
causes, whilst others as a matter of mere reflex flittered from one fashionable cause to another. No example of a veritable large-scale conta-
gion of empathy is as poignant and pathetic as that mass of Russian
students who, caught up in a wave of 1860s populism (*narodnichestvo*),
rushed to the countryside to join themselves to "the real people."

Causes on behalf of victims provided ideological community and righteousness for their advocates. Ideology is identity in the changing modern world. Identity with victims defines one's allies, one's enemies, one's outrage and one's hope.

Romanticism made victims and their suffering an abiding part of our sensibility, determining our moral discourse with ourselves and the world. Romanticism, furthermore, gave great and revitalized value to suffering, sacrifice, and martyrdom—and, at many points, grafted itself to, and even substituted itself for, a Christian view of a life based on the principle of self-sacrifice. The following discussion of Marx, Dostoevsky, and Nietzsche will underline romanticism's close relationship to suffering and victims as fundamental elements of modern conscience.

MARX: THE REDEMPTIVE SUFFERING OF
THE PROLETARIAT

In one sense, Marx was an ally of Bentham. Despite the profound differences of generations, nationality, class, and philosophical inheritance that separated them, they were both secular to the bone. It was the pains and pleasures, the actions and possibilities of earthly humanity that mattered to them. Neither attributed a personal or a transcendental value to human suffering. Both whole-heartedly supported the dismantling of the old order and welcomed the rationalization and urbanization of life as the road to a new and happier human order. They were both heirs of the Enlightenment.

Marx was one of the secular Enlightenment's most militant children.[34] His ideals were in main derived from eighteenth-century rationalism. Unlike Bentham, Marx was influenced by the contemporary writings of French socialism and German idealism (especially as formulated by Hegel). As a youth he was profoundly romantic. His classic hero was Prometheus on his rock; his contemporary hero was the revolutionist at his barricades. Marx never rejected the romantic theme of humanity saving itself. His narrative—the story line of his rhetoric—turned on the theme of suffering redeemed.

However, God, Christ, and the saints and all the religious sentiments about human suffering were for Marx vestiges of a dark feudal order. Revealing the mixture of Enlightened rationalism and romantic sensibility (especially the late eighteenth-century German *Sturm und Drang* movement, which put a premium on the tormented individual), the young Marx repeatedly returned to the heroic theme of humanity struggling to attain humanness.

A student of idealist philosopher Hegel (1770–1831), Marx also believed that humanity attained itself across history and through struggle. Like Hegel, Marx did not look upon history as an irrational slaughter bench, to use Hegel's own words, "as butchery," as a disordered process in which human suffering and sacrifices are of no value, but saw all its events, even when evil has triumphed and empires are brought low, "as means towards a final end which we believe to be the true result of world history, its substantive destination, its absolute final end."[35] Unlike Hegel, Marx did not conceive of history as the process across which humans come to full consciousness.

Dissenting from Hegel's spiritualization of history but not the purposefulness Hegel attributed to history, Marx saw consciousness following rather than preceding human material development. Marx believed that the emerging order of industrial capitalism would destroy all past orders of human production and give humanity a new relation to nature and itself. Industry would liberate humanity from the toil, drudgery and fatalism and all the rest of the pain and suffering associated with human servitude to nature.

Marx argued that the promise of the Industrial Revolution could not be realized as long as capitalism commanded industry, since it subordinated the promise of industry and humanity to its economic interests. According to Marx, capitalism's nemesis and humanity's victim-liberator-savior is bred within and to be born out of the industrial capitalist order itself. It is the working class, the proletariat. Suffering the worst abuses and injustices of the new industrial order, the proletariat is emptied of all past religious beliefs, family ties, and cultural traditions. All that remains for them is the revolutionary awareness that they have lost everything; yet they, the enslaved majority, can retake everything. Born of absolutely wronged innocence, the proletariat's righteousness is unimpeachable. They are history's greatest and most universal victim. Their revenge would not be, Marx prophesied, a transitory slave's revolt, but the revolution for the new humanity.

The core of Marx's moral indictment of capitalism was based on the notion of the wronged innocence of the proletariat, the new worker of the spreading industrial capitalist order. Marx assumed a labor theory of value; that is, it was labor, not nature, land, scarcity, ingenuity, or other goods, that was the source of human wealth. On an elemental level, as testified to by the young Marx's writings of the 1840s, the labor theory of value meant not just the work embodied in a product, but all the suffering—the pain, abnegation, struggle, and misery—workers endured to make a living, as well as all the sacrifice of their energy, consciousness, imagination, and potential required for them to survive in the capitalist order. Marx wrote in *Wage Labour and Capital* (1849):

Labour is the worker's own life-activity. . . . And this life-activity he sells to another person in order to secure the necessary means of subsistence. Thus his life activity is for him only a means to enable him to exist. He works in order to live. He does not ever reckon labour as part of his life, it is rather a sacrifice of his life.[36]

The proletarians, thus, work against themselves, to use Marx's dialectical language; that is, in the abstract language of his 1844 *Manuscripts*, the proletariat's alienated labor reverses human essence and existence by reducing labor, human essence, to being only a means for existence. At the core here is a type of suffering theory of value: the proletarian's worth is reduced to the condition of victimized labor in the capitalist system.

By raising his horror and revulsion at the condition of the worker to a metaphysical level, Marx revealed the rising expectations of nineteenth-century society. What had been the situation of the vast majority of humanity since time immemorial, which every peasant knew—you will live by the sweat of your brow—became in Marx's work justification for putting philosophy in the service of class revolution. Marx argued that not only was the proletariat cheated in the exchange of their labor (their life energy and blood) for wages but that their being itself was stolen by the capitalist system. The workers' lives themselves were purchased by the boss's wages; their surplus labor was transformed by the capitalist into profit, which permitted the capitalists to purchase yet more factories and workers to exploit human suffering.

The process of capitalist exploitation, according to Marx, turned the proletarian into an emptying vessel by suffering, making the proletariat, in a theological sense, a kenotic Christ. Unconsciously, Marx drew a parallel between the saint and the worker. As the saint prepared himself through ascetics, a "holy emptying" to house God's spirit, so collectively the proletariat's entire being was negated by the discipline of the factory of "ascetic capitalism." All that remained for the proletariat, according to Marx, was revolution, or more precisely, a consciousness as a class that everything had been taken from them and that revolution was the sole means to regain it. With Hegel's slave as its predecessor, Marx's proletariat bore the necessity and the right of revolution.

For Marx, the proletariat's struggle, like Christ's agony on the cross, carried all humanity's promise. "The proletariat," born of the most universalized suffering in human history,

has a universal character because of its universal sufferings and lays no claim to no particular right, because it is the object of no particular injustice, but of injustice in general. This class can no longer lay claim to a historical status, but only to a human one. It is finally, a sphere that cannot emancipate itself without emancipating these other spheres themselves. In a word, it is the complete loss of humanity and thus can only recover itself by a complete redemption of humanity.[37]

Marx justified revolution. "The categorical principle," Marx proclaimed, "is to overthrow all circumstances in which man is humiliated, enslaved, abandoned, and disposed."[38] Doing quintessentially what contemporary advocates of victims do, Marx ethically equipped the proletariat for revolution. He entitled the proletariat with righteousness, attributed to the proletariat absolute innocence and unquestionable potential, argued that their suffering alone mattered, and prophesied that only their revolution mattered.

The proletariat, after the successful revolution, would be, Marx promised, a new species of humankind. Like a Prometheus liberated from his rock, the proletariat would be God; they would command all their energy, intelligence, imagination, and potential to their own ends. They would be free of the past, its myths, moralities, and values; they would no longer exist as a class or in a specialization. They would transcend all divisions between the private and public spheres of life. Between their potential and being, dreams and reality, there would no longer be any discrepancies. Unlike humanity in the past, especially the peasant, whom Marx despised, the new humanity would suffer no more.

What religious and social reactionaries most railed against, Marx proclaimed as an ideal: humanity attains humanity. It exists by and for itself alone; only its work and activity matter. In the future, Marx idealized, not only the ruling classes and their dead and their religions would be banished, but even the source of religion itself, which for Marx arose from a heartless world and soulless circumstances, would be eliminated. Humanity would no longer need to cry out in misery.

DOSTOEVSKY: SUFFERING AS GOD'S CALLING

Voicing a different tradition of romanticism as a rhetoric of suffering, Dostoevsky (1821–81) believed none of what Marx preached. In fact, the axis of his mature works turned around an opposition to Marx and Bentham and their followers' reduction of the meaning of human suffering to earthly calculation.[39]

Suffering is the heart of Dostoevsky's work.[40] His sensibility was shaped by romanticism's new and extended sympathy for the poor, women, children, the brokenhearted, the solitary, and even "the insulted and the injured," to mention the title of one of his early works. Dostoevsky even showed the century's growing sensibility to animal suffering. On the eve of the murder he is to commit, Raskolnikov, the protagonist of *Crime and Punishment* (1866), even dreams of the terrible killing of a horse: a cart overloaded with drunken people made it impossible for the horse to pull, however hard she tried. Her drunken master beat in her skull with a crowbar.

In his story "The Grand Inquisitor"—which forms the heart of Dostoevsky's greatest work, *The Brothers Karamazov* (1880)—godless Ivan asked his holy brother, Alyosha, how could there be forgiveness on this earth, when people did such cruel things: a mother responding to the crying of her child by locking her in a privy and then later, when the child cried, smearing feces in her face, or a landlord feeding a child to his dogs, right in front of the child's mother.

For Dostoevsky life was either frost or furnace. His art was intimately linked to the knowledge that his father was possibly murdered by his peasants. It was inseparable from his exile in Siberia; his epilepsy, which grew worse with age; his financial and psychological anxiety as a writer, made worse by his compulsive gambling; and his resentful dependence on others, especially women. Most horribly, it was possibly linked to his own perverse attraction to young children and his possible corruption of a child, which he, as he read the New Testament, took to be the unforgivable sin. All his works bear the romantic stamp. Dostoevsky's main characters are extreme in their sufferings. They embodied great innocence or evil; they lived by hate or forgiveness; their lives are turbulent. Their individuality is inseparable from their suffering.

His dark heroes are like the fallen angels who so intrigued the romantic mind. They invariably are tormented by secret suffering. They are lacerated by the memory of the suffering they have caused or suffered. Svridrigailov of *Crime and Punishment,* Raskolnikov's dark double, molested a child. Raskolnikov killed a pawnbroker and her sister. Subconsciously Ivan directed his bastard brother, Smerdiyakov, to the murder of their father. Upper class Katerina Ivanova, also of *The Brothers,* offered herself to Dmitri (Alyosha and Ivan's brother) for having saved her father's career, only to be rejected by Dmitri for the more sensual and lower class Grushinka. A young boy in *The Brothers* died of grief, having seen his father towed about by his beard by Dimitri.

Most of Dostoevsky's characters do not find forgiveness. They are murdered or commit suicide. Even when they ask for forgiveness and forgiveness is extended to them, they are too proud to forgive themselves what they have suffered or the suffering they have caused. Evil binds them to their own individuality; suffering turns them upon themselves. They cannot open themselves to God's love. They cannot accept the humiliating suffering they have caused or witnessed.

Opposing Dostoevsky's dark heroes are his saints. They are the simple, the innocent, and the downtrodden. Most often they are women. In all cases they are always humble and meek Christians. For instance, the hero of *The Idiot* (1869), Prince Myshkin, is truly Christ-like. He returns from an asylum in Switzerland to Russia to face the fatal attraction that Rogozhin and Nastasia Filippovna have for each other. Suffering fills the lives of Dostoevsky's saints. It empties them of their earthly pride and vanity, and this emptying *(kenosis)* makes them Christ-like, a vehicle of God's ministering grace. Their suffering propitiates sin and obtains forgiveness.

In Dostoevsky's major novels, earthly saints confront with love and understanding proud and isolated individuals, his fallen angels. Their confrontation establishes the main axis of Dostoevsky's major works.

In the most important of his early works, *Notes from the Underground* (1864), Dostoevsky asserted the abiding place of irrationality and suffering in human experience in direct and irreconcilable contradiction to the West's claims to progress, rationality, and happiness. (To a degree Dostoevsky shared the view of reactionaries like Joseph de Maistre, who contended that God required human suffering in propitiation.[41]) Dostoevsky's underground man describes himself as "a sick and spiteful man." A bureaucrat of forty, he lives by resentment. He cannot—Dostoevsky has the underground man confide to the reader—restrain himself from sticking out his tongue at the Crystal Palace, that structure of steel and glass built in London for the Great Exhibition of the Works of Industry and All the Nations of 1851 that symbolizes the spirit of the new age of humanity. The underground man despises the Crystal Palace and the humanitarianism, rationalism, utilitarianism, and comfortable and painless society it stands for. Explicitly criticizing Bentham, Mill, and Buckle, the underground man contends that the world of science, industry, prosperity, and peace amounts to nothing other than an ant-heap conformity. Asserting the ultimate painfulness of the painless world, he argues that a world without suffering is a world without consciousness. The underground man wishes to smash things and cause suffering.

In vaudeville, for instance, suffering is inadmissible. I know that. In a crystal palace it's unthinkable; suffering is doubt, negation, and what kind of crystal palace would it be if doubt were possible in it: And I am convinced that man will never give up true suffering—that is, destruction and chaos. Why suffering is the sole root of consciousness. Though I declared in the beginnings that consciousness, in my view, is man's greatest misfortune, I know that man loves it and will never exchange it for any satisfaction. Consciousness, for example, is infinitely nobler than two times two. After two times two, there would be nothing left, not only to do, but even to learn.[42]

Dostoevsky's underground man lives alone and by his resentments. He lives in a small and dreadful room. He takes the smallest and pettiest slights to heart. He finds fine society revolting and obscene. People are a constant source of humiliation to him. He needs people, thus he hates them. The smallest and slightest insults, even unintentional ones, hurt him and consume him with the desire to get revenge. (In his mind he is forever getting even by insults, slaps, and even duels, for which he had no capacity whatsoever.) He believes nothing good can come from another human being.

Even when a prostitute, Liza, takes pity on him and truly offers her heart to him, he denies her. He cannot reciprocate. Even after truthfully confessing to her his miserable condition, he is compelled to drive her away. Her tears cannot purify him. He chooses, as if possessed, the conceits of his own selfish mind over the redemptive suffering offered him. He cannot accept the humiliation of love born of true and emptying suffering, but instead chooses the lacerating suffering of unsatisfied pride.

This exchange between the loving prostitute and the perverse civil employee—so starkly set forth in the *Notes from the Underground*—was repeated in all of Dostoevsky's following works. In *Crime and Punishment,* the major work of Dostoevsky that followed *Notes from the Underground,* the young prostitute Sonya sees good in anguishing Raskolnikov, who has killed an old pawnbroker and the pawnbroker's sister (a religious friend of Sonya's) in order to escape the sacrifice that his own sister intends to make for him by marrying a well-to-do bourgeois. Raskolnikov fights the unjudging, accepting, simple, and what he feels to be the profoundly humiliating love of Sonya. Making her love all the more unacceptable, Sonya has prostituted herself to save her family, as Raskolnikov's own sister has planned to do through an unwanted marriage. Raskolnikov, student, intellectual, wants to believe he killed the pawnbroker because he is a superman. He has the right to kill and stand beyond the law, because the strong make the law by their actions. Sonya's love says no one stands beyond human suffering, kindness, forgiveness, and the need of God's pity. Eventually Raskolnikov yields to Sonya's love, telling her at one encounter, "It wasn't you I bowed down to. I bowed down to all suffering humanity."[43] Following Sonya's advice to accept suffering and redeem himself by it, Raskolnikov bows down and embraces the earth itself, asking for forgiveness.[44] Raskolnikov confesses his crime. Seven years later in Siberia, during the spring thaw, he finally accepts Sonya's love.

This theme of the spiritual encounter of the proud and the humble is repeated without such happy endings throughout Dostoevsky's work.[45] Dostoevsky drew certain conclusions regarding suffering, which set him in profound opposition to Bentham and Marx and the secular forces of his era. Suffering, for Dostoevsky, was inescapably part of the human condition. Men and women must live and transact their own affairs and their relations to God with and through suffering. Zossima, the religious elder of *The Brothers,* who perhaps more than any other character voices Dostoevsky's high spiritual wisdom, counsels the women who have lost their children to weep as they must but also to trust in heaven where their suffering will bring reunion and joy. To those who

wish holiness, he counseled, "Be glad as children, the birds of heaven.
. . . There is only one means of salvation, then take yourself and make
yourself responsible for all men's sins, that is the truth."[46]

Dostoevsky—Christian and romantic that he was—insisted that suffering is the road to salvation. It is the way beyond the self. It moves
the person toward sorrow and contrition and toward forgiveness and
hope. Some people are given the grace to put their suffering in the
service of God and others. This suffering is an extension of Christ's
suffering. It helps redeem the world.

Throughout his works Dostoevsky returned to the theme of suffering as redemptive. In metaphor after metaphor, Dostoevsky suggested—and apparently literally believed—that the shedding of tears of
sorrow was required to cleanse man and the world. In his vision everyone belongs to a community whose redemption depends on all others.
Suffering is a necessary price for man's communal redemption. Ultimately, his characters carry forward the agonies of Israel, the salvation
of Christ, and the mission of the church.

This view of the world set Dostoevsky in radical opposition to Bentham and Marx, whose universes were prayerless, without means of
supplication. Dostoevsky belonged, and chose to belong, to a world in
which the living still suffered and prayed and carried on a discourse
with the dead. Spurred on by romantic sensibility, Dostoevsky embraced a Christian world view, as was formulated by a newly revitalized
Russian Orthodox spirituality.

For Dostoevsky, Bentham represented the archetypical bourgeois.
Borrowing what had already become a prevalent aesthetic and social
stereotype of the bourgeois in Bohemia, Dostoevsky depicted Bentham
as a spiritless, soulless, passionless bourgeois.[47] In turn, in conformity
with the era's spiritual anatomy of the bourgeois, Dostoevsky depicted
the bourgeois as a narrow, tight, unimaginative person who heartlessly
calculates all things. He does not know love, feel, or care about human
suffering; the idea of sacrifice exceeded his imagination. He doesn't
suffer. He doesn't sympathize with suffering; he is at home on his little
island of personal and familial happiness. The bourgeois, indeed, was
for Dostoevsky and his romantic contemporaries the antithesis of love,
art, grace, blood, heart. This moral anatomy of the bourgeois still ex-
cites the moral outrage of radicals of the political left and right.

Dostoevsky diagnosed another spiritual form of godlessness at work
among the socialist revolutionaries, who belong to the family of Marx.
Dostoevsky considered their quest to transform the world as a willful
rebellion against God and his creation. The revolutionary (be it Raskolnikov the schismatic, Ivan the atheist, or Stavrogin the skeptic and
Kirilov, who madly identified himself, humanity, and God) seeks to go
beyond conscience, morality, the law, and God. He wills a new order

of human existence. Yet his new order of existence, in whose name the revolutionist kills and commits suicide, promises no new community, but instead conceals the proud and solitary will of the individual to be prince of his own world. He belongs to the kingdom of Satan.

Dostoevsky's view of the antithesis of the earthly kingdom and that of the community of the suffering innocents and Christ not only ultimately separated Dostoevsky from Bentham and Marx but made Dostoevsky a reactionary. Before the choice, which every nineteenth-century Russian intellectual was compelled to make—the choice of whether or not the Russian people should imitate the West or remain true to what they took to be their own inheritance, Dostoevsky chose the side of Pan-Slavism. As a young man under the repressive regime of Nicholas I (1825–55), Dostoevsky, who had identified himself with the Westerners and believed that Russia, like Europe, should have a constitution, free its serfs, and allow a free press, discovered that such sympathies could mean prison, exile, or death. He discovered the truth of what Herzen said: "It is a strange thing that almost all our day-dreams ended in Siberia or the scaffold and hardly ever in triumph."[48] In his mature years, following his own return from Siberia, Dostoevsky rejected progressive European ideals and came to favor Russian nationalism and Orthodox Christianity.

As Russia increasingly became for him an object of religious faith, Europe with all its values and institutions became a matter of passionate negation.[49] Europe stood for godlessness—for materialism, calculation, and individualism, for willfulness and revolution—for what he took to be the essence of Bentham and Marx; Russia conversely, Dostoevsky contended, embodied true Christian suffering and faith. The Roman Catholic church and socialism, quintessentially representative of the West for Dostoevsky, were judged to be power hungry and rationally authoritarian. Dostoevsky even went so far as to assert that even Europe's workers had become capitalists. In Dostoevsky's vision, which contradicted Mazzini and so many western European social romantics' pre-1848 dreams of a European community, Europe was dead. It had lost the meaning of brotherhood, the principle of sacrifice, and the promise of redemption.

Dostoevsky spoke of the spirituality of Russia's redemptive mission. His language was that of the European romantics who spoke of victim-savior peoples. He shared an epochal sensibility with the radical Jules Michelet, who described revolutionary France as those who "watered with blood the tree [liberty] that she had planted;" or one of the voices of failed nationality, Mickiewicz, who described Poland crucified as "the Christ of Nations"; or Mazzini, who also conceived of a suffering Italy, which upon regaining its own state would help redeem humanity.[50]

This faith, which today continues to motivate national and social movements and their preoccupation with the historical rights and mission of victims, contradicted Bentham's and the philosophes' vision of the rational and progressive movement of humanity to its maturity. The articles of this faith—so obviously Jewish and Christian in their messianic quality—saw the peoples of the world as suffering and meriting a unique destiny in which they attained a land, a government, a community, and a strength that, in the first half of the nineteenth century, only England and, to a degree, France had.[51] This faith, whose appeal, of course, was only to literate intellectuals, called for a merging of one's fate with the destiny of one's people and promised nation. Like the early church, the tree of early nationalism, too, was watered by martyrdom. This was the purest of suffering since it carried the full and conscious sacrifice of one's life. It bore the measure of sincerity and earnestness. Priest and democrat, Felicité Lamennais wrote after the fall of Warsaw in 1831, "Heroic people, people of love, rest in peace in the tomb which the crime of some and the cowardice of others have dug for you. But don't forget: that the tomb is not void of hope, it is surmounted by a cross, a prophetic cross which announces: you will be reborn."[52] Everywhere the romantic revolutionist faith reached out to embrace, not just to reach, the poor, women, and children, but also the Jew, the Greek, the Italian, the Pole, the German, all people whose suffering is worthy of historical redemption.[53]

In the world of post-1848, when nationalism (especially in eastern Europe) became increasingly exclusive, Dostoevsky attributed a singular holy mission to Russia—to Russia, alone. He affirmed that its unique suffering as a God-bearing nation separated it from the West. He even argued that Russia was saved by its social and economic "backwardness." Organized around the communal village *(mir)*, the Russian peasant was free of the West's selfish individualism and in his heart still carried a pure image of Christ and of Mary.[54] Free of European egoism, Russia, Dostoevsky chauvinistically contended, had a mission to all humanity. "Russia," Dostoevsky declared, "in conjunction with Slavdom, will utter to the whole world the greatest word ever heard, and that word will precisely be a covenant of universal human fellowship."[55]

Dostoevsky mythologized Russia as a new Israel and a new victim-savior of mankind. He who knew so much about human suffering enrolled himself in what ultimately was an exclusionary community of suffering, in whose name armies would march throughout the world. Dostoevsky, who so valued compassion, ended up without being aware of it serving modern nationalism, which, as no other doctrine, has accounted for so much suffering and death in modern history.

Messianic nationalism historicized Jewish and Christian doctrines of redemption. The failures of the cosmopolitan revolutions of 1848 and the military unifications of Italy and Germany made doctrines of nationalism hard and exclusive. One nation's fulfillment and happiness now seemed to mean another nation's suffering. Claims of innocent suffering became inseparable from the nations' identities and peoples. The issue of victims (who they were and what their rights were) became first a matter of politics. In the name of victims, parties were formed that lay claim to the destinies of Europe and the world and armies were set to marching.

NIETZSCHE: BEYOND SUFFERING

Friedrich Nietzsche (1844–1900), who disliked nationalism in all its forms, read and appreciated Dostoevsky near the end of his life.[56] He who so resembled Dostoevsky's disbelievers and rebels recognized in Dostoevsky a kindred spirit. They were unhappy men. They were complicated and contradictory men. Dostoevsky sought Christian simplicity and Nietzsche hid behind irony. Both were romantics, even though Dostoevsky mocked easy sentimentality and Nietzsche constantly sought to ally himself spiritually with Voltaire against Rousseau. Well in advance of Freud, Nietzsche and Dostoevsky explored the irrationality of the human spirit.

Both were, so to speak, "psychologists of contemporary civilization." However, in their prescriptions, they parted company. Dostoevsky, who had great empathy for the nonbeliever and the atheist, called for a total surrender to God's love, whereas Nietzsche (who expresses for us the last third of the nineteenth century) sought to go beyond God and human suffering, casting his lot with the person, who by will and art, will make the man who is worthy of being. Nietzsche was not unlike the young Raskolnikov, who believed that the good is what the strong wills it to be. Humility, which Dostoevsky saw as a cure, Nietzsche saw as the disease, and the will, which Nietzsche saw as restoring man's health, Dostoevsky diagnosed as the path to destruction. Each man was the other's doctor.

Nietzsche spent his mature intellectual life seeking to free European humanity from the sensibilities that, according to him, made it a weak and sniveling people. Nietzsche attacked the doctrines of inflated nationalism and distrusted all those who claimed to sympathize with suffering humanity. He numbered among his special enemies liberals, sociologists, reformers, philanthropists, and others friends of "suffering humanity."[57]

In the young Nietzsche's romantic eyes, which were shaped by his appreciation of early Greek theater, creation requires destruction. Tragedy's purpose is to destroy the myths, the ideals, and the culture that restrain life. Tragedy, according to Nietzsche, liberates one to make oneself a work of art. For Nietzsche, humanity must create, yet its creations are never permanent: life demands that art be destroyed.[58] From his earliest writings, Nietzsche judged suffering to be the price humanity pays for life and art.[59] For Nietzsche, tragedy and destruction pervade all nature and history. The sublime subjugates terror; the comic releases us from the tedium of the absurd.[60]

This aesthetic and highly cultivated romantic consciousness separated Nietzsche from his age. It gave him a sense of being on "a mountain peak of lonely contemplation where he will have few companions."[61] He called his age spiritless: "Every culture that has lost myth has lost, by the same token, its natural creativity. . . . Only a horizon ringed about by the myths can unify a culture."[62] He judged his age to be without myth, thus devoid of culture; an age of abstract law and abstract government; "a culture without any fixed and consecrated place of origin, condemned to exhaust possibilities and feed miserably and parasitically on every culture under the sun. . . . Here we have our present age, the result of a Socratism bent on extermination of myth."[63] Nietzsche prophesied: "Socratic man has run his course."[64] "All that is now called culture, education, civilization, will one day have to appear before the incorruptible judge, Dionysus."[65]

This tragic aesthetic consciousness inspired Nietzche's thoughts on history. In *The Use and the Abuse of History* (1873), Nietzsche directed history to the same therapeutic ends as he had tragedy. History should destroy what blocks life and foster what ignites the will. "I hate everything," Nietzsche quoted Goethe to say in the first line of his *Use and Abuse of History* "that merely instructs me without increasing or directly quickening my activity."[66] Elsewhere Nietzsche described history "as an enormous heap of indigestible knowledge-stones."[67] In place of this useless history, Nietzsche proposed a critical history, a history that instructed that for life forgetting is as important as remembering. "Everything," Nietzsche remarked, "that is born is worthy of being destroyed."[68] Critical history, Nietzsche argued, should bring "the past to the bar of judgment, interrogate it remorselessly, and finally condemn it. Every past is worth condemning."[69]

Nietzsche's critical history praised Goethe's conscienceless man of action: "He . . . is without conscience, he is also without knowledge: he forgets most things in order to do one, he is unjust to what is behind him, and only recognizes one law—the law of that which is to be."[70] Already at this stage, Nietzsche can be understood to be supporting the myth of the superman—the man who will be the life force of a new order. He owes God and the dead nothing, and he is indifferent to the suffering, the conscience, and the principles of the living.

In the *Genealogy of Morals* (1887) Nietzsche took direct aim at his age's conscience, the source of his era's antilife impulses. In advance of

Freud by a generation, Nietzsche understood that the nature of society itself results in repression. "All instincts," Nietzsche wrote, "that are not allowed free play turn inward. This is what I call man's interiorization; it alone provides the soil for the growth of what is later called man's soul."[71] To be a member of any society, Nietzsche argued, is to have inside oneself a set of ideals about the good, the true, and the beautiful, which serve as an inner censure of all one's instincts. All civilization meant repression according to Nietzsche; contemporary civilization, in his opinion, had the most destructively repressive conscience.

In Nietzsche's view, one source of the repressive-guilt morality was the growth of rational individualism. As if he were speaking in advance for a host of twentieth-century thinkers, Nietzsche wrote in the *Gay Science* (1882) of the dread of being the solitary individual. "During the longest and most remote periods of the human past, the sting of conscience was not at all what it is now. . . . Nothing was more terrible to feel than that one stood by oneself. To be alone . . . was not a pleasure but a punishment; one was sentenced to individuality."[72]

Nietzsche considered "slave morality" as another source of the contemporary guilt. Slave morality came to birth in the resentful person, a creature who, too weak and fearful to compete with others, seeks by thought the nobility that he cannot have in action. The resentful man—that "diminished, hopelessly mediocre, and always savorless contemporary type"—teaches weakness, "the ethics of pity."[73] He kills the strength of others with sermons about the pervasiveness of suffering. Sympathy, empathy, charity, and equality—these were the composing elements of the ethics of pity, which Nietzsche so despised. In the socialist's infatuation with the downtrodden, in the reformers' cosmic altruism, Nietzsche found enemies of the vital and of the strong. If they had their way, everyone would be reduced to his smallest, most pitiable, and suffering self.

Slave morality was, according to Nietzsche, the result of a negative rebellion. The slave, according to Nietzsche, unlike the aristocrat, was created out of opposition. Noble life filled him with envy, jealousy, and resentment. Guilt, morality, and conscience were his favorite means to attack the noble. The slave only had for a life his dark broodings about life; he had nothing to affirm but his resentment. This was his value.

Priests—whom Nietzsche considered "the greatest haters in history"—are the ideologues of the slaves.[74] Bad conscience is their profession. Of all the groups who were responsible for the introduction of slave morality into the spirit of the West, the Jews were most responsible, according to Nietzsche. He called them "the most priestly people of all." Nietzsche contended that all attacks on the powerful and the great seem trivial compared to what the Jews have done, that "priestly people who succeeded in avenging themselves on their enemies and oppressors by radically inverting all their values, that is by an act of the most spiritual vengeance."[75] Nietzsche described their inversion of morals: "It was the Jew who, with frightening consistency, dared to invert the aristocratic value equations good/noble/powerful/beautiful/ happy/favored-of-the-gods and maintain that only the poor, the powerless, are good; only the suffering, sick, and ugly, truly blessed."[76]

In addition to slave morality and repression, Nietzsche postulated another source of the guilty conscience. Taking his cue from the German word *Schuld* (which has debt at its root in the verb *Schulden*, which means to be indebted), Nietzsche argued that all archaic and primitive peoples conceived their transactions as involving a creditor and a debtor. Nietzsche saw the debtor's conscience formed around a recognition of what he had been given and what he must give in return. The debtor's state of being beholden was recognized not only by the creditor's right to find his remuneration among the debtor's goods (including wife and children) but his additional right to have his compensation by exercising cruelty on another. One purpose of punishment, according to Nietzsche, is payments of damages to the injured.[77] Nietzsche sought to find the creditor's compensation in punishment in that well known German concept, *Schadenfreude:* one gains pleasure in another's suffering. It is especially pleasurable to cause that suffering since it testifies to one's power.

In diametrical opposition to "contemporary bleeding hearts," the allies of suffering, Nietzsche affirmed that violence and suffering were intrinsic to human experience. "There is no feast without cruelty, as man's entire history attests. Punishment, too, has its festive features."[78] "To speak of right and wrong," Nietzsche contended, "makes no sense at all. No act of violence is intrinsically 'unjust,' since life itself is violent, rapacious, exploitative, and destructive and cannot be conceived otherwise."[79] Nietzsche did not hesitate to draw the least democratic, non-utilitarian, and antiprogressive conclusion that sacrificing humanity to a single stronger human species would be progress.[80]

Bloody sacrifice, Nietzsche contended, was essential to the spiritual self-definition of archaic peoples. "Early societies were convinced that their continuance was guaranteed solely by the sacrifices and achievements of their ancestors and that these sacrifices and achievements required to be paid back."[81] With this debt acknowledged to their ancestors, who existed in their minds as powerful spirits, "some major act of 'redemption,' some gigantic repayment of the creditor" had to be made to them.[82] Their survival and well-being depended upon it. In this sense of indebtedness, Nietzsche found a kind of logic at work that created more and more powerful ancestors who eventually were transformed into gods.[83] Nietzsche concluded: apropos the emergence of collective guilt in archaic man, "he had inherited from the tribes, together with the tribal gods, a burden of outstanding debt and the desire to make final restitution."[84]

If Nietzsche were to succeed in his genealogy of modern conscience, he had to find the "missing links" between the sources of morality he deciphered in archaic man's collective sense of indebtedness, the aristocratic concept of good and bad, and the slave revolt in morality. For Nietzsche, Christianity was the missing link. Within it slave morality and the sense of indebtedness were joined, thereby creating the religion of the sick conscience. Nietzsche wrote: "Then suddenly we come face to face with that paradoxical and ghastly expedient . . . *God's sacrifice of himself for man*. The creditor offers himself as a sacrifice for his debtor out of sheer love . . . *out of love for his debtor*."[85]

Christianity, Nietzsche defyingly asserted, was the perfect religion for the resentful person. Using his moral logic, Nietzsche argued: all suffering, weakness, miserableness throw the Christian upon his God; all his abnegation and self-denials are understood to win him heaven. Contrariwise, he sees all who yield to their instincts, flesh, or will to be of the Devil and destined to face judgment and hell. With Christianity, Nietzsche asserted, Israel triumphed over classical nobility. The weak and debased took their vengeance against the noble.

Nietzsche asked: "What could equal in debilitating narcotic power the symbol of the "holy cross," the ghastly paradox of a crucified god, the unspeakably cruel mystery of God's self-crucifixion for the benefit of mankind?"[86] "Did not Israel attain the ultimate goal of its sublime vengefulness precisely through the bypath of this 'Redeemer,' this ostensible opponent and disintegrator of Israel?"[87] The Romans, whom Nietzsche considered to be the "most noble people," succeeded to a degree in counteracting and containing the Jewish-Christian fanaticism through their influence on the church, but the German Reformation and the English Reformation again brought forward, with all its virulence, this spiritual disease of eternal guilt and everlasting punishment—"this most terrible sickness that has wasted man thus far."[88] Christianity, for Nietzsche, was based on the hatred of life, with its hopes of a life beyond, its bloody phantasmagoria of the sacrificial animal, the redemptive deed, the holy legend, and its asceticism. It, too, was the creator of the new slaves, teaching equality by virtue of all having claim to an everlasting soul.[89]

The French Revolution was, in Nietzsche's opinion, a result of this Christian doctrine of equality. And these new slaves of equality were, in Nietzsche's interpretation, the weak and the resentful; "the maggot man . . . , the 'tame man,' the hopelessly mediocre and insipid man [who] has already learned to feel himself as the goal and zenith, as the meaning of history, as 'higherman.' "[90]

Nietzsche held Christianity to be responsible for more than the prevalent antilife, "herding-animal morality." Nietzsche judged it to be the deepest source of those sickly reformers, liberals, democrats, and especially socialists, who inherited from it their fetish-like concern for suffering, that fashionable "ethics of pity," that "tragic empathy" for the downtrodden. All this, in Nietzsche's words, was but a secularized *"la nostalgie de la croix."*[91]

In liberalism, socialism, and democracy, Nietzsche saw the results of Christianity.[92] He described liberals, democrats, and socialists as sharing a mutated Christian faith:

At one in their tenacious opposition to every special claim, every special right and privilege (this means ultimately opposition to every right, for when all are equal, no one needs "rights" any longer); at one in their distrust of punitive justice (as though it were a violation of the weak, unfair to the *necessary* consequences of all former society); but equally at one in their religion of sympathy, in their compassion for all that feels, lives, and suffers (down to the very animals, up even to "God"—the extravagance of "sympathy, for God" belongs to a democratic age); altogether at one in the cry and impatience of their sympathy, in their deadly hatred of suffering generally, in their almost feminine incapacity for witnessing it or allowing it; at one in their involuntary beglooming and heart-softening, under the spell of which Europe seems to be threatened with a new Buddhism; at one in their belief in the morality of mutual sympathy, as though it were morality itself, the climax, the attained climax of mankind, the sole hope of the future, the consolation of the present, the great discharge from all obligations of the past; altogether at one in their belief in the community as the deliverer, in the herd, and therefore in "themselves."[93]

In direct relation to his criticism of what he took to be the weak and the morally repressive, Nietzsche lent his philosophy to the strong and the virulent. He took his heroes from early Greece and the Italian Renaissance. He valued men who acted beyond morality, who shaped their age by their desire and will. All moral limits demean the man Nietzsche idealized. He conceived of atheism as a type of "second innocence." In the death of God, which was preached as the good news of his era, Nietzsche saw the birth of a new man: a man who is "beyond good and evil," who does what power and spontaneity command.[94] This new man was for Nietzsche, Zarathustra, Dionysus, the Antichrist, the superman. Nietzsche, in his madness, took himself to be the John the Baptist of the new man, the man who was beyond morality and suffering.

Nietzsche wrote to cover over his own sickness and suffering. Nietzsche asked himself, like Dostoevsky's Svridrigailov, "Am I monster or victim?"[95] His sickness was inseparable from his isolation. Nietzsche was never married. His relations with females were limited and confused, and after his resignation from the university in 1876 for reasons of health and his break with the composer Wagner, Nietzsche's friendships were diminished in quality and number. His works brought only a few readers. Afflicted by a worsening case of syphilis and in the grips of an intensifying hypochondria, Nietzsche ever more desperately sought his own cure by reading, writing, medicine, long walks, and the constant changing of residences, which led him from one lonely boarding house to another. There was a desperateness to his search for peace and health.[96] Madness settled upon him, and more and more, as a paretic—a sufferer from syphilis—he mistook his deepening madness for truth. Indeed, in the 1880s before his final collapse, Nietzsche resembled a Dostoevskyan character. Like Raskolnikov, the more helpless he became, the more he conjured heroic deeds and chased singular transforming ideas to cure himself and transform the world. One day in January of 1899, he emerged from his apartment to see a man beating a horse. He, who in his writing was so indifferent to suffering, was overwhelmed by this experience. Thereafter, his madness could not be concealed; in his letters to friends he spoke of himself as God and the assassin of emperors. He wrote letters to the pope and the king of Italy, signing himself, "The Crucified."[97] Nietzsche was brought home and put under the care of his mother and sister for the next decade, during which time he never regained his lucidity.

Tragically, he, who was so sensitive and had suffered his whole life so much, was among the most intellectually violent of his era. He strove to be hard and indifferent; he took weakness, suffering, and pity to be bad—sympathy, an unwanted inhibition on the spirit of the strong. He conceived of concern for victims as only an impediment to action. He was not alone in contending that suffering and pity should finally have no place in the orders of life and culture.

His writings joined him to all those who believed in the power of the deed and of biological forces. He was spiritually on the side of those who in Darwin's name annexed continents, articulated universal theories of racial superiority, preached the good as the survival of the fittest. He was—if only by extrapolation—on the side of those who in almost every sector of life preached that will, action, and war were the means to settle what words could not. Nietzsche was a vitalist, a sort of protofascist—a man who saw suffering and death as necessary consequences of action by strong men. He was not without parallels to the anarchists who chose to define themselves and the world by their singular deeds.

Indeed, at the turn of the century, the extremes could have been no greater between the varied parties and philosophies that sought to cure all suffering and even to remove all pain from civilization and even nature and those who preached the rights of the powerful to do what they wished, contending that would best serve society, the economy, the nation, and the race. In some sense Nietzsche belonged to the activists—and it is not entirely accidental that among his first readers were the youths whose commitment to vitalism and heroism led them to welcome the First World War. This war would end a century of humanity's most glorious experiment in word, feeling, and action to enlarge the human heart and to end human misery.

NOTES

1. For a provocative French work on Western humanity's growing attack across two centuries against bad smells, see Alain Courbin, *The Foul and the Fragrant: Odor and the French Social Imagination* (Cambridge, Mass.: Harvard University Press, 1986).

2. Edward Tannenbaum, *1900: The Generation Before the Great War,* (New York: Anchor Press/Doubleday, 1976), 9–10.

3. E. J. Hobsbawm, *Industry and Empire* (New York: Penguin Books, 1969), 79. Also useful for a survey of Europe at the turn of the century and the vast transformations underway are Tannenbaum, *1900* and Eugen Weber, *Peasants into Frenchmen: The Modernization of Rural France, 1870–1914,* (Stanford: Stanford University Press, 1976).

4. C. P. Hill, *British Economic and Social History, 1700–1982* (London: Edward Arnold, 1985), 194–95.

5. For a recent and thorough discussion of mortality in England at the turn of the century, see N. L. Tranter, *Population and Society, 1750–1940* (London: Longman, 1985), 64–91.

6. Tannenbaum, *1900*, 18.

7. Hill, *British Economic and Social History,* 65.

8. Martin Pernick, *A Calculus of Suffering: Pain, Professionalism, and Anesthesia in Nineteenth Century America,* (New York: Columbia University Press, 1985), 7.

9. Lydia Mez-Mangold, *A History of Drugs* (Totowa, N.J.: Barnes & Nobles, 1986), 160.

10. This is one of the essential arguments of Pernick's *A Calculus of Suffering.*

11. Guy Williams, *Age of Miracles: Medicine and Surgery in the Nineteenth Century* (Chicago: Academy Publishers, 1987), 1.

12. For a discussion of the place and function of miracles in the nineteenth-century French Catholic church, see Thomas Keelman, *Miracles and Prophecies in Nineteenth Century France,* (New Brunswick, N.J.: Rutgers University Press, 1983.) For a recent historiographical essay on the relatively recent retreat of religion and superstition—*"soeurs ennemies"*—as the primary means for treating all human needs and maladies, see Eugen Weber, "Religion and Superstition in Nineteenth-century France," *Historical Journal* no. 2 (1988): 399–423.

13. Eugen Weber, *France: Fin du Siècle* (Cambridge, Mass.: Harvard University Press, 1986), 2, 21.

14. Ibid., 2–3.

15. Gertrude Himmelfarb, *The Idea of Poverty: England in the Industrial Age* (New York: Vintage Books, 1983), 534.

16. Ibid., 533–34.

17. Cited in Richard Altick, *Victorian People and Ideas* (New York: Norton, 1973), 10–11.

18. John Spargo, *The Bitter Cry of Children* (Chicago: Quadrangle Books, 1968), x–xi. For a general study of social reform and the progressive period and the new sensibility, see Allen Davis, *Spearheads for Reform: The Social Settlements and the Progressive Movement, 1890–1914* (New York: Oxford University Press, 1967) and Robert Bremner, *From the Depths: The Discovery of Poverty in the United States* (New York: New York University Press, 1956).

19. Cited in Marvin Kohl and Paul Kurtz, "A Plea for Beneficient Euthanasia," *Beneficient Euthanasia,* ed. Marvin Kohl (Buffalo, N.Y.: Prometheus Books, 1975), 223.

20. James Turner, *Reckoning with the Beast: Animals, Pain, and Humanity in the Victorian Mind* (Baltimore: Johns Hopkins Press, 1980), 131.

21. Keith Thomas, *Man and the Natural World: A History of the Modern Sensibility* (New York: Pantheon Books, 1983), 185.

22. Ibid., 139.

23. Ibid.

24. Harriet Ritvo, *The Animal Estate: The English and Other Creatures in the Victorian Age* (Cambridge, Mass.: Harvard University Press, 1987), 1–3.

25. Thomas, *Man and the Natural World,* 180. For a survey of a contemporary text on animal rights (rights which a few people have extended even to plants and trees), see Tom Regan, *The Case of Animal Rights* (Berkeley: University of California Press, 1983).

26. For Victorians and their views of and relations to animals, see Ritvo, *The Animal Estate,* reviewed by Stephen Jay Gould, "Pussycats and Owls," *The New York Review* (March 3, 1988), 7–9.

27. Thomas, *Man and the Natural,* 185.

28. Ibid.

29. For information on the humane movement, see Charles D. Niven, *History of the Humane Movement* (New York: Transatlantic Arts Inc., 1967), esp. 79–96.

30. Ibid., 87.

31. For an introduction to romanticism, see Franklin L. Baumer, *Modern European Thought: Continuity and Change in Ideas, 1600–1950* (New York: Macmillan, 1977), 268–301; George L. Mosse, *The Culture of Western Europe: The Nineteenth and Twentieth Centuries* (Boulder, Colo.: Westview Press, 1988), 237–50; Eugen Weber, ed., *Paths to the Present: Aspects of European Thought from Romanticism to Existentialism* (New York: Dodd, Mead & Company, 1960), 15–124; and Howard E. Hugo, ed., *The Portable Romantic Reader: The Age of Romanticism (1756–1848) Mirrored in Poetry and Prose from England, France, Germany, and America* (New York: Viking Press, 1957).

32. Eric Hobsbawm, "The Invention of Tradition," in *The Invention of Tradition,* eds. Eric Hobsbawm and Terrence Ranger (Cambridge: Cambridge University Press, 1983).

33. For a short essay on Rousseau, see my *Ethics, Living or Dead* (Tuscaloosa, Ala: Portals Press, 1982 and Marshall, Minn.: Venti Amati, 1982); for the attitudes of early bohemia, see Jerrold Seigel, *Bohemian Paris: Culture, Politics, and the Boundaries of Bourgeois Life, 1830–1930* (New York: Viking, 1986).

34. The following pages on Marx are based on my *Ethics, Living or Dead?*

25–34. Useful on Marx are Karl Löwith, *From Hegel to Nietzsche: The Revolution in Nineteenth Century Thought* (New York: Holt, Rinehart, Winston, 1964); Sidney Hook, *From Hegel to Marx* (Ann Arbor, Mich.: University of Michigan Press, 1962); Jean Hyppolite, *Studies on Marx and Hegel* (New York: Basic Books, 1969); and Shlomo Avineri, *The Social and Political Thought of Karl Marx* (Cambridge: Cambridge University Press, 1968). A convenient collection of young Marx's writing is Lloyd Easton and Kurt Guddat, eds., *The Writings of the Young Marx on Philosophy and Society* (Garden City, N.Y.: Doubleday, 1967). Among generally useful works on Marx are Isaiah Berlin, *Karl Marx* (Oxford: Oxford University Press, 1978); John H. Jackson, *Marx, Proudhon, and European Socialism* (New York: Collier Books, 1962); George Lichtheim, *Marxism: An Historical and Critical Study* (New York: Praeger, 1961); Robert Tucker, *Philosophy and Myth in Karl Marx* (Cambridge, Mass., 1961). Also, see David McLellan, *Karl Marx* (New York: Penguin, 1976); and Melvin Rader, *Marx's Interpretation of History* (New York: Oxford University Press, 1979).

35. Cited in Carl Frederich, ed., *The Philosophy of History, The Philosophy of Hegel* (New York: Random House, 1954), 14.

36. Cited in Avineri, *The Social and Political Thought of Karl Marx*, 107.

37. Cited in McLellan, *Karl Marx*, 28–29.

38. Ibid., 28.

39. For useful guides to Dostoevsky, see Nicholas Berdyaev, *Dostoevsky* (Cleveland: Meridian, 1957), Donald Fanger, *Dostoevsky and Romantic Realism* (Chicago: University of Chicago Press, 1965), Joseph Frank's *The Seeds of Revolt* (Princeton: Princeton University Press, 1976), Vyacheslav Ivanov, *A Study in Dostoevsky* (New York: Noonday Press, 1963), and David Magarshack, *Dostoevsky* (Princeton: Princeton University Press, 1967). Additionally see Anna Dostoevsky, *Dostoevsky, Reminiscences* (New York: Liveright, 1977), Ronald Hingley, *Dostoevsky: His Life and Work* (New York: McGraw-Hill, 1978), and George Panichas, *Burden of Vision* (Grand Rapids: Eerdmans, 1977).

40. Suffering marks Dostoevsky's personal life. Literary and financial quarrels with fellow writers and editors supplied him with intimate knowledge of scandal, envy, pettiness, and resentment. Living on the edge of scarcity, Dostoevsky hungered for recognition, and his life frequently was characterized by a desperate frenzy to gain it. Dostoevsky's intimate relations were marked by great ambivalence. He had the darkest, most divided feelings about his father, whom he believed was killed by his own peasants. He wrestled with his feelings about his mother. He was both thankful for how much she had given him and greatly resentful for how much she expected from him. Dostoevsky also felt a crucial sense of unpayable debt to his sister and his wife. The model for Raskolnikov's sister was Dostoevsky's own sister, whose marriage was to the advantage of Dostoevsky and his older brother, Michael. Dostoevsky experienced an overwhelming sense of indebtedness to his young wife, Anna, who for the last fifteen years of his life was his Sonya. She bore his children, prepared his manuscripts, and stood firm when he suffered the grief of a child's death, raged over a rejected manuscript, and alternately was taken by feverish fits of gambling and long bouts of remorse. Dostoevsky also resented Anna's love. Her love made him feel like he was a child, a sinner, and a parasite. This resentment not only showed in his characters like Raskolnikov, but it was also

expressed in his fiction by his attraction for the femme fatale (another romantic bugaboo). Other personal experiences confirmed Dostoevsky's belief that only the loving embrace of the mother gave life worth. He stood helplessly by when his children died. He knew life was filled with pain and suffering that could not be escaped, injustices that could not be rectified, situations against which human will was impotent. As a young man, he had stood before the tsar's sham firing squad. As a mature man, he was under the sentence of increasing epileptic seizures, which made death seem terrifyingly near, ever unpredictably present. The comfort of a woman's love was, in Dostoevsky's view, solace for human limits.

41. Stressing how much suffering and violence was inescapably part of man's earthly experience, Joseph de Maistre, reacting against the French Revolution while anticipating Darwin, wrote, "Above the numerous animal races is man whose destructive hand spares nothing which lives: he kills to nourish himself . . . to attack, to defend, to learn, to amuse himself; he kills in order to kill. He has need of everything, and nothing resists him." Translated from the second volume of *Les Soirées de Saint Petersbourg*, (Bruxelles: Goemaere, 1852), 23.

42. Feodor Dostoevsky, *Notes from the Underground*, trans. Mirra Ginsburg (New York: Bantam Books, 1974), 39.

43. Feodor Dostoevsky, *Crime and Punishment*, trans. Sidney Monas (New York: Signet, 1968), 315.

44. Ibid., 407.

45. Dmitri in *The Brothers Karamazov* accepts the redeeming love of the two women as well as his brother Alyosha and accepts his punishment for his father's death as justified and essential for his restoration, whereas Stavrogin in *The Possessed*, and Rogozhin and Nastasia Filipovna in *The Idiot* are not saved from themselves by the offer of redeeming love.

46. Feodor Dostoevsky, *The Brothers Karamazov*, trans. Constance Garnett (New York: Vintage, 1955), 384.

47. For two characterizations of the bourgeois as a category of modern cultural and social criticism, see esp. part I of Seigel's *Bohemian Paris* and my *Mounier and Maritain: A French Catholic Understanding of the Modern World* (Tuscaloosa, Ala: University of Alabama Press, 1975), 29–54, passim.

48. Alexander Herzen, *My Past and Thought*, trans. Constance Garnett (New York: Vintage, 1973), 65.

49. For Dostoevsky's fierce attack against the West and its values and institutions in general and France in particular, see his *Winter Notes on Summer Impressions*, trans. Kyril Fitzlyon (London: Quartet, 1955), 70–94.

50. Mickiewicz is cited in Hans Kohn, *Pan-Slavism: Its History and Ideology* (New York: Random House, 1960), 40; Jules Michelet's quotation is from his *The People* (Chicago: University of Illinois Press, 1973), 185.

51. For a discussion of "the unhappy consciousness," which drove romantics to seek hope in messianic historical visions, see Martin Malia's *Alexander Herzen and the Birth of Russian Socialism* (New York: Grosset & Dunlap, 1965), 290–2, passim.

52. Cited in Hans Kohn, *Pan-Slavism*, 38.

53. Michelet, representatively of the pre-1848 empathetic romantic nationalism, asked, "How could those great souls of nations, with their vivid genius,

their history rich in martyrs, and abounding sacrifices of certain immortality, ever perish? When one of them is momentarily eclipsed, the whole world is sick in all its nations, and the heart of the world which responds to nations' aches with pain. That suffering I see in our own heart, my reader, is Poland and Italy," *The People*, 182.

54. Dostoevsky, *Diary of the Writer*, vol. 1 (New York: Octagon Books, 1973), 202–23. For a discussion of the theme of Holy Russia, see V. V. Zenkovskii, *Russian Thinkers of the West* (Ann Arbor: University of Michigan Press, 1953), esp. 154–70.

55. *Diary of the Writer*, vol. 2, 578.

56. The section on Nietzsche is based directly on my *Ethics, Living or Dead?*, 53–70. For Works by Nietzsche, see *Complete Works*, ed. Oscar Levy, 18 vols. (New York: Russell & Russell, 1964). For Works on Nietzsche, see Frederick Copleston, *Frederick Nietzsche* (New York: Barnes & Nobles, 1975); Karl Jasper, *Nietzsche and Christianity* (New York: Gateway, 1961); Walter Kaufmann, *Nietzsche*, 3rd ed. (Princeton: Princeton University Press, 1968); Lev Shestov, *Dostoevsky, Tolstoy and Nietzsche* (Athens: Ohio University Press, 1970); and Stefan Zweig, "A One-Man Drama," in *Master Builders* (New York: Viking Press, 1939), 443–530. Also on Nietzsche, see R. J. Hollingdale, *Nietzsche: The Man and His Philosophy*, (Baton Rouge, La.: Louisiana State University Press, 1973), and J. P. Stern, *Frederick Nietzsche*, (New York: Penguin, 1979).

57. See Geoffrey Clive, ed. *The Philosophy of Nietzsche* (New York: New American Library, 1965), 404–405.

58. This conception of life as a work of art, and its important place in Nietzsche's thought, testifies to the profound influence upon Nietzsche of Swiss cultural historian Jacob Burckhardt; especially influential was Burckhardt's *Civilization of the Renaissance*, 2 vols, (New York: Harper & Brothers, 1958).

59. Friedrich Nietzsche, *Birth of Tragedy* (New York: Doubleday/Anchor, 1956), 50–51.

60. Ibid., 52.

61. Ibid., 138.

62. Ibid., 136.

63. Ibid., 137.

64. Ibid., 124.

65. Ibid., 120.

66. Friedrich Nietzsche, *The Use and Abuse of History* (New York: The Bobbs Merrill Company, 1957), 3.

67. Ibid., 23.

68. Ibid., 21.

69. Ibid.

70. Ibid., 9.

71. Friedrich Nietzsche, *The Geneaology of Morals*, trans. Francis Golffing (New York: Doubleday/Anchor, 1956), 217–18.

72. Friedrich Nietzsche, *The Gay Science*, trans. Walter Kaufmann (New York: Vintage, 1974), 175.

73. Ibid., 176.

74. Nietzsche, *Genealogy of Morals*, 173.

75. Ibid., 167.

76. Ibid., 167–68.

77. Ibid., 213.

78. Ibid., 198.

79. Ibid., 208.

80. Ibid., 210.

81. Ibid., 222.

82. Ibid.

83. Ibid.

84. Ibid., 223.

85. Ibid., 225. Emphasis is mine.

86. Ibid., 169.

87. Ibid., *Basic Writings of Nietzsche,* ed. and trans. Walter Kaufmann (New York: Modern Library, 1968), 471.

88. Ibid., Golffing, 226.

89. For a significant expression of Nietzsche's attack against Christianity, see his *The Will to Power,* ed. Walter Kaufmann (New York: Vintage Books, 1968), 85–219.

90. Nietzsche, *Genealogy of Morals, Basic Writings of Nietzsche,* 479.

91. Nietzsche, *Genealogy of Morals,* trans. Francis Golffing, 150.

92. Karl Jaspers, *Nietzsche and Christianity* (Chicago: Henry Regnery, 1961), 39.

93. Geoffrey Clive, ed., *Philosophy of Nietzsche* (New York: Signet, 1965), 404–5.

94. Friedrich Nietzsche, *Beyond Good and Evil, Basic Writings of Nietzsche,* 329.

95. Dostoevsky, *Crime and Punishment,* 541.

96. No single essay so well develops the pathos of Nietzsche's last years as Stefan Zweig's lengthy piece on Nietzsche, "A One-Man Drama," 443–530.

97. Christopher Middleton, ed., *Selected Letters of Nietzsche* (Chicago: University of Chicago Press, 1969), 344.

6

A Century of Victims: Europe's Responsibility for a World's Suffering

Our village, ever more planetary and ever more patriotic—the two things go together—lives in the age of nationalism, separatism, irredentism and tribalism. Its darker features are known as segregation, racism and xenophobia. Universalization of subjects = tribalization of subjects.

"Ideology" is what remains when the acropolis has been razed, the walls have been destroyed and the plane trees have been cut down. Modern ideologies are homelands for the homeless.

Regis Debray, *Critique of Political Reason*

In the course of the nineteenth century, Europe took upon itself great responsibility for the world. It accepted the philosophes' burden to make humanity happy.

At the end of the last century, there was no doubt that, insofar as Europe was the great source of change in the world, non-Western peoples were either Europe's beneficiaries or victims. Predictably enough, in the following century, Europe and its oldest and most powerful child, the United States, were to be taken before the court of world conscience and accused for all the suffering caused to as well as the unrealized possibilities of the world's peoples.

It could be conceded on Europe's behalf that some of the things it did were good, that all of its motives (especially those of the missionary and the philanthropist) weren't entirely bad, that indigenous forces too, accounted for change; or (to make the great incalculable argument) that the peoples of the world were on the whole happier and had higher expectations than before the coming of the West. Nevertheless, not one of these defenses exempted Europe from being singularly tried as the source of suffering in the world. By virtue of its power, the world in toto had become its victims.

The First World War belied Europe's strength, rationality, and altruism. As colonialist, imperialist, white man, modern man, European, Englishman, American, or some other subspecies of the West, the European was judged to be guilty of the world's suffering. Accusations already common in the nineteenth century in the hearts of the leaders of the non-Western world became, for many, standard rhetoric in the twentieth century. In yet more extreme ideologies of the third world (like that expressed in Franz Fanon's *Wretched of the Earth,* to emerge later in the century), revolution was not only justified, but the very act of killing a white man was idealized as the first act of self-definition and freedom.[1]

After the Second World War, which further diminished Europe's power and stripped it of its empires, the American increasingly took the place of the European before the tribunal of world victims. America was tried, especially by "the intellectuals of the world," for not only all it did and didn't do, but all Europe had once done or not done. Ironically such serious public discourse, which operated so much in the religious language of blood, sacrifice, martyrs, guilt, and innocence existed as the majority of Europeans' and Americans' first interests were in family and self. Indeed, the majority of Westerners, thanks to the revolutionary increase in material goods, were learning in ever greater numbers and with growing sophistication to calculate their increasing pleasure against their diminishing pains. The age of war and revolution, and depression, atrocity and holocaust, was also the era of leisure, the automobile, and the consumer. So two entirely different moral calculuses assembled themselves side by side in twentieth-century western civilization: one in the private realm counted with ever more subtlety and distinction pleasures and pains, as Bentham had taught; whereas the other, in the public realm, taught, forgetful of constitutional and democratic origins, an atavistic language of blood, sacrifice, and victims.

EUROPE AT WAR

Around the bloody sacrifice of the First World War, European nations unleashed, organized, and directed—by word and deed, myth, propaganda, and police—great conformities of resentment, hatred, and anger.[2] Each nation made itself a holy community of suffering by martyring so many in its name. Consecrated by the deaths of millions, each nation claimed itself to be a repository of holy victims. Nations—which Bentham, the philosophes and their heirs had hoped would lead men and women to a more rational, humane, and happy world—turned humanity over to mass death and martyrdom, hatred, revenge, and yet other impulses whose satisfaction lay far beyond reason, persuasion, and compromise.

Young men had to be induced to sacrifice their lives for the nation. Peasants and lower class peoples, who knew little or nothing about the nation or the national society to which they were supposedly joined, were recruited and asked to kill and die for a project they neither understood nor believed in. They were the war's victims. Newly created citizens were asked to surrender their first loves and interests, the things they had worked and sacrificed for, for the nation's good. Society, as a whole, had to be convinced that the war was a holy and important mission, worthy of sacrificial death. Governments had to find justification for such staggering sacrifices.

The need to justify such a sacrifice brought elemental laws of human exchange into play. The more states asked their peoples to sacrifice, the more the states had to promise to give them in return. As the war dragged on, the sacrifice of men, materials, ideals, and even hope itself became greater. Accordingly, the debt owed to the people mounted ever higher.

The twentieth-century political life and discourse was given over in spiritual mortgage during the First World War. Each state had accumulated a terrible debt of innocent blood to repay.

An elemental agreement occurred at the heart of the war. The more people paid for the war with their sufferings—their losses and disillusionments—the more they came to feel that they belonged to the nation and the nation belonged to them. The war was democracy's savage crucible. In it people and nation were fused together. In many instances, those who served and died, came from families and regions that had just taken up a national identity. The market, railroads, public schools, party politics, or yet some other modernizing and nationalizing force had just led them beyond their local and regional identities to a national identity. Many were initiated into a national consciousness by the war itself—a bloody baptismal rite.

For the entire society—soldiers, peasants, workers, teachers, and merchants alike—the war was a rite of passage into national life. In Europe and America entire new groups enrolled themselves for the first time in the national ethical community. The national unity that literacy, public schools, newspapers, political parties, and railroad tracks had begun only decades before the war, the war completed.[3] Nationality became universally a part of conscience in the West. (New citizens came to believe that what they gave in work, suffering, or sacrifice of life itself to the nation the nation owed them in return. With the war, one of the oldest laws of ethical discourse took hold of twentieth-century public life: blood demands blood.

The war put military sacrifice at the center of national life. All participated in the sacrifice. The veterans and legionnaires became the high priests of this new church. The war called forth millions of "soldier-Christs." These martyr-founders, these fallen soldiers, became more powerful in their deaths than they had been during their lives. Cults, shrines, and memorials were erected in their names; vengeance was called for; wars were justified; and new armies were set marching. Official cults of gratitude for suffering were formed; victims, real and manufactured, multiplied in the millions.

The war was proclaimed by some to be the holiest national sacrament. It established new elders. The conception of the nation at war was now more influential than the philosophes' ideal of humanity's progress, which, in the aftermath of four years of carnage, appeared a utopian ideal from a remote past.

Pacifists cautioned against the cruel gods of war. But these pacific voices, echoing the philosophes, were unheard against the bloodthirsty sirens of the heroic dead.

With the war, the rhetoric of Europe's public discourse became consumed with the irresolvable domestic and, above all, international questions of who suffered what, at whose hands, and what was owed in return? The strongest accusations were those leveled on behalf of the betrayal of innocent suffering. In the name of innocent suffering, party criticized party, class criticized class, nation criticized nation. While those of the right constantly spoke of the betrayal of the nation and its people to foreign doctrines and interests, those of the left spoke of the exploitation of the worker and the people by capitalism. Even when supporting the violent overthrow of government, each side claimed to represent innocent suffering. In the interwar years, Europe, led by its intellectuals, put itself on trial. Accusation, guilt, and self-hatred multiplied, and the older and less heroic, but more rational, politics of the middle class gave way to the politics of the extremes. Intellectuals of both the right and left, in the tradition of the philosophes, served as the new priests of words. They defined themselves and articulated their causes in reference to preferred successions and sacred suffering and martyrs of chosen causes.

Fascists thrived in the aftermath of the Great War. Their moral rhetoric flourished—indeed it was born out of the theme of innocent suffering betrayed. Their first accusation was that of the betrayal of the nation's soldiers. The fascists and their nationalist allies charged that the saviors of the fatherland, the pure and heroic youth who had given everything for the fatherland, returned home, if at all, to find themselves without work, their families most often in trouble, and society in political and moral disorder. They found that those in control—the reigning bourgeois—were indifferent to their sacrifice. They claimed that they had given everything and, in turn for their suffering, received nothing. Their sacrifice, they contended, constituted the moral essence of the nation.

Nowhere was the accusation of betrayal of innocent blood more powerful than in Germany, where a defeat of unimagined proportions was suffered, and in Italy, where victory seemed to cost as much as defeat. For both the Fascists of Italy and the Nazis of Germany, no indictment against the postwar liberal democratic governments could be considered too strong. They believed themselves to speak on behalf of a moral power greater than any elected government. With transcendental gods to accept the sacrifice of the war, and unwilling to allow each hearth and local community to absorb its own suffering, they asserted—and this was the moral essence of fascist politics—that the nation should vindicate the fallen soldier and the betrayed people.

Nazis argued that their soldiers—their young Christs—were not beaten on the battlefield itself but betrayed by statesmen at home. For this betrayal of German blood they held liberal, socialist, and Jewish politicians guilty. The soldiers and the nation had not lost. They would not forsake their fallen comrades, in whose deaths they believed resided more honor than all the principles of democracy and liberal constitutions, as well as the principles of orderly and pacific civil life. Resentment and hatred were aimed in almost every direction; the desire for revenge and the willingness to shed blood took root in the hearts of many, the most cynical and calloused attacks against democracy were vindicated. Ernst von Solomon, a founder of the German *Freikorps* (an active paramilitary group composed of radical right-wing veterans, students, and others) asserted that the returning soldiers would always "carry the trenches in their blood."[4]

The war legitimized the most hateful languages of the nineteenth century: great new numbers of people were enrolled in believing that social reality was class against class, nation against nation, peoples against peoples, race against race. Even at the outset of the war, the most civilized men began to use freely the words *blood, nation,* and *sacrifice.* For instance, the eminent German statesman and member of the Catholic Party, Matthias Erzberger, wrote on October 21, 1914, in *Der Tag,* "If a way was found of entirely wiping out the whole of London it would be more humane to employ it than to allow the blood of a single GERMAN SOLDIER to be shed on the battlefield."[5]

The war proved fertile ground for the languages of Darwinism, imperialism, and exclusive nationalism. In the course of the war, statesmen from every nation echoed the sentiments of the German Social Democrat Philipp Scheidemann who, upon examining the Treaty of

Versailles, which was imposed upon Germany, wrote: "We must hold together. We must stick together. We are one flesh and one blood, and he who tries to separate us cuts with a murderous knife into the live flesh of the German people."[6]

The language of blood, which both Hitler and Mussolini, both war veterans, spoke so well, had powerful resonances in postwar Europe and its newly formed democracies. Now, it could be taught that only one's own gods and blood mattered; every party had its holy victims— its dead—whom it would have nation and world honor exclusively. Before this most primitive yet modern language, manipulated by the most cynical and brutal politics, the languages of liberalism and conservatism paled, appearing morally puny. (After all, the middle class does not suffer the way real soldiers do!) Constitutional languages of rights and duties seemed equally remote, precious, and cultivated in a time when, to quote Yeats's poem, "The Second Coming," "a blood dimmed tide is loosed," and "innocence is drowned."[7]

In the postwar period, a collision between the representatives of veterans groups and those of workers unions became inevitable. They were, at least for the intellectuals who represented them, two different moral solidarities. They had different cults of suffering and they derived different worldviews and rights upon the basis of sacrifices made and things owed. It was as if legions of Christ-soldiers battled legions of Christ-workers (les sans culottes de Nazareth). While veterans found their heroism in the fighting of the war and saw it as the great test of national sacrifice and honor, labor's explanation denied the war its moral value. The war, for the spokesmen of labor, was not a matter of valor, heroism, or sacrifice. It was a destructive waste of life and things. It was started, fought, and continued out of the capitalists' selfish interests. Labor did not conceive of the war as the uplifted chalice of the nation; instead, labor judged the war to be a gigantic death mill into which the few fed the ignorant and suffering many. While labor was divided over its assessment of the Russian Revolution, its martyrs were those who fell for the workers' cause. It would erect no shrines and cults to those who fought the nation's glorious battles.

Labor's antinational view, which profoundly limited its appeal over the long haul, not only to the nation at large, but even to the rank and file of its own members who were not immune to the notion of national sacrifice, struck the veterans' groups, nationalists, and fascists alike as sacrilegious. For them, labor's view desecrated what they took to be the nation's highest sacrament: the valiant test of arms and the ultimate sacrifice of innocent men.

The struggle between the veterans of war and labor marked the entire period from 1919, through the Spanish Civil War and into the Second World War itself. More than a struggle of parties and individuals, it was a war of moral views. Each group had a different view of who suffered and of what constituted just compensation. In the name of victims, they warred over the present; labor, to simplify the division between them, still sought justice and hoped for earthly happiness, while war veterans, not immune to getting their share of benefits, wanted recognition and spiritual vindication. They contested for power and the benefits it gives.

Their battle, on one front, was a battle of ideologies. In the victorious and defeated nations alike, both the representatives of veterans and labor attacked the middle class and its constitutional rule, which was established for all European nations at Versailles in 1919. Both groups judged constitutional democracies to be motivated by selfishness and to lack compassion. After all, hating the middle class (the bourgeoisie) was an old-time European business: accusing the middle class of lacking heroism, imagination, and heart, and claiming that it did not really belong to the real people was a well-practiced art by the time of Marx, Dostoevsky, and the foundation of the first bohemia of the 1840s.[8]

Already before the war, some European thinkers spoke of the middle class and the rich as the betrayers of both the nation and the poor. In the formation of Fascism, Mussolini and Hitler adroitly attacked the established order by joining nationalistic and socialistic attacks on the ruling middle class: national socialists in Italy, Germany, and elsewhere spoke of how the rich, the capitalists, the Jews, the Bolsheviks, and the cosmopolitan intellectuals conspired to exploit the blood of the real nation.

These powerful indictments of the European democratic and constitutional traditions, whose headwaters lay even beyond the First World War, became gigantic and raging currents in the European world during the years 1929 to 1933. During these crisis years everything that was hoped for Europe in the nineteenth century failed. Democracy survived only in England, France, and of all the new democratic states founded in 1919, Czechoslovakia; a free and open world economy fell to a world of separate and independent state-run economies, autarchies; and world government, embodied in the League of Nations and promising world peace among free states, was already understood by keener minds to be impotent in the face of a new and frightening stage of international anarchy.

This "mood of cosmic questioning," caused in great part by the First World War and by the events of the period 1929–33 transformed itself into an intellectual anxiety over human destiny. This existential anxiety over humanity's fate and the West's destiny fused together, transformed, radicalized, and universalized nineteenth-century criticisms of bourgeois society and politics. No past criticism of European life went unvoiced; no past attack against some aspect of European society or culture was considered entirely without some truth regarding the contemporary order. Dostoevsky and Nietzsche, Proudhon and Marx, Burke and De Tocqueville, Sorel and Péguy were equally, and often simultaneously, made guides to what was thought to be a crisis of civilization.[9]

The 1930s became a climate of extremes. The most excessive and irrational ideas were given legitimacy in direct proportion to which the traditional order appeared to have failed. There was no place in this world for the middle class utilitarians and followers of Bentham, who conceived of society as a matter of individuals and groups of individuals seeking to diminish their pain and increase their pleasure. The repudiation of moderate discourse and a constitutional framework became common to much of the political rhetoric of the era. The new languages spoke of survival, sacrifice, heroism, and the creation of new civilizations and orders of humanity.

Across Europe, especially nondemocratic Europe, political leaders called for sacrifice. But this was not sacrifice in any personal, familial, or religious realm; it was sacrifice in the service of the nation. The leaders of Fascist Italy, Nazi Germany, and Bolshevik Russia went the furthest in the language of blood and sacrifice. Ironically, they who were to slaughter so many claimed themselves to be victims of great historical injustice, declared themselves to be locked in a life-and-death struggle for the new order, which they claimed they were creating. With powerful means of communication and unprecedented forms of coercion, they lay claim to total and absolute control of their societies. Mussolini contended that in the nation

individuals and generations are bound together by moral law, with common traditions and a mission which, suppressing the instinct for life closed in a brief circle of pleasure, builds up higher life, founded on duty, a life free from the limitations of time and space, in which the individual by self-sacrifice, the renunciation of self-interest, by death itself can achieve that purely spiritual existence in which his value as a man consists.[10]

At the same time, on a scale and with an intensity beyond anything Mussolini ever conceived, Hitler was developing National Socialism, the German version of Fascism. National Socialism attacked the conscience and all its sources of independence. It tolerated no institutional, social, or spiritual opposition to the state. Law, parties, churches, professions, labor organizations, intellectual traditions, press, institutions, and the market were all molded in accordance with the party's everchanging ends. No spiritual independence of mind, art, or culture was permitted. (The Nazis, for example, raided the theaters where *All Quiet on the Western Front* was showing. They obviously wouldn't tolerate the pacifist thesis that Germany's youth had been senselessly sacrificed in the war for the good of the fatherland.) "The prolific German mother," to cite another example of Nazi intervention into culture, was declared by official propaganda "to be accorded the same place of honor in the German Volk community as the combat soldier, since she risks her body and gives her life for the people and the Fatherland as much as the combat soldier does in the roar and thunder of battle."[11]

Europe's democracies, weakened and indecisive up to the final hour, again had to go to war to save everything they valued from states whose power was unlimited and whose vision was irrational. For five years Europe and the world were again locked in war—and the language of sacrifice and blood again prevailed. On some immense scale, suffering would fall on great parts of humanity; a new bloody baptism had occurred; again there would be all sorts of victim-martyrs. Again blood debts were owed, and again, much of the future had been mortgaged to the fighting of a war.

THE WEST APPRAISED AFTER ANOTHER WAR

The Europe that emerged from the war was not only physically shattered but also almost morally broken. No doubt, throughout Europe, heroes had risen; they had fought the worst tyrannies unto death. They had done what only the best can do: at the risk of their lives they fought for the cause of freedom. The martyrs of the resistance, those who had suffered at the hands of Nazi violence, were the moral source of a new order.

Yet, the martyrdom of these heroes (many of whom formed the youth of the Communist party and the newly emerging Christian Democratic parties) did not deny the overwhelming sense that Europe appeared to have failed tragically the highest historical missions given to it in the eighteenth and nineteenth centuries. It had not secured justice, freedom, democracy, or happiness for the world; indeed, it had dragged the world into its inequalities, racism, nationalism, and wars.

In even the most academic quarters, Europe was surveyed from the point of view of its failure. Each national history was told as a story of failed revolution—*una revoluzione mancata*.[12] Every movement, be it liberalism, nationalism, Marxism, socialism, or conservatism—was surveyed in reference to its decisive weakness, fatal flaw, its hideous mutations, or its tragic exploitation. Europe was increasingly viewed, even by Europeans themselves, from the point of view of the third world peoples—and the negative judgment was repeated, became commonplace, a matter of standard rhetoric. Europe had exploited and failed the peoples of the world. While not attaining a universal consensus, a common portrait depicted Europe as a victimizer of the world. Europe had not brought the happiness it promised but instead had brought suffering to the world.

Germany, the heart of the fascist beast, was judged to be the quintessence of evil. Nazi Germany had systematically killed millions of protesters, enslaved and killed millions of those whom it took to be inferior peoples. It had ruthlessly exterminated opponents of every sort at home and abroad. It had grotesquely experimented with human beings for the sake of its science. It had sought—and in large part almost succeeded in—the genocidal destruction of the Jews. Its atrocities, often technologically articulated, went beyond previously known measures of brutality and perversity. It carried out its mass murder with a systematic and technological efficiency that only a disciplined, industrial, and nationalistic modern society could achieve.

In their lachrymose narratives of victimization, many critics made Nazi Germany the essence of Europe. And up until very recently, there were bountiful ideologists, especially common in the United States, who assume that Europe and the West can be spiritually reduced to Nazi Germany.

Marxism, too, of course, continued to supply in the postwar period a view of a Europe as victimizer. Behind everything European, from its politics to its most sophisticated arts, there was to be found, so the Marxist critique ran, the dominant interest of class. In all things the Marxist sniffed self-interest and caught the scent of plunder. The core moral indictment made by Marxism, however sophisticatedly developed, essentially argued that first Europe sucked the blood of its own and then the blood of the world.

Outside of Europe, established and fledgling nationalist movements ignited whole continents against Europe as victimizer—as racist, colonialist, imperialist. In a singularly unique way, Gandhi transformed Christian nonviolence to fit the political ends of India's independence. He made willingness to suffer and be a victim a means to power, which became in the course of the century an increasingly common means for the weak to deny moral legitimacy to the established order.

The postwar world abounded with accusations about the West, in the form of colonialist, missionary, capitalist, and white man, as the primary cause of all innocent suffering. This indictment became the age's dominant moral rhetoric. It became the moral spine of third world ideologies.

European intellectuals themselves were not immune to this language. Indeed, intellectuals of the left especially took to it. Already long accustomed to over a century of practice to the dramatics of self-accusation and inflamed in the postwar period by mutual incrimination about collaboration and prosympathy and communist sympathies, European intellectuals pushed their language to extremes. They appeared to try to make their words equal the seriousness of recent events. In the guise of existentialism, they depicted the world as absurd; pondered the most perplexing questions of suffering innocence; and asked when it was right to kill, to shed absolutely innocent blood for a cause. The speeches of Dostoevsky's most extreme characters and Nietzsche's most radical aphorisms became common fare in the existential writings of the postwar period.[13]

Europe's confidence in its role as leader of humanity was in large part shattered. Claude Levi-Strauss spoke for many near the conclusion of his 1955 *Tristes Tropiques* when he wrote: "For those of us who are earth-bound Europeans, our adventurings into the heart of the New World have a lesson to teach us; that the New World was not ours to destroy, and yet we destroyed it; and that no other will be vouchsafed to us."[14] While Europe did not retreat from colonies gracefully or even always willingly, the older languages of the Christian missionaries and late nineteenth-century imperialism no longer provided Europeans with an easy conscience about its mission to humanity.

European conscience was not without its buffers. The great majority of Europeans were preoccupied with putting together what they could of their lives and property after six years of a war in which civilian suffering through deprivation, conscription, bombings, and mass migrations had reached awesome proportions. Many others knew that they had risked their lives in fighting Fascism, while yet others, especially identified with the labor movement, could claim that all along they had fought all forms of European colonialism and imperialism. On this point, Marxism served many well who wished to protest their innocence, for it served to put one on the side of the downtrodden of Europe and the world. Leaving aside the problematic tangle of judging the Russian Revolution and Soviet actions before, during, and after the Second World War, Marxists could claim that they were on the side of victims everywhere and at all times. Thus, they had no blood on their hands.

The need to reestablish national economies and governments relieved the majority of European politicians and those involved in politics from the depths of self-hate that reached new levels of fashionability in the postwar period. Collaborators were tried, as was the case in France. Constitutions and parties were established; in France, Italy, and Germany this meant particular attention to founding democracies based not only on Christian principles, but on the initiation of Christian Democratic parties, which were to dominate postwar politics. Likewise, in each Western European society there were simply too many pieces to be picked up for uninterrupted self-interrogation. Guilt over failed responsibilities was overshadowed by the specific tasks that individuals, families, and governments had before them to put themselves and their world back together again.

What else buffered European conscience in the postwar period was the simple fact that responsibility for the world no longer belonged to Europe. Power had gone elsewhere. Britain could no longer maintain its great empire. France's weaknesses, which had manifested themselves since the Franco-Prussian War of 1870, were now manifest to all. Italy had a democracy to rebuild. Germany was disarmed and divided.

Power and responsibility had passed elsewhere. Like the rest of the world, now Europeans—not without a good deal of hypocrisy—could hold others, primarily the Americans and Russians, responsible for the world as they went about their business.

In the aftermath of the war, the majority of Western Europeans and peoples of the world looked to the United States as the center of the world. On this basis many Europeans assumed that the United States was now solely responsible for the West. With it rode the promise or failure of Western civilization, as well as moral culpability for all suffering carried by the white man, colonialism, capitalism, and the West. The all-embracing ideologies of the nineteenth century, which made mankind the source of its redemption or damnation, now focused on the United States. The United States had great power and great redemptive myths that allowed it to take upon itself the role of savior of humanity.

NOTES

1. For two brief surveys of and primary sources representative of ideologies of the third world, see Paul Sigmund, ed., *The Ideologies of the Developing Nations* (New York: Praeger, 1967) and Donald Hodges, Robert Elias, and Abu Shanab, eds., *National Liberation Fronts, 1960–1970* (New York: Morrow, 1972).

2. Early pages of this section on the First World War involving the nationalization of conscience are based on my *Guilt and Gratitude: A Study of the Origins of Contemporary Conscience* (Westport, Conn.: Greenwood Press, 1982), 99–103.

3. For a generally useful volume on the transformation of traditional peoples into modern national citizens, see Edward Tannenbaum, *1900: The Generation before the Great War* (New York: Doubleday, 1976) and Eric Hobsbawm, *The Age of Empire, 1875–1914* (New York: Pantheon Books, 1987); for a specific work on this transformation in France, see Eugen Weber, *Peasants into Frenchmen: The Modernization of Rural France* (Stanford: Stanford University Press, 1976).

4. Cited in Marvin Perry et al., eds., *Sources of Western Tradition, From the Scientific Revolution to the Present*, 2 vols. (Boston: Houghton Mifflin, 1987), vol. 2, 256.

5. Cited in ibid., 246–47.

6. Cited in ibid., 249.

7. W. B. Yeats, "The Second Coming," *Collected Poems* (New York: Macmillan, 1969), 184–85.

8. For Europe's hate of the bourgeois see my *Mounier and Maritain: A French*

Catholic Understanding of the Modern World (Tuscaloosa, Ala: University of Alabama Press, 1975) and Jerrold Seigel, *Bohemian Paris: Culture, Politics and the Boundaries of Bouregois Life* (New York: Viking, 1986).

9. Amato, *Mounier and Maritain,* 111–12.

10. Cited in John Weiss, *The Fascist Tradition* (New York: Harper and Row, 1967), 424–25; emphasis is mine.

11. Cited in Amato, *Guilt and Gratitude,* 104.

12. For an important development of the concept of *revoluzione mancata,* see A. William Salomone, "The Risorgimento between Ideology and History: The Political Myth of *rivoluzione mancata,*" *American Historical Review* 68 (October 1962), 38–56.

13. Aside from the numerous works of Sartre, Camus, Mounier, Malraux, Ponty, and many others, especially useful for intellectual life in the post-World War II period in France are Raymond Aron, *The Opium of the Intellectuals* (New York, 1962); Victor Brombert, *The Intellectual Hero* (Philadelphia: Lippincott, 1961); Michel-Antoine Burnier, *Choice of Action: The French Existentialists on the Political Front* (New York: Random House, 1968); Roger Garaudy, *Perspectives de l'homme: existentialisme, pensée catholique, marxisme* (Paris: Presses Universitaires de France, 1961); Herbert Luthy, *France Against Herself* (New York: Praeger, 1955); and my *Mounier and Maritain.*

14. Claude Levi-Strauss, *Tristes Tropiques* (New York: Atheneum, 1969), 392.

7

America: Its Victims

There is tremendous moral capital in suffering, even if you aren't suffering anymore.

Jessica Benjamin, "Victimology"

What happens to our established moral categories when victims act like oppressors, and they outnumber the rest of us?

Thaddeus Radzilowski, conversation on March 15, 1988

Americans emerged from the Second World War believing that their victory was, above all else, a moral one. They did not dwell on the moral ambiguities surrounding their use of the atomic bomb, which had brought the war to a swift conclusion. America, they could believe, had defended the cause of democracy against the forces of tyranny. It was home to countless immigrants. It started the successful rebuilding of Europe and Japan. It had risen, so Americans easily believed, above self-interest. It was an exceptional nation, which, since its founding, had traversed a singular path through world history and bore a unique relationship to the happiness of the rest of humanity.

America's willingness to shoulder the suffering of the world by saving it from the shackles of Communism and by being the instrument of economic development is explained by the myth of American exceptionalism. This myth, which in measure immunized America from the guilt inherent in being responsible for the world's suffering, affirmed America as the promise to the rest of humanity.[1]

America's redemptive myth was not that of other nations, such as Russia, Poland, or France. Their myths contended that their suffering, like that of Christ on the cross, helped purchase their redemption. By contrast, the American redemptive myth does not have its analogy with the suffering Christ, but with the newly born Christ. In this child humanity witnesses the beginning of a new order of freedom and redemption.

The American myth, so obviously religious in its origin, had its beginnings with Puritans, who believed that by leaving England in 1620 they were escaping the corrupt Old World in order to establish a holy commonwealth in the New World. The Puritans believed themselves to be the new vessel of God's redemption of humanity, the fulfillers of the millennium toward which all history was directed. The migration from England to America was interpreted as a release from the Babylonian captivity and the beginning of a new Jerusalem.

This belief in innocence, which forms the marrow of American self-definition, is inseparable from the myth of the American as the new Adam. The American is the new Christian. Free of the old church—its saints and Mary, its sacraments and priesthood—the American establishes himself in a new promised land and there erects, like a city on the hill, a new beacon for humanity.

Ernest Tuveson calls this American way of thinking about itself millennial-utopianism.[2] America is the place where God will establish the millennium, the thousand-year reign of Christ. It is utopian because it supposed that rightly motivated people, blessed by God's grace, and exercising supreme control, would establish the Kingdom of God on earth.

While Augustine had taught that the Kingdom of God is a transcendent reality, American utopianism reverses Augustine's position and proclaims an imminent kingdom established within history itself. For Augustine, the millennium was understood allegorically. The city of man could never, in Augustine's thinking, become the city of God, unless human nature itself was miraculously transformed. In the seventeenth century, however, Augustine's allegorical understanding of the millennium gave way to the idea that history itself would regenerate human nature. This unwarrantedly optimistic understanding of the powers of historical transformation carried with it the progressive corollary that in all things, Americans were the special beneficiaries of God's providence; Americans were humanity's tutor in the pilgrimage to perfection.[3]

These modified religious myths, which taught freedom from the past and total transformation in the future, merged with powerful secular myths, which since the Renaissance and into the Enlightenment had opened up to Western imagination the possibility of a new man and a new human order. The promise of newness resided, at least implicitly, in Renaissance humanism's search for real Greek and Roman texts and the attempt to implement classical civic ideals; in science's search for the rational and knowable principles of the order of nature and creation; in the discovery of a new world of peoples and cultures; in the Enlightenment's articulation of a new mental, moral, and social order of humanity.

Each of these idealizations about innocence and renewal found a place in speculations on the promise of America, which had already taken the place of Europe's promise. "In the beginning all the world was America."[4] And the hero of this New World adventure would be "an individual emancipated from history, happily bereft of ancestry, untouched and undefiled by the usual inheritances of family and race; an individual standing alone, self-reliant and self-propelling, ready to confront whatever awaited him with the aid of his own unique and inherent resources."[5]

With this self-glorifying myth of a redeemer nation, which assured America power and innocence, the United States committed itself to saving the world. This commitment, which the United States passionately but only temporarily made under Woodrow Wilson during the last two years of the First World War and the Treaty of Versailles, was irrevocably made after the Second World War by a set of decisions that made the entire globe a matter of America's perpetual interest. Until the Vietnam War, America successfully maintained its belief in its own innocence, newness, and righteousness. Its myths assured against the grave ambiguities that always accompany the practice of power, especially the power that had the primary responsibility for representing the interests of the West—democracy, freedom, and capitalism—throughout the world.

It is not possible to attain a neat distinction between the religious and secular elements feeding American consciousness. Although the philosophers of the Enlightenment sought to eclipse Christianity, as we saw in chapter 6, they also drew heavily upon that which they sought to overcome. Love toward God was translated into love toward humanity; the vicarious suffering of Christ became the idea of human perfectability; and the hope of eternal life became the hope of being remembered by future generations.[6] The philosophers removed humanity from the position of having to wait for the promise of felicity in another life by making the promise realizable in the present. Suffering could be ameliorated in the here and now by human action; pain in almost all its forms was increasingly understood to be inimical to humanity. Happiness, human power, and progress became increasingly synonymous. An historically attainable state of felicity became a fixture in the American mind, and the United States itself became the incarnation of the ideals proclaimed by the eighteenth-century philosophers. As such, America is both the new Israel proclaimed by the religious myth and the new earthly leader of humanity.

These mythic American assumptions were incarnated in President John F. Kennedy.[7] Kennedy, above all else a child of the eighteenth-century Enlightenment, preached American power and know-how. He defined the world as a set of problems, which intelligent, determined, and courageous Americans could resolve. In his 1961 inaugural address, he linked America's mastery of history with the completion of humanity. He invited all humanity to judge America's performance. He made pledges to the poor, to disarmament, to the cooperative exploration of space, to the eradication of disease and hunger, to an economic revolution in America, and to the support of the arts. He called American youths to join his Peace Corps and to take up the struggle for the millennium. America, by Kennedy's prescription, would be responsible for humanity; it would have all humanity share in America's promise of happiness. There was no suffering or wrong it would not fight; no good it would not pursue. John F. Kennedy pressed the myth of America as the ally of humanity to its limits, and in doing this, he made Americans more susceptible and vulnerable to the world's suffering than ever before. He led them to confront suffering that America, alone or in concert, could never reverse, prevent, or cure.

Lyndon Johnson, who took up the mantle and the liberalism of the slain martyr-president, John F. Kennedy, ran in 1964 as the peace candidate, vowing not to send American troops to southeast Asia.[8] Falling victim to his generals' bad advice that the war was winnable and persuaded by the argument that since World War II, Americans had invested too much in the defense of freedom to concede Southeast Asia to Communism, Johnson led America into the Vietnam War. In majority Americans understood themselves to be on a humane mission there. They expected gratitude. As the war expanded and victory receded, they received criticism. America, critics said, was causing not curing suffering in Vietnam. A challenge to the claim of American exceptionalism arose in the form of antiwar protests and then youth and university protests.[9] Defeat confronted the nation with its finitude, its limits. The painful recognition grew, though bitterly fought by many, that America was not a city on a hill set above the conflicting forces of world history. Instead it was thoroughly enmeshed in them. Racial violence at home and violence in Vietnam challenged America's claim to innocence.[10]

Ironically, the polemical language of exceptionalism was turned upon itself by the protesting youth of Students for a Democratic Society.[11] While fervently dissociating themselves from official America by word, alliance, and dress, they equally fervently—even religiously—insisted that

America should be judged by its own highest moral ideal. They found betrayal and moral failure in every corner of the nation. They held America to its highest claims, as impossible as they were. They judged American liberalism to ring hollow when measured against the realities of life for black citizens and against the national investments in the prolongation of the Cold War. They went so far as to say that America had become an engine of death, the victimizer of victimizers. Their convoluted chauvinistic logic, which contained no small quantity of self-hate, argued that insofar as all was not perfect in the world and human existence, America was guilty.

The protesters of the 1960s, who were by belief children of the Enlightenment philosophes, believed intensely in their own capacity for happiness, the potential goodness of America, and the capacity of humans to remake the world. They were profoundly ahistorical.[12] They believed in a world without suffering. This belief made them profoundly naive, profoundly American—and because they were so American, they strove to disassociate themselves from the dirty America of war, racism, poverty, and injustice and dared to claim that they were in the process of forming nothing less than a counterculture.[13]

By 1968 protesters attacked the founding myths of official national culture. They polemicized that far from being a savior-nation, America was a scourge to humanity. Victims of every sort, even those most tangentially related to America's power and history, were cited to demonstrate America's evil. In a much different way, the assassinations of Robert Kennedy, Malcolm X, and Martin Luther King, Jr. became the symbols and the proof of American evil.

The old history of America was based on the myth of an innocent nation. The new history started with the assumption that America was a victimizer. The new history set victims in judgment. Native Americans, blacks, women, labor, immigrants, and the poor and other victims of America and the third world constituted a new and blaming conscience.[14] Violence and oppression were not understood as temporary aberrations of American history but its abiding elements. The new historians—and they were joined by sociologists and anthropologists—put America on trial, as European historians had put their nations on trial in the 1920s, 1930s, and after. American history, said these moral revisionists, had its roots in imperialism and genocide. Innocent suffering and victims were summoned to judge America.

By 1968 America was morally challenged as it had never been before. Every past accusation against industrialism, racism, and imperialism was vented against America as it foundered in Vietnam. The war in Vietnam allowed America's critics to stand the myth of America's innocence on its head. They depicted America as being racist, the exterminator of the Indians, the exploiter of all nonwhite peoples, the first user of the atomic bomb, and finally, the enemy of life itself. America was understood to be alien to sexuality, nature, the ecological system, and the biosphere itself.

Critics went so far as to hold America responsible for all the unrealized good they could imagine. America was held accountable for the wrongs and suffering that could be understood to be the result of "relative deprivation" (somebody not having what somebody else does). At the extremes, America was tried for failing to be both Christ and Prometheus; for not, as romanticism would have it, absolutely embracing suffering and its victims; for not being perfectly rational in confronting the world's problems, as Bentham prescribed; for not creating the happy world of which the philosophes dreamed; for all the real and imagined failures of community since the Industrial Revolution; and finally, for not achieving the painless world that the comfortable and to an extent guilty middle class wanted for themselves and all sensate creatures. They angrily judged America for all the sights of pain and suffering that still reached them. They would, if they had their way, repress all suffering.

There was more. America was also tried for all the suffering that would or could possibly result from nuclear war. Having militarily arrived at the paradoxical position of preparing itself to risk everything in order to save itself, America was vulnerable to almost every universal moral accusation. Ironies and ambiguities surrounded the notion of America as savior-nation when America conceded that it was willing to endanger all its citizens in order to purportedly defend them, to destroy humanity for the sake of its freedom. Might not the destruction of humanity, the earth, and life itself one day be set at the feet of this new Christ-nation, critics asked. Making such accusations was a giddy business. Some critics even mistook their indictments for profundity and prophecy. Others sought their own innocence in accusation and identity with real, conjured, and even hypothesized victims.

VICTIM LANGUAGE AND OFFICIAL VICTIMS

The language of victims, spoken by blacks, Native Americans, women, Latinos, the unemployed, the disadvantaged, animal rights advocates, representatives of wildlife, and others, became a part of standard public discourse, as did the poor, hungry, and the oppressed of the third world. This language escalated and it became a means for seeking moral dominance and contending for power.

It was a means to control opinion and to use the most powerful of all instruments, the state, for the speakers' own ends. Victim language predicated a Manichean moral world view in which America—its government, society, and culture, its corporations and citizens—was always guilty, and those who were exploited, unfulfilled, or simply against official America were the victims.

Victim language was fashioned into standard rhetorics and thrived as never before as Americans' hopes for a better world grew and their revulsion to pain and suffering was magnified and as more distant peoples became Americans' companions in the daily news. Victim language served several functions. In some instances, it faithfully rendered wrongs the majority had done to a minority. In other instances, it defined and, in some sense, even created groups in reference to a holy and ennobling suffering. In all instances, it allowed its users a dramatic and superior moral posture, serving their desire for power. (It was especially useful in controlling significant elements of the liberal wing of the Democratic party.) As once the upper classes, especially the nobility, defined the good, now victims—the downtrodden, the oppressed, the humiliated—were equated with the good.

Contradicting what would seem both a natural and necessary desensitization to pain and suffering taught by the experience of ages, heightened sensitivity was proclaimed to be a precious good; caring became an obligation; and compassion, ever more conspicuously flaunted, was assumed to be readily available in the human heart. At the extremes even those who committed crimes against the property and person were welcomed into the fold of victims. In fact, their crimes themselves became proof that they themselves, not the victims of their crimes, were the true victims of the system.

Predictably, all victims of the period were not equally fashionable. The suffering of blacks and Native Americans and select third world peoples, for instance, had a higher "moral currency" in the 1960s and 1970s than that of white rural, laboring, and ethnic groups. Likewise, the suffering of women received infinitely more attention than the suffering of the working class, men, children, animals, and fetuses throughout the 1970s. One standard that defined what was chic in this moral universe was the measure of how far a group was defined to be spiritually distant from the stereotypic white Protestant male, who was defined as not suffering at all and, in fact, being the prime mover of suffering in the world.

The suffering of any particular group of victims had accordion-like possibilities. A group's innocent suffering could be related to specific conditions of wrong and particular remedies that could be sought in a specific court ruling or piece of legislation. Contrariwise, a group's suffering could be made universal and global. The more the proponents of a group specifically defined a group's suffering and appropriate compensation for it, the more their motivation could appear crass and political; whereas, the more they universalized their group's suffering, the more they ran the risk of losing themselves, their followers, and their audience in confusing historical and philosophical arguments and complicated proposals to what seemed vastly complex and intractable situations.

BLACKS AND WOMEN

With America's power and prosperity on the rise, yet its legitimacy made dubious by the requirements of the continuing Cold War, advocates found fertile grounds to fashion suffering victims into dramatic moral selves with moralizing rhetorics. In the 1950s and 1960s American blacks emerged as America's premier victims. A myriad of nonviolent civil rights protests throughout the American South, which spanned almost a decade, equaled in moral power Gandhi's movement for Indian independence. Religiously inspired and well-disciplined, the Civil Rights Movement expressed to the nation blacks' willingness to sacrifice themselves for equality before the law. Showing another face of their victimization and protest, urban blacks, beginning in 1964—the very year of the passage of the Civil Rights Act—and continuing during the next several years, rose up with destructive and angry violence.

Blacks challenged conscience in a way Native Americans did not. Native Americans stood as a great moral threat to all claims of American goodness and innocence. They were lied to, poisoned, killed; their land was taken away, their way of life destroyed; and taken as a single people, they were irreparably injured by white diseases, commerce, land-hunger, technologies, and cultures. The injury they suffered was beyond reparation and compensation. The disordered life of the great majority of Indians stands as direct consequence of the triumph of American civilization. The fate of Native Americans was that of indigenous peoples everywhere across the globe. What they suffered was frightfully typical of what all traditional, archaic, and primitive peoples suffer in the modern world. Their destruction was joined to the destruction of nature itself by encroaching civilization. In light of the growing ecological sensibilities of the 1960s and 1970s, the Indian's plight was understood to be everyman's plight, and the plight of life itself. The destruction of Indian cultures in North and South America revealed the disastrous and irreversible consequences of "the Columbian exchange" itself.[15] The Native Americans, as victims, became a way for their advocates and allies to fear and judge a changing world.

However, for a variety of reasons, black suffering more than Native American suffering captured American conscience in the 1960s.[16] There were many more blacks than Native Americans. They posed a more direct threat to American order and reputation than Native Americans did. They had far more allies in the universities and the Democratic party. They were far more articulate about their suffering, problems, needs, and wants than the Native Americans. Furthermore, the blacks possessed a rich literature and tradition of protest that was amplified by the Civil Rights Movements and urban rebellions.

Blacks' claim to being victims of white civilization could not be easily put aside. They had suffered great injustice. Slaves in the past and second rate citizens, radically discriminated against, in the present, blacks had suffered every type of cruelty, exploitation, and injustice. Their moral claim against America and its government was not restricted to a given abuse or a fixed period of time and correspondingly could not be compensated or indemnified with a fixed sum of money by payment to a definite number of victims, as was the case of the government's essentially symbolic bill of intended compensation of $20,000 during ten years to each Japanese American interned during the Second World War. Their claim remained immeasurable—unpayable until, in Lincoln's own words, "every drop of blood drawn from the lash shall be paid."[17]

The heart of their moral claim for special and preferential legislation was their innocence and the wrong they had suffered at white hands. Whipped, raped, lynched, families split apart and sold at auction blocks—they had everything taken from them. American blacks could be depicted as were Hegel's slaves, Marx's proletariat—beings to whom nothing remained but the right to revolt.

The linkage of blacks to victim status made "blackness and victimization status virtually synonymous."[18] Black identity was a moral identity; it was a "righteous suffering owed." Blacks became the archtypical victims. Blacks hold a special place in the liberation theologies. More than one radical theologian speaks of a black Christology.[19]

Victim status gives powerful moral leverage. It is a means of controlling much of society's diffuse guilt. Consequently, it has been tempting for blacks to fight among themselves over the right to represent black suffering. Disagreements over such issues as responsibility for crime or economic development is invariably transformed into a set of conflicting moral charges about loyalty to a sacred moral inheritance. For instance, in a disagreement over the role of the government in helping blacks, black Democrat Congressman of Michigan, John Conyers, accused black Republican, William Lucas of Michigan not only of being an Uncle Tom and, though biologically black, not "in the spirit of Martin Luther King or the civil-rights movement," but "went so far as to compare Lucas with some Jews who led their brothers and sisters into the ovens of the Holocaust."[20]

Showing how important it is for the underdog to claim the moral high ground, one black scholar, Na'im Akbar, who spoke at Wayne State University, was reported to contend that it is a "simplistic notion of slavery which makes it easy for people to compare their holocaust to our holocaust. They don't understand that going to the ovens knowing who you are, is damn well better than walking around for 100 years not knowing who you are. . . . Our holocaust in America is worse than the holocaust in Europe."[21]

Blacks—no doubt like any oppressed group seeking their full rights in society—have historically used righteous innocence in two ways. "They have bargained with it, granting white society its innocence in exchange for entry into the mainstream; or they have challenged it, holding that innocence hostage until their demand for entry (or other concessions) was met."[22] In the Civil Rights Movement, blacks invited white society to join them in doing what was right. They permitted whites to form a mutual moral community with them. Together they would suffer and sacrifice for the good. No doubt, what was so uplifting about the Civil Rights Movement was that it provided all its participants with the sense that they were part of a community suffering for the right.

Yet, in the course of the 1960s, especially after the death of Martin Luther King in the spring of 1968, much black rhetoric became exclusionary. Advocates of black power, the Black Muslims, and others argued that blacks were a unique and separate people unto themselves. In the name of their past suffering under slavery and its consequences, they indicted white society universally. The most extreme interpretations against white society were global and violent, and all discussion of black violence and black racism of black against black were sharply suppressed.

Of all radical black intellectuals of the late 1960s, Eldridge Cleaver—criminal, rapist, self-educated author, journalist for *Ramparts*, 1968 Peace and Freedom party candidate for the presidency of the United States, and secretary of information of the Oakland Black Panthers—best expressed the state of militant black radical consciousness. Cleaver sought to establish a countermythology to official culture. In Cleaver's polemics, the white man, "Pig America," and the evil West were combined as one universal oppressor and victimizer. According to Cleaver's Muslim beliefs, the whites formed "a race of devils, created by their maker to do evil, and make evil to appear as good. . . . The white race is the natural, unchangeable enemy of the black man, who is the original man, owner, maker, cream of the planet Earth."[23] White history was, in his view, the uninterrupted tale of the rapacious drive to dominate. According to Cleaver, all colored peoples know the purpose of white police and armies. They have lost their lands to the whites and had their bodies broken by white rule. Centuries of white dominance have led blacks to despise themselves.

For Cleaver, psychological analysis did not suffice. Power, he argued, is essential for respect. Upon that premise Cleaver conjured a possible coalition including "all" the oppressed peoples and victims of the third world and the enemies of America and the West. He included the radical white American youth, who, he believed, knew the true enemy and had shown a true willingness to fight. Cleaver wrote:

There is in America today a generation of white youth that is truly worthy of a black man's respect. A young white today cannot help but recoil from the base deeds of his people. On every side, on every continent, he sees racial arrogance, savage brutality toward the conquered and subjugated people, genocide; he sees the human cargo of the slave trade; he sees the systematic extermination of American Indians; he sees the civilized nations of Europe fighting in imperial depravity over the lands of other people—and over possession of the very people themselves. There seems to be no end to the ghastly deeds of which his people are guilty. GUILTY. The slaughter of the Jews by the Germans, the dropping of the atomic bombs on the Japanese people—these deeds weigh heavily upon the prostrate souls and tumultuous consciences of white youth. The white heroes, their hands dripping with blood, are dead.[24]

In course of the 1960s the blacks had made America their classroom. Blacks became the eye of white conscience. (National television brought scenes of their victimization as they were set upon by police dogs and sprayed by firehoses and their churches were dynamited and the bodies of their innocent supporters were exhumed. There seemed to be substance to James Baldwin's prophetic message: that the fate of America was inseparable from the fate of its blacks.

Women became America's second victims in the 1970s. The architects of the multifaceted women's movement modeled themselves on the blacks, arguing that they too, regardless of their own social background and education, were victims of the white male and his system. Along with the blacks, they defined themselves abstractly and universally, as Marx had once defined the proletariat, as victim-liberators.

Women, the leaders of their movement claimed, had a special insight into oppression. Like the slave and domestic, women saw their oppressor up close: they knew his inner and private ways. (After all, the rhetoric went, who knew him better than they who slept with him, bore him, raised him, nurtured him, lived with him?) They knew, so they argued, his violence, rapaciousness, greed, and cruelty. Shaping their description of the white man upon the European intellectuals' portrait of the quintessential bourgeois, women knew men to be, above all else, insensitive to the suffering of their victims.

Beyond claiming to have intimately experienced the heel of the patriarchal tyranny, feminist advocates contended that women also knew the sharp difference between domestic myths and the reality of their lives. Their list of grievances was inexhaustible. They were given the least meaningful and the most degrading work (work belonging to the biological and domestic orders). They were not considered individuals, but as belonging to a group that was superficial, sensual, emotional, and hysterical—anything but the dignified creatures that men claimed to be.

The women's movement was inseparable from a range of rhetorics, polemics, ideologies, and new theories and histories.[25] Exercising a singularly important influence on the movement was Betty Friedan's earlier critique of "the feminine mystique" as an ideology that romanticized domestic life.[26] This mystique, Friedan argued, had the painful consequences of infantilizing women and transforming the suburban home into a comfortable prison. Countless formal and informal tribunals heard charges of sexism, and issues from rape to indifference were tried on the principle of what women suffered at men's hands.[27] The more moderate, so to speak, of the militants rallied around antidiscrimination causes and affirmative action. They were older, from the middle class, and they sought to work essentially within the political process. The most extreme feminists, who were usually younger and outside the establishment, identified themselves with lesbian separatism.

If the women's movement had a single association it was the indisputably white, middle class, National Organization of Women (NOW), founded in 1966. Demanding women be allowed to develop their full potential and judging anything short of it to be unfair and a matter of suffering, NOW developed a bill of rights in 1967 that called for widespread antidiscrimination laws at the federal and state level, rights assuring women control over their own reproductive lives, policies of maternity leaves, and reforms of welfare to help poor women. In 1973, with the ruling of the *Roe v. Wade* Supreme Court case, abortion became and remained the acid test of NOW membership. The rights of women over their own body exceeded for them any rights, interests, or suffering that abortion might have for the fetus, the father, or society.[28]

The most radical intellectual proponents of the women's movement, like Mary Daly, articulated "metapsychologies" and "megahistories" of the counterculture.[29] They articulated their indictment of maleness in universal historical terms. Not only did they reject any connection between God and maleness, but the entire course of Western history was conceived as resting on the universal prejudice of male superiority. While arguments among most advocates turned on the issue of the source of this prejudice—especially whether it was purely environmental and cultural or was rooted in biology—the most fervent, identified the problem and the source of the suffering as sexual differentiation itself. The most militant feminists misanthropically regarded the male as universal oppressor and counseled that women should entirely separate themselves from men.

A more conciliatory attitude dominated the majority of middle-class feminist circles in the 1970s and 1980s, as women in ever greater numbers successfully entered the work force. In this period, men and women entered into some of the most complex contracts imaginable as they tried to negotiate equality at home and a fulfilling life outside of home. They would share pain and pleasure equally; they would carry Bentham's calculation into the household itself. Men learned more about child rearing and cooking and sharing domestic duties, while women were expected to make the work place a kinder place, and it was predicted that they would be less likely to lose their identity in their work. It was even argued idealistically by proponents of the women's movement that as men became more sensitized to their wives and daughters, they would become equally sensitive to the poor, the downtrodden, nature, and even themselves. Their revolution, they contended, would help humanity. The world, it was openly prophesied, would thank the movement for the world that would result from the women's revolution.

The public at large had become sensitized to the suffering of women as it never had been before. Women's suffering became a major industry: in print, on screen, in the lecture hall, and in discussion groups everywhere women's problems, pains, and suffering were set forth, along with charges of discrimination and demands for retribution and compensation. Feminist advocates made women the second official victim of the nation. They established an orthodoxy of innocence and suffering.

AFFIRMATIVE ACTION AND OFFICIAL SUFFERING

The convergence of the woman's movement and the black movement occurred during the heart of the 1960s. Blacks and women established themselves at the center of the American political discourse as its premier official victims. More than other groups, including Native Americans, Hispanics, and Asian Americans, blacks and women provided the dominant images of injustice and the primary moral language for seizing power. They demanded from the government reparations like victims of wars.[30]

Affirmative action, whose roots in the United States are in efforts to end discrimination and to achieve equality of opportunity in the 1960s, came into existence in the early 1970s.[31] In 1972 Congress gave additional powers to the aggressive Equal Opportunity Employment Commission, which began immediately "to put pressures on states and cities to follow patterns of proportional representation in employment."[32] Latinos, Asians, Vietnam-era vets, Native Americans, and others, shared with blacks and women the category of suffering and of having been discriminated against. Affirmative action sought not just to offer protection against discrimination but to define a preferential status for victims in the job market. Affirmative action spread from federal government to state government, from the employment sector to admission to universities and other institutions. Starting with the McGovern Rules of 1968, proportional representation of minorities became the rule of the Democratic party.

Affirmative action officially articulated the type of suffering that should be compensated. It did this in accord with the individualism of a career-conscious middle class. It identified the suffering that merited compensation with new opportunities for victims in the job market. (Indeed, its assumptions were highly debatable: wherever we find inequality of opportunity in the present we are observing the consequence of past injustice; wherever representation in good jobs is unequal, we are witnessing the result of injustice and the need for action to remedy this imbalance.) Responding to the employment desires of groups and especially individual leaders of coalition groups, the framers of affirmative action asserted that compensable suffering involved racial, sexual and, in a very narrow yet confused sense, certain types of ethnic suffering. Suffering that resulted from an individual's memership in a social class or in the class of illiterates did not per se count. Furthermore, supporters of affirmative action do not acknowledge the existence of any factors such as wealth, literacy, age, place of origin, nationality, or family inheritance that might disqualify a member of their group from preferential status. No matter how educated, how rich, or how much success an individual has had, the individual keeps minority status. Once you were granted membership into the official family of "suffering victims" it is assumed that no good fortune (such as where and to whom you were born) or great success (such as achieving a wonderful education and making ten million dollars) spared you the ravages of discrimination or negated your right for preferential status.

As James Fishkin, a sympathetic critic of affirmative action, contested, there are serious discrepancies in affirmative action's moral philosophy.[33] First, providing compensation for historical wrongs suffered is not the same as establishing conditions for equal opportunity. Second, group compensation by sex, race, and ethnic origin, determined independently of an individual's citizenship, historical experience, family background, class, and literacy, fails the theoretical test of justice as well as the practical goal of establishing equality of opportunity. While not examining the complex historical and social question of identifying victims and the proper heirs of victims, Fishkin correctly saw the central dilemma: the least changeable and most private institution, the family, more than anything else determines an individual's well-being and success in society. As long as the family remains the primary human unit of prospering and suffering in the world, proponents of equality of opportunity and education will never achieve the level playfield they claim they wish. Consequently, Fishkin argued, unless one makes the totalitarian argument that in the name of equality it is best to destroy the family, there will always be a world in which there is inequality. Some will suffer less than others because they have been better loved and educated. Their head start cannot be erased.

At the core of affirmative action is an ambivalence over the question of whether intervention is to compensate past suffering, fight present injustices, secure equality of opportunity, or realize a just society, in which pain and suffering will be banished. Its proponents have been increasingly tempted to define a just society, in the most abstract and utopian sense, namely as a society in which an equal proportion of the whole is found in each of the parts. Adding a corollary to Bentham's utilitarianism, they would have the majority composed of equally pro-portioned groups, enjoying equal pleasure.

Affirmative action has ultimately failed to convince significant groups of Americans of its justice. Even those who are willing to overlook its definitional confusions in matters of race, culture, and ethnicity, in ad-dition to the inevitable practical abuses associated with its immense clas-sificatory and bureaucratic schemes, must in candor question whether the benefits of affirmative action go to the suffering or to its upwardly mobile exploiters. Some even argue that affirmative action is a trumped-up program that does little to change basic unfairness in this society and pays off the ambition and greed of the self-declared middle class advocates of blacks, women, and other minorities. By giving power and jobs to the middle class advocates of the suffering downtrodden, affir-mative action amounts to organized and moral greed. Thomas Sowell, a controversial black professor, argued that preferential treatment, a legacy of the Civil Rights Movement, yielded benefits for *the advantaged in the name of the disadvantaged* not only in the United States but across the globe.[34] Sowell wrote:

In Uganda, the first major boycott of the Asians was organized and instigated by African businessmen who competed with Asians, and by the more educated Africans who stood to gain by replacing Asians in the civil service. In various cities and localities in India, strident (and sometimes violent) demands for pref-erential hiring of disadvantaged locals, over migrants from other parts of In-dia, have repeatedly been led by newly educated people seeking middle-class jobs. Much the same story could be told, with local variations, of the French separatists in Quebec, and preferential treatment in Thailand, among others. Those who believe in the essential brotherhood of man have little reason to be surprised to see similar patterns emerging in the United States.[35]

Ethnic leaders of white European backgrounds made expected criti-cisms of affirmative action. They responded most vehemently to the ideological advocates of affirmative action who turned them into white exploiters and did not hesitate to add moral dogmatism to their racism by asserting a priori that (as was recently contended in *Thought and Action,* the NEA higher education journal) "Caucasians are not victims of past discrimination."[36] They argued that not only was black and minority suffering unjustly elevated and compensated but that the suffering of their own people was entirely discounted, even though they too had been exploited, oppressed, and discriminated against.[37] The discrimination and oppression the Jews and the Irish suffered extended over centuries; southern Italians, Portuguese, Greeks, and others too had experienced considerable legal and social racial discrimination for their dark skins and alien ways. Ethnic Americans resented the assumption that their cultures and experiences were not only denied any special value but also the implication that they and their ancestors belonged to the white exploiting class of America.

Ethnic leaders argued that the vast majority of their peoples arrived after the Indians were removed from the land, Mexican territories were taken, and slavery was ended. This blood was not on their hands. They argued that their peoples were categorized independently of how they were treated in America and what they had done since arriving in America, even if it included martyring themselves in America's armies, creating its unions, or serving other causes of justice. Ethnic leaders found it profoundly insulting to be labeled exploiters and victimizers by upper class members of the press, the government, and the courts and to be told that the suffering of their parents and grandparents did not count. They could not accept as just the proposition that their children, who had only just arrived at the doors of opportunity, should automatically be placed behind the children of officially defined minorities. From their point of view, affirmative action, along with busing and proportional political rerpesentation, was an official national apology made by the rich at their expense. Adding to their anger and resentment was the sense of being hustled by "professionals in the suffering business."

In considerable numbers, American Jewish leaders shared these criticisms of affirmative action. While they in majority found their political home in the liberal wing of the Democratic party, they were understandably adverse to quotas. Quotas posed a threat to their admission into areas of employment and education in which they had become highly successful. Moreover, quotas ominously suggest an authoritarian society in which individuals are given fixed and established identities. Exacerbating Jewish-black relations (which have often turned on problems of local control in communities and schools in large eastern cities) has been the tendency of many black leaders, since the 1960s to identify explicitly with Islam and with anti-Israeli causes in the Near East.

Behind this loomed the comparison: our slavery versus your Holocaust—who suffered the most?

Jews and ethnics of middle and working classes were unwilling to concede the moral power of innocent suffering to the exclusive and official control of any group. They knew that things had not been given to them on a silver platter. They knew that they had paid a price to get where they were. They did not accept the notion that they had not earned what they had or that what they had, had been purchased at the expense of the blood of others. They would not allow themselves to be defined by the hour's guilt, anymore than they would acknowledge themselves to be former princes of Europe, slave owners of the South, or heirs of the robber barons of American capitalism. Simply put, they knew what suffering meant—and they were not going to allow someone else to define the worth of their family's sacrifice.

More than one critic has concluded that affirmative action is dividing rather than unifying the nation. The tendency for many of its advocates to turn it into a quota system as well as the numerous cases of reverse discrimination that inevitably occur support the critics' contention. Small groups of blacks themselves have turned away from affirmative action and explicitly sought to do without its benefits so that their accomplishments might not be understood as being the result of the help of others rather than their own ability and work.[38]

Even some elements in the liberal wing of the Democratic party began to realize in the late eighties that a claim to exclusive control of suffering alienates more voters than it wins. In the 1988 election for the presidency, even black candidate Jesse Jackson began to expand his conception of who suffers.

Jackson, a Baptist minister and member of the Civil Rights Movement who became a well-to-do speaker and Democratic politician, began his ascent to public life by identifying himself with the suffering of the Civil Rights Movement and its immense moral inheritance. He specifically attached himself to the martyrdom of Martin Luther King. (In fact, it is alleged that in the wake of King's assassination in Atlanta, Jackson returned to Chicago wearing a bloody shirt, allowing the world to believe mistakenly that Martin Luther King died in his arms.) Jackson's whole career is inseparable from his having wrapped himself in the holy, bloody shirt of black suffering. In turn, ideologue and Christian minister that he is, Jackson reduces the history and experience of all blacks in America, their familial, cultural, social, regional, and national background, to a single narrative of victim. He makes the innocent suffering caused by discrimination the universal black identity, and he makes this identity a standing moral claim upon society.

Jackson has consistently preached that truth is with those who suffer. Jackson, not unlike romantics of ages past, contends that those who do not suffer are not real. In context, this amounts to saying, "If you are not black, or poor, you somehow are not real." Jackson is explicit about black's special kinship with suffering: "It's like you're talking to a white man who thinks everything is fine. . . . And the black man is thinking, 'Can't you see my pain?' "[39] Jackson holds that the experience of blacks is spiritually superior to that of whites. "The privileged," he said, "haven't any story."[40]

In his first run for the presidency, Jackson, like a good nineteenth-century democratic nationalist, already began to extend suffering's net. He abandoned his prolife position and supported abortion in order to court middle class NOW members and women voters. Months into his failing campaign, which already had ideologically joined poor whites to blacks (upon the basis that they were fellow victims in poverty), he belatedly invited, without much success, the Hispanics to join the "Rainbow Coalition."

By the start of his surprisingly successful 1988 campaign for the presidency, Jackson had expanded his suffering narrative and the Rainbow Coalition to include not only women, blacks, Hispanics, and white workers, but all the poor whites, the farmers, the unemployed, the displaced, homosexuals, AIDS victims—all whom he deemed to suffer or who were attuned to the politics of the suffering. He had launched a redemptive political campaign, which would put government in the service of the suffering needy. By the time he arrived at the 1988 Democratic convention, he was willing to concede that even the white ethnics, like Democratic candidate Dukakis, have suffered, although he pointed out that they came to America by choice, not on slave ships.

Although rooted in a politics of suffering's rights, Jackson was beginning to understand that majorities, not minorities, elect candidates. His attempt to build a political coalition around themes of compensable suffering and new opportunities (absolutely consistent with the sensibility of the middle 1960s) tests the outer limits of how successful a political rhetoric of victims can be in America.

The language of victims continues to have powerful vibrancy in this country. The word victim, once a religious term and until very recently used primarily to describe individuals or groups abused by nature or government, has come to form in our world the standard language of hypercomplaint. The dialect of victimology is increasingly utilized not only to express real and significant injustices but to level charges for unachieved expectations and unrealized imagined potentials. National associations of victims multiplied at rapid rates throughout the 1970s, including not only groups for victims of crime (the right's reply to the left), but groups for victims of sexual abuse, victims of the child welfare system, dental victims, and those injured by the new laws of child abuse. Increasingly, the language of victimology was used not only to describe all those injured by nature and by the state but those injured by family, environment, and the whole of society itself, inferring that where there is wrong, there is "blame and claim." As a political language, victimology frequently fails because it defies the important American moral theme of success through hard work and individual initiative. In addition to sounding the crybaby and beggar, victimology can even sound subversive and anti-American. While the majority of Americans will tolerate significant criticism of their government and society, they will not countenance a language of total and uninterrupted blame. They believe that their own and their nation's efforts have amounted to something. They also are susceptible to a resentment borne by the sense that their sacrifices for family, community, and nation have gone unacknowledged: hence the potential moral power of a term like the moral majority, which implies that sacrifice and courage does not belong to vocal minorities alone.

No doubt, part of the appeal of Reagan was his old-fashioned moral homeliness. He closed what seemed to be "a values gap" between the common people and their ideals and those in power.[41] He allowed Americans to feel good again after years of guilt, self-accusation, and shame under Johnson, Nixon, and Carter. With Reagan, Americans stopped being so hard on themselves. Those who engaged in the endless recitation of what was wrong with America and all the suffering it was causing were at least temporarily isolated on a moral peninsula of their own. (The word *liberal* has become one of the moral descriptions of that peninsula.) Reagan, not without precedent, made criticism itself seem anti-American. The language of American exclusivity and innocence had returned. President Bush benefited from this reversal.

In the 1960s, 1970s, and 1980s, profound segments of American society began to argue that their nation was no longer holy, innocent, and beneficent. Guilt-inducing suffering became bountiful; it poured in on the American conscience. It became increasingly common to see groups giving themselves the moral status of victim. And it is not uncommon to see the same groups allocate to themselves the most powerful moral tactics of nonviolence (willingness to suffer and be victims of evil) for fighting relatively insignficant issues. For example, recently at St. Cloud State University, in Minnesota, two of its activist groups, People Educated and Committed to Equality (PEACE) and Non-Violent Alternatives (NOVA), joined forces to protest celebrating Columbus Day at the university. A founding member of PEACE, Steve Gareri, was quoted to say "Christopher Columbus was not a hero, but just another person who raped and pillaged Indians." A counterpart in NOVA, Bary Sands, outdid Gareri: "Columbus may be a hero to the minority who supported Hitler."[42] A year earlier at St. Cloud State, a group of feminists declared a hunger fast to force the university to remove copies of *Playboy* and *Penthouse* from the student union. The university's president, Brendan McDonald, acquiesced. The same university, in May 1989, advertised for an instructor/assistant professor of human relations whose qualifications required knowledge of:

1. institutional/structural oppression and the political-economic foundations.
2. institutional oppression based on racial or ethnic group, gender, age, sexual orientation, religion, disability, physical appearance, etc.
3. global oppression and human rights issues including neocolonialism, militarism, and the U.S. role regarding human rights in the world.
4. the interrelationships among these different types of oppression.[43]

Also, moved by the fashionable and often self-serving bug of guilt, Robert Carothers, the chancellor of the Minnesota State University System, to which St. Cloud belongs, set aside a certain number of academic positions only to be filled by select minorities, or no one at all.

Others scurried after morality and righteous innocence in other ways for other reasons. Some people, like the intellectuals of the past two centuries, are filled with self-hatred and thus morally migrated from self, family, and background by identifying themselves with distant victims and vigorous critics of what is presently defined as the system. Others, not adverse to using the moral power of ideas for self-interest, commandeered suffering. Specifically, with affirmative action some people made their own suffering officially compensable, and thus bureaucratically empowered themselves to get what they can, proving Charles Peguy's truism: "Everything begins in mysticism and ends up in politics."[44]

Affirmative action itself is only a single chapter in the place of suffering and victims in contemporary American life. For below it are yet deeper and more perplexing questions about our own suffering and that of others, the voice of the blood of our brothers. We, citizens of the world's most powerful nation, do not know what our suffering is; whether we should suffer at all; to which communities of suffering we belong; for what suffering we are responsible; to what sacrifices we are indebted; and what sacrifices should command our politics. With such elemental questions unanswered, we cannot set the moral boundaries of our world—and politics remain profoundly confused.

NOTES

1. For a recent discussion of the place of American exceptionalism in American historiography, see David Noble, *The End of American History and Capitalism, and the Metaphor of Two Worlds in Anglo-American Historical Writing, 1880–1980* (Minneapolis: University of Minnesota, 1985), which I reviewed in *The*

Annal of the American Academy of Political and Social Science 465 (January 1988): 207–8.

2. Ernest Lee Tuveson, *Redeemer Nation: The Idea of America's Millenial Role* (Chicago and London: University of Chicago Press, 1968).

3. Reinhold Niebuhr, *The Irony of American History* (New York: Charles Scribner's Sons, 1952).

4. Cited in Robert Bellah, *The Broken Covenant* (New York: Seabury Press, 1975), 5.

5. R. W. B. Lewis, *The American Adam* (Chicago: University of Chicago Press, 1955), 5.

6. Carl Becker, *The Heavenly City of the Eighteenth-Century Philosophers* (New Haven and London: Yale University Press, 1969), 130.

7. For a view of postwar America and the Kennedy presidency, see Carl Degler, *Affluence and Anxiety: America Since 1945*, 2nd ed. (Alenview, Ill.: Scott, Foresman, and Company, 1975); William Leuchtenberg, *A Troubled Feast: American Society Since 1945*, updated ed. (Boston: Little, Brown and Company, 1983); and Zbigniew Brzezinski, *Between Two Ages: America's Role in the Technocratic Era* (New York: Viking, 1970), as well as Henry Fairlie, *The Kennedy Promise* (New York: Dell, 1974); David Halberstam, *The Best and the Brightest* (Greenwich, Conn.: Fawcett Crest Book, 1969); and Richard Walton, *Cold War and Counter-Revolution: The Foreign Policy of John F. Kennedy* (Baltimore: Penguin, 1972).

8. Excellent for the Johnson presidency and his desire for respect and gratitude are Halberstam, *Best and Brightest*, and Doris Kearns, *Lyndon Johnson and the American Dream* (New York: Signet, 1976).

9. Standard historical introductions to the 1960s include: Ronald Breman, *America in the Sixties* (New York: Harper Colophon, 1968); Harold Hayes, *Smiling through the Apocalypse* (New York: McCall Publishers, 1969); Godfrey Hodgson, *America in Our Time* (New York: Doubleday, 1976); William Leuchtenberg, *A Troubled Feast* (Boston: Little, Brown, 1973); and Ronald Lora, *America in the 60's* (New York: Wiley, 1974).

10. For works critical of America as a creation of myth, see and compare Garry Willis, *Reagan's America* (Garden City, N.Y.: Doubleday, 1987), Noble, *The End of American History*, Niebuhr, *The Irony of American History,* Joseph Amato, *Guilt and Gratitude* (Westport, Conn.: Greenwood Press, 1982); and Connor Cruise O'Brien, "Purely American," *Harpers* (April, 1980), 32–34.

11. The following statement of the SDS is the "Port Huron Statement," found in Massimo Teodori, ed., *The New Left: A Documentary History* (New York: Bobbs-Merrill, 1969), 163–72. The standard history of the SDS is found in Kirkpatrick Sales, *SDS* (New York: Vintage, 1974).

12. Michael Lerner, one of the protesting youth in 1968, writing twenty years later argued that the basic assumption of the New Left was the individualistic notion that one can become anything one wants to be. The movement thought it could bring about a new humanity in a single generation. The assumption of the old left, stemming from the New Deal, had been that if we bring about fundamental change in society, the new society will itself create new people. The new left turned that idea on its head, arguing that new individuals will create a new society. This belief resulted in intense self-blaming as people within the movement inevitably failed to embody and live up to the higher and in

many cases nonsensical ideals they embraced. People began to burn out and drop out as they discovered in themselves the old and familiar evils of egoism, greed, sloth, and so on. The unexpurgated evil within caused resignation and hopelessness about the possibility of creating fundamental change. Self-transformation as the necessary presupposition for the transformation of society led quite naturally into the depoliticization and self-absorption of the 1980s. Michael Lerner, "The Legacy of the Sixties for the Politics of the Nineties," *Tikkun* (Jan/Feb. 1988): 44–48.

13. See Theodore Roszak, *The Makings of a Counter-Culture* (Garden City, N.Y.: Anchor, 1969). The attempt to articulate an opposing culture (not without historical analogy to those who called for new cultures and civilizations in the 1920s) is expressed in such works as Roszak, *Sources* (New York: Harper Colophon, 1972); Robert S. Gold, ed., *The Rebel Culture* (New York: Delta, 1970); Jeff Nuttall, *Bomb Culture* (New York: Delacorte Press, 1968); and Mel Howard and Thomas Forcade, eds., *The Underground Reader* (New York: Plume Books, 1972).

14. A single example of this whole new historical literature focusing on the suffering of the underdog, which ultimately has its origins in romantic historiography but has become a veritable academic enterprise since the 1960s, is Jacqueline Jones, *Labor of Love, Labor of Sorrow: Black Women, Work, and the Family from Slavery to the Present* (New York: Basic Books, 1985). For a textbook that embraces the principle of American history as a matter of oppression and underdogs, see Peter Carroll and David Noble, *The Free and the Unfree: A New History of the United States* (New York: Penguin Books, 1977).

15. For global views of the Western destruction of human and biological orders, see Alfred Crosby, *The Columbian Exchange: The Biological Consequences of 1492* (Westport, Conn.: Greenwood Press, 1972) and John Brodley, *Victims of Progress* (Menlo Park, Calif.: Cummings Publishing, 1975).

16. For one revealing statement of Indian cultural criticism of white society, see Vine Deloria, *We Talk, You Listen* (New York: Macmillan, 1970).

17. Cited in Lance Liebman, "Ethnic Groups and the Legal System," in *Ethnic Relations in America,* ed. Lance Liebman (Englewood Cliffs, N.J.: Prentice-Hall, 1982), 173.

18. Shelby Steele, "On Being Black and Middle Class," *Commentary* 85 (January 1988): 44.

19. An example of special theology for blacks is Theo Witvliet, "In Search of Black Christology," *Cross Current* 37, no. 7 (Spring 1987): 17–32.

20. Glen Loury, "Who Speaks for American Blacks," *Commentary* 83 (January 1987): 36.

21. Na'im Akbar cited in Krystal Miller, "Akbar: US Blacks Need to Explore Heritage," *The South End* (February 11, 1987): 3.

22. Steele, "On Being Black," 49.

23. Cleaver, *Soul on Ice.* (New York: McGraw-Hill, 1968), 66.

24. Ibid., 82.

25. For a critical survey of feminist scholarship, see Jean Bethke Elshtain, "The New Feminist Scholarship," *Salmagundi,* no. 70–71 (Spring–Summer 1986): 3–49; a useful survey of the woman's movement is found in Linda Kerber and

June DeHart-Mathews, eds., *Women's America* (New York: Oxford University Press, 1987), 415–66.

26. Betty Friedan, *The Feminine Mystique* (New York: Norton, 1963).

27. Most prominent of the legal cases was the 1984 Sears case, which featured the EEOC charging Sears with sexual discrimination in its work force; men, it was alleged, held positions superior to those held by women. Sears counterargued that it could not be responsible for what positions women chose to apply for. For a self-defense of her testimony on behalf of the EEOC, see historian Alice Kessler-Harris, "Equal Employment Opportunity Commission vs Sears, Roebuck and Company: A Personal Account," *Radical History Review* 35 (1986), 57–95. For a criticism of the EEOC's case and Kessler-Harris, see Carol Iannone, "The Barbarism of Feminist Scholarship," *The Intercollegiate Review* 23, no. 1 (Fall 1987): 35–42.

28. A useful consideration of feminist politics and abortion is Kristin Luker, *Abortion and the Politics of Motherhood* (Berkeley: University of California Press, 1984).

29. For an example of Mary Daly's work, see her *Gyn/Ecology: The Metaethics of Radical Feminism* (Boston: Beacon Press, 1978).

30. For an example of an explicit discussion of reparations, see James Bolner, "Towards a Theory of Reparations," *Phylon* 29 (Spring 1968): 41–47 and Boris Bittker, *The Case for Black Reparations* (New York: Random House, 1973). For an introductory discussion of black scholars who, like Glenn Loury, William Wilson, and Thomas Sowell, challenge older and established black scholars' notions that the poor social and economic condition of the blacks is primarily a consequence of discrimination and assert that these conditions are more a result of social class and family stability rather than skin color and are even willing to accuse (as Loury specifically does) black leaders for making the wrongs of the past excuses in the present, see Jacob Lamar, Jr., "Redefining the American Dilemma," *Time* (November 11, 1985): 33, 36.

31. For short introductions to affirmative action, see Nathan Glazer, *Affirmative Discrimination: Ethnic Inequality and Public Policy* (New York: Basic Books, 1975) and James Fishkin, *Justice, Equal Opportunity and the Family* (New Haven, Conn.: Yale University Press, 1983), reviewed by Joseph Amato in *The Annals of the American Academy of Political and Social Science* 473 (May 1984), 218–19.

32. Glazer, *Affirmative Discrimination*, 205.

33. See esp. Fishkin, *Justice, Equal Opportunity, and the Family*, passim, and Glazer, *Affirmative Discrimination*, 196–221.

34. Thomas Sowell, *Civil Rights: Rhetoric or Reality?* (New York: William Morrow, 1984), 110; emphasis is his.

35. Ibid., 110–11.

36. E. Gareth Honchlander and Cynthia L. Brown, "Asians in Higher Education: Conflicts over Admissions," *Thought and Action* 3, no. 2 (Fall 1989): 14.

37. For a critique of white ethnic views, see Robert Weaver, "The Impact of Ethnicity upon Urban America," *Ethnic Relations in America*, 98–100. *In Ethnicity and the Work Force* (Madison: University of Wisconsin System/American Ethnic Studies Coordinating Committee/Urban Corridor Consortium, 1985), 46, Winston Van Horne and Thomas Tonnesen argue simplistically that white ethnics

were quick to pick up native racism and discriminate against blacks throughout the labor force. For a more complex historical analysis of the complex relations and interrelationships between blacks and whites and the existence of black nativism, see Jay Rubin, "Black Nativism: The European Immigrant in Negro Thought," *Phylon* 36 no. 31 (Fall 1978): 193–202 and Thaddeus Radzilowski, "The Competition for Jobs and Racial Sterotypes: Poles and Blacks in Chicago," *Polish-American Studies* 33, no. 2 (Autumn 1975): 5–16.

38. Abigail Theinstrom, "Permaffirm," *The New Republic* (July 31, 1989): 17–19.

39. Cited in Wal Harrington, "The Puzzle Named Jesse Jackson, Prophet, Preacher, Politician, Performer—Or All of These?" *The Washington Post National Weekly Edition* (March 9, 1987): 7.

40. Ibid., 9.

41. For a discussion of Reagan's exploitation of the value gap, read Christopher Lasch's "Reagan's Victims," a review of John White's *New Politics of Values* (Hanover, N.H.: University Press of New England, 1988) in *The New York Review* (July 21, 1988), 7–8.

42. *St. Cloud Chronicle*, October 10, 1 and 3.

43. *Minneapolis Star Tribune* (Sunday, May 14, 1989), 5K.

44. Charles Péguy, *Basic Verities* (New York: Pantheon, 1943), 109.

8

Universal Victims and the Limits of the Politics of Suffering

---

Political considerations permit us to think that we have the "general solution" because they permit us to do away at one stroke with all human reality and the search for truth.

Jacques Ellul, *The Political Illusion*

There is an elemental moral requirement to respond to innocent suffering. If we were not to respond to it and its claim upon us, we would be without conscience and, in some basic sense, not completely human. And without compassion for others and passion for the causes on behalf of human well-being, what is best in our world would be missing.

The good mother and father respond to their child's suffering. Friend helps friend. The good citizen responds to the needs of his community. Many of our most important idealizations of ourselves depict us ministering to suffering. The higher religions themselves prescribe brotherhood between all humans: the strong should help the weak; no one in need should be treated as a stranger. There is for those of us in the West the additional impulse to respond positively to the suffering of the victim, not just blame or banish him for his misery. Insofar as our heritage is Judaeo-Christian, we believe God often wants—even requires—suffering. Repeatedly, the Old and New Testaments teach that suffering is our path to God, and God appears to us in the form of the suffering stranger. Christians are taught that Christ is every victim.

Contemporary ethical thinkers like Richard Taylor, Jonathan Bennett, and Philip Hallie, consider it a fundamental moral responsibility to come to the aid of those in distress.[1] Taylor concludes (moving in the direction of Schopenhauer and Eastern religion) that empathy for one's fellow creatures, humans and animals alike, is the first condition for ethical life. Others, with more or less rigor, have argued that morality is inseparable from elemental intuitions about fairness and justice, intuitions that require us to be receptive to fellow humans and their suffering.

On a more naturalistic plane, ethical thinkers like David Hume and Adam Smith and their followers found the root of our capacity to do good in some sort of sympathy between creatures.[2] As the trapeze artist moves across the wire above, so we, to choose an example from Hume, safely on the ground below totter and sway within our souls. Without arguing from abundant evidence from the animal kingdom or seeking to assign some definite place to fellow feelings in our nature and our psychological development, fellow feelings occupy not only an idealized but also a natural place in our being.

The acknowledgment that we must be responsive to the innocent suffering of fellow creatures does nothing to settle the arguments about what types of suffering we should respond to, what grounds we should use to choose between the contradictory claims of different victims, and why and how to respond appropriately to victims. On this matter there can be, Bentham not withstanding, no calculus of innocent suffering or fixed catalogue of victims or certain table of remedies, compensation, and indemnification.

The matter of our responsibility for the suffering of others raises a set of philosophical questions that constantly demand to be asked but will never yield fixed answers. First, there are questions about whose suffering has what kind of claim upon us. For example, does one have special responsibilities for certain forms of suffering by virtue of one's position, such as being a parent or citizen? Is one particularly responsible for certain types of suffering by virtue of one's immediacy and proximity to the victim? Or is one more connected to and, hence, more responsible for certain suffering as a consequence of one's membership in communities shared with the victim or in communities that have injured the victim? Or yet, does membership in a community implicate one in collective responsibility for suffering caused by one's own kind, and does membership in the human community itself, to ask a philosophical question of contemporary interest, entail some sort of obligation to future generations of unborn humans?[3] And, to ask yet one more question, how in our age does one cast oneself, except with prejudice and violence, as a member of a single community, class, or nation? With such complexity surrounding our moral responsibilities and identities, there can be little surprise that our reason fails to supply clear direction to the often irregular, confused, and fashionable surges of our senses of empathy and responsibility for the array of changing victims around us. This is especially true in light of the contradictory cultural impulses that would have us deny and repress all sight and awareness of pain and suffering and simultaneously would have us be open, sensitive, and compassionate to all pain and suffering. Correspondingly, we are impossibly instructed to love all victims and care about all fellow suffering of sensate creatures, and at the same time to hate victims for intruding with their misery upon our isolated world of real and fantasized happiness with messages about what may be the ultimate cheapness of human life and the certainty of human death. Invariably, caught up in the contradictions of modern sensibility, the modern commitment to openness, and the modern world's flood of universal information, we find victims are too numerous either to love or to forget.

A second set of questions, which is also accountable for our problematical relation to suffering, turns around the matter of defining suffering and victims. While there is no doubt, as the law itself makes abundantly clear, that we presume victims to be those who wrongly suffer harm and injury, the question still remains of whether they can be classified into hierarchies of serious suffering and deserved attention. Are there, to ask this question in other and more pleading language, types of suffering that express more violence or embody greater innocence, thereby creating purer, nobler, and more deserving victims? The history of the American government's arguments about and reasons for compensating North American Indians should in itself convince us of the complexity of defining and compensating victims for the wrongs they directly or indirectly suffered. Should we assign greater victim status to children than to adults and to victims of natural catastrophes rather than victims of political actions? How do we measure and arbitrate rights and compensation when confronted by competing groups of victims? Then, too, there is the matter of seeking to weigh suffering of one's fellow citizen against that of the nonstranger or valuing the suffering of a group in the present against those who have suffered atrocities in the past or those who may, unless something is done, in all likelihood suffer disaster in the future. Of course, there is no courtroom in which we decide the multiplicative claims of victims.

If, in order to restrict victims' confusing claims upon us, we argue that we are responsible for the suffering caused by injustice, there still remains the perplexing question of defining injustice. Must we, only to hint at this perplexity, distinguish—as it seems we must—between the injustices of man, nature, and God? Are we not compelled to distinguish between that suffering for which there is remedy and that which by its nature defies all remedy? Borrowing distinctions from Chaim

Perelman to underline how complex it can be to define who actually suffers injustice, we can ask individuals or groups that have not received the same thing as others or been rewarded according to merits, works, needs, rank, or legal entitlements.[4] (A similar set of distinctions in the matter of distributive justice offered by Nicholas Rescher allows us to argue that injustice and its victims are those who do not receive or are not compensated in reference to equality, needs, ability, effort, sacrifice, and productive contribution or yet in relation to a common good, public interest, or welfare of humanity.[5])

This approach to suffering, which includes exceptionally difficult but also preliminary questions and distinctions about justice, permits no calculus of suffering and victims. And it is both too restrictive and technical for popular civic discourse as well as the various rhetorics and ideologies that sustain our popular views of victims and their rights.

More ample definitions of suffering and victims are often articulated in reference to being denied what are defined to be basic human rights or needs. Secure footings for these rights and needs have been sought throughout modern Western history in what is taken to be the terra firma of human nature. Accordingly, victims (those who suffer or have suffered) are those who are defined in relation to a denial of needs and rights to which nature entitles them.

Without intending to make arguments on behalf of historical relativism, human nature invariably proves to be more malleable and elusive than any fixed lists of human needs and rights. The most superficial reading of modern history convinces one that supposed human necessities and rights of one place and period are not those of another place and period. Surely in the West rights and needs have been expanded and differentiated as human material conditions have improved and, correspondingly, human aspirations have geometrically multiplied. Surely, we have both opened ourselves, by a new sensibility and greater information, to whole new worlds of pain and suffering, while at the same time, due to greater aspirations and political and technological power, we are determined to eliminate pain and suffering on an historically inconceivable scale. Accordingly, in a most paradoxical movement of the modern mind, victims are to be acknowledged and disposed of in ever greater numbers. Increasingly, the measure of justice has been replaced by the ideal of happiness, and happiness has been linked not just to satisfying human nature but to even satisfying idealized human potentiality. In its most utopian impulse—an impulse that increasingly pervades modern sensibility—victims are defined not only as those who have suffered great wrongs or are not accorded life's basic necessities, but also as those who have not received the compassion, understanding, affection, and opportunities that the prospering middle class and its intellectuals conceive as essential to having a full and happy life.

As André Béjin interestingly pointed out, pleasure for ever increasing numbers is inseparable from the quality and process of sexual enjoyment. Sexologists, orgasmotherapists, and sex therapies and the whole range of literature, talk shows, and other theories of intimate and personal identity form in his words "a sexual therapy market and a pleasure establishment."[6]

This inflation of expectations for earthly sensual happiness has made us ever more sensitive to our own pains, hurts, deprivations, and sufferings, in addition to those of fellow humans as well as animals. It parades before us ever greater numbers of victims. As we more greatly differentiate our pleasures, so at ever greater length we differentiate our pain and suffering, with the consequence that everybody potentially becomes victim and victimizer in this world in which everyone is defined has having the right to happiness. Governments, courts, and bureaucracies (as recent American history well testifies) freshly define legions of victims, whose suffering, as a matter of our moral duty, we are first to acknowledge and then by justice, reform, and even revolution, to banish from this paradise.

This increasing and paradoxical sensitivity to suffering, which is at the spine of the reformist impulses, accounts for among other things the softening of civilization. Nietzsche was right. Concern for others (particularly the weak and the downtrodden) and the guilt associated with it turns warriors into courtiers. It makes power taboo; it surrenders culture to moralizers. Also, this immense opening to suffering and victims has the ironic consequence of making us uncertain of how to value our own suffering and that of others. Intensified by the dissolution of older communities, confusions over what suffering is, who victims are, and what our responsibility to them is undermine our identity. Without a capacity to define orders of suffering and hierarchies of victims, we cannot structure our moral place in the order of things.

However, our confusion over suffering and victims is not merely a philosophical perplexity or a cultural quagmire. It takes us to the heart of contemporary political experience and rhetoric. Twentieth-century events have turned on the formation and obliteration of whole peoples and groups. Contemporary democracy turns on contentions about suffering and the distribution of pain and pleasure.

If the utilitarians had their way, the principle of utility, which equates with the rational and the good, would serve to distribute the most pleasure, or the least pain, to the greatest number. However, their quest for a rational order appears utopian when measured against the pervasiveness of indifference, the yet unregistered suffering of distant peoples and groups who have not yet entered our worlds of information and feeling, and the demand for blood that continues to form the discourses of revolutionists and contemporary and national leaders alike. In a relatively recent photograph from a cemetery in Tehran, a parade of Iranian troops circle in praise the Fountain of Dead, a large red-colored-water memorial to the nation's military dead. They serve the Ayatollah and his revolutionary government's belief that the more people who die for their cause, the stronger their cause will become.[7]

Governments must justify blood split on behalf of the nation. As witnessed to by the 1987 incident of the USS *Stark*, in which thirty-seven American sailors patrolling the Persian Gulf were killed by the mistaken attack of an Iraqi plane, governments must elevate the deaths of their servants beyond politics itself to the mythic level of heroes and martyrs, even if the deaths are clearly the near predictable result of a failed policy or a mistaken calculation or the almost certain statistical consequence of normal operations. Governments must honor their constituencies of holy dead.

In the spring of 1985, Ronald Reagan inadvertently demonstrated how closely groups' identities can be tied to past suffering and how strongly they react when these identities are not honored. On April 11, the White House announced that during his forthcoming trip to Germany Reagan planned to lay a wreath at a German military cemetery at Bitburg for German soldiers who fought Americans and other Allied troops in World War II. Reagan and his advisors radically underestimated how this act, which they took to be an act of reconciliation, would anger Americans. Both American veterans and Jews found Reagan's intention tantamount to dishonoring all who fought, died, and suffered at the hands of Nazi Germany. The White House's attempt to mollify representatives of veterans and Jews, as well as the majority of the U.S. House of Representatives, by laying a second wreath at a Nazi concentration camp to commemorate the victims of Nazi Germany did not suppress criticism. Reagan's attempt to defend his visit by making the German soldiers victims of Nazism too only further fueled the debate: "There is nothing wrong with visiting that cemetery," Reagan argued, "those young men are victims of Nazism also. . . . They were victims just as surely as the victims of the concentration camp."[8] On the same day, in Washington, Elie Wiesel, speaking at the National Civic Day of Commemoration of the Holocaust ceremony urged "Secretary of State Schultz to 'tell those who need to know that our pain is genuine, our outrage deep' and expressed 'pain and shame' to learn that 'the President . . . plans to visit a cemetery in which there are a good number of SS graves.' "[9] A few days later at the White House, Wiesel implored Reagan not to visit the cemetery: "That place, Mr. President, is not your place. Your place is with the victims of the SS."[10]

Reagan, who had sought to stress reconciliation with Germany and the promise of future partnership between the United States on the occasion of the fortieth anniversary of the end of the Second World War, had discovered that suffering forms moral kingdoms of martyr-victims that demand special recognition. No kingdom has been as morally powerful in post–World War II America as the Holocaust.[11] Holocaust (the Greek word to describe an offering consumed wholly by flames) has come, not without argument even among the Jews themselves, to fashionably suggest an unimaginably unique suffering providing special moral entitlements in contemporary political discourse.[12]

For Israeli and American Jews, the Holocaust was a founding moral event of untold suffering that justified the founding of Israel as well as the entire range of Israeli policies and acts.[13] On an even more comprehensive scale, the Holocaust serves as the point from which Jews can morally survey the entire past and classify all present society. It forms the great court of wronged innocence, in which Jews can judge religions, nations, cultures, and individuals. The Holocaust is understood to be the logical and, in some measure, unavoidable consequence of all preceding forms of anti-Semitism, from the subtlest prejudices to the most cold-blooded and massive acts of murder. Anti-Semitism, in the hands of the most militant, is assumed to be part of the enduring substratum of Western history.[14] Instead of being understood as a type of historical accident, a unique and singular action of Nazi Germany, the Holocaust is understood as the historical culmination of all past anti-Semitism. Christian beliefs and superstitions, medieval patterns of discrimination and pogroms, as well as nineteenth-century ideologies of anti-Semitism and modern doctrines of race, empire, and nationality, are all understood to have their final end in the Holocaust.

Some Jewish thinkers consider the Holocaust are providing a singular vantage point of wronged innocence against which they can judge everything else. It is—has consciously been chosen by Jews to be—their Crucifixion: the great sorrow they must mediate.[15] Non-Jews are tried by two questions: what did they do (collectively or individually, directly or indirectly, by commission or omission) to further anti-Semitism? What did they do to stop the Holocaust? The most severe judges find everyone guilty who did not risk his and his family's lives to save Jews from the Holocaust.[16]

The subject of the Holocaust—a term that became popular in the mid-sixties and shows the human tendency to translate its most important experiences into religious metaphors—constitutes an immense debate amongst Jews. The Holocaust in the Jewish community is the subject of political, cultural, religious, and even aesthetic polemics, as Phillip Lopate observed.[17] At issue are such provoking moral-historical questions as the uniqueness and exclusivity of the Holocaust as a Jewish

experience, who shared what sorts of responsibility for the extermination of the six million Jews, and who has a valid right to speak for and
commemorate the dead of the Holocaust.[18] Also, in debate among Jews,
is the issue of Jewish collaborators—who did exist in considerable numbers—and the matter of who, if anyone other than the Jews themselves,
has the right to judge these collaborators.[19] Elie Wiesel, who as much
as anyone is understood to be speaking for the survivors and cynically
can be considered to be the head of "the Holocaust industry," said in
his acceptance speech of the Nobel Prize in 1987 that receiving it pleased
him and frightened him: "It frightens me because I wonder: do I have
the right to represent the multitudes who have perished? . . . It pleases
me because I may say that this honor belongs to all the survivors and
their children, and through us, to all the Jewish people with whose
destiny I have always identified."[20] In his 1980 Nobel Lecture, Pole
Czeslaw Milosz described his own anxiety regarding the Holocaust and
historical truth:

When the meaning of the word Holocaust undergoes gradual modifications, so
that the word begins to belong to the history of the Jews exclusively, as if among
the victims there were not also millions of Poles, Russians, Ukrainians, and
prisoners of other nationalities. He feels anxiety, for he senses in this a fore-
boding of a not distant future when history will be reduced to what appears on
television, while the truth because it is too complicated, will be buried in ar-
chives, if not totally annihilated.[21]

The Holocaust raises complex historical issues of national and international law, particularly insofar as it raises questions of punishment
and compensation.[22] It is central to American-Israeli relations.[23] The
Holocaust provokes arguments about who has the right to commemorate and pray for the Holocaust dead. The issue of who has the right
to commemorate the Holocaust took focus in the 1980s in a conflict
between Catholics and Jews. Without reconstructing the history of the
entire affair, which has taken a series of surprising twists and turns,
representatives of the international Jewish community pushed the Car-
melites to withdraw their convent and their cross from the perimeters
of Auschwitz, contesting the right of Catholics to establish a convent in
a place of Jewish sacrifice and commemoration. Beyond the contradictory reply of church officials, many Catholics pointed out that great
numbers of Catholics, especially Poles, and others aside from Jews were
murdered at Nazi Auschwitz before it became an extermination camp
for Jews, and they also asked whether everyone does not have the right
to pray where they wish.[24] Museums have been erected and are being
erected to keep the Holocaust memory alive—the most well known is
the Yad Vashem in Israel. The most recent to open, in the fall of 1988,

is the five-story United States Holocaust Museum, which is to be located in Washington, D.C., between the Jefferson Memorial and the Washington Monument, near the heart of the National Mall. Whole literatures surround the nature of being a survivor of and witness to the Holocaust. Forming a paradigm of real suffering, writers and thinkers say, no doubt pseudodramatically, that after the Holocaust there can be no art and denigrate their own experiences as superficial and unworthy of expression.

In *The Survivor* Terrence Des Pres revealed the power of the Holocaust as the ideal of innocent suffering when he wrote: "Odd as this sounds, there is among us an envy of suffering. It increases with education, and it reveals the bitterness felt when history renders our own pain trivial."[25] A contemporary Japanese-American writer further testifies to the hold of the Holocaust on contemporary conscience when he wrote of his internment experience during the Second World War:

I have never liked to talk about the internment. In the past, when asked by white friends about the experience, I told them things were not so bad. Compared to what happened to the Jews, I said that the Japanese experience was not worth talking about. [However] it occurred to me at the Smithsonian [sponsoring an exhibition on the Japanese-American experience] that I did not like talking about the experience because I thought it was so bad, but because it was not bad enough. . . . I envied the survivors of Japanese prisoner-of-war camps for the stories of brutal mistreatment they had to tell. I even envied the Jews for what they suffered in the German concentration camps.[26]

While the Nazi destruction of the Jews has become for Westerners the archetypical expression of the suffering innocent, there is still to be remembered, for instance, the genocidal war the Nazis conducted against other peoples and nationalities and other victims, like the handicapped and the Gypsies; Pakistan's destruction of three million Bengalis; the Turkish slaughter of a million Armenians; Pol Pot's destruction of three million Cambodian people; the Soviet purges of peasants (twenty million in all) and Ukrainians of the 1930s; or other immense horrors of this bloody and cruel history.

The assertion of the moral primacy of the Holocaust has not been free of controversy; its privileged moral status has not gone unchallenged.[27] Controversies between Jews and Arabs, especially over Palestinian rights, and Jews and blacks, especially associated with control of the inner city as well as affirmative action, turn on the issue of who has suffered what at whose hands and what present rights and benefits should be derived from past suffering. Often at stake between these groups are demands that, exceeding requests for fairness and justice, lay claim to mercy, compassion, and even love.[28]

Although essentially ignored by the public at large, one of the most revealing debates over the merit of past suffering in general and the Holocaust in particular exists between Polish Americans and Jewish Americans. Both groups cannot be separated from their conception of being a suffering, abused, and homeless people. Both find a large part of their worth in their suffering and their recent suffering at the hands of the Nazis. Milosz, revealing the Polish experience, said, "It is possible that there is no other memory than the memory of wounds."[29] Revealing a similar moral identity with the remembrance of suffering, Wiesel remarked. "Memory is our shield, our only shield."[30]

From a common, though not universally shared, Jewish point of view, Poles were long-standing anti-Semites, who failed to do what they could for the Jews during the Nazi occupation. Indeed, they cooperated with the Nazis in the Holocaust. The Polish reply to this accusation in these terms: they too were listed for extermination as an inferior people by Hitler. They stood in the way of his vision of an eastern Europe enslaved to his new Germany. They, too, suffered immense civilian losses, amounting to what some have considered "a forgotten holocaust." Moreover, Poles argue, Jews historically were more at home in Poland than anywhere else in Europe up to the Second World War, and that, while not perfectly, Poles did much to defend their Jewish neighbors and aid the Warsaw ghetto against Nazi oppression. They furnished the Germans with fewer collaborators than the Jews themselves. From the Polish point of view, to be accused of being a victimizer of the Jews not only impugns their honor, but denies them a place among the innocent, courageous, and tragic victims of the Second World War. They suffered under and fought against Germany from the outbreak of the war, not only within the regular Polish army and Home Army but in the services of other nations (like the British RAF) as well as an independent army, which landed at Normandy with the Americans, British, Canadians, and French.

Debates between Poles and Jews have not only fed mutual stereotypes but have reached the center of American academic life. (In one recent and notable case these debates decided an academic appointment.[31]) Even though few debates equal in historical complexity that between Pole and Jew, debates over suffering occupy national political lives in the twentieth century. Answers to questions of who suffered what and at whose hands are often transformed into standing rhetorics and become part of a work-a-day democracy's language. Saying one cares about the suffering of others has become a cheap way to counterfeit decency in a world in which taking measure of one's responsibilities is a complex matter. "A good heart" is an insufficient substitute for responsibility. Claiming that one is moral by simply asserting that one is on the side of victims against victimizers (whoever the victims be) is a moral sleight of hand, as is the claim that one's victims alone are really victims. This denies conscience and politics the rational deliberation they require.[32]

PERPLEXITIES AND DILEMMAS OF RESPONSIBILITIES

Even though justice requires us to respond to innocent suffering, there are impediments to responding: resentment leaves little room for empathy. Resentment is a powerful emotional force. In the twentieth century, it has directed whole peoples to concentrate on what they don't have or on what others do have.

Past ages taught us that survival requires being indifferent to pain and suffering; life doesn't afford people—at least the vast majority— the luxury of taking upon themselves the misery of others. Then, too, there is the basic fact that resentment plays such a powerful part in human experience. Furthermore, at all times it serves the healthy well not to dwell upon the sick. There is always a standing need to repress some suffering, to leave it without meaning, to live beyond, around, despite it. As, following Jesus' command, the dead should bury the dead, so the suffering should care for the suffering. There is always available a greater amount of suffering than we can fathom. Only professional literary mourners and idle and secure audiences have time and means to cultivate vicariously and multiplicatively the suffering of distant others. Melodramatics aside (upon which nineteenth- and twentieth-century literatures and their aficionados commonly dwell), no one's empathy is infinite. Anyhow, as a practical peasant might remark, a large heart doesn't spare a man or his neighbor pain or work.

However, these reasons do little to dike the rising rivers of suffering that come from every quarter. Victims have their sources in political repression, poverty, and the very processes of nationalization and modernization.[33] Equally important, the growing power of the media makes ever greater numbers of faces of the suffering strangers familiar to us.[34] Strangers ask us as citizens, believers, or fellow humans what we have done for them. Victim-strangers can cut to the core of our feelings. Their pain can seem to be direct and immediate; we cannot repress it. At other times their pain and suffering seems only momentary, and we banish it without even allowing it a trace in our memory.

The majority of pictures of the world's suffering brought to us by the evening news is more a matter of entertainment than anything else. Daniel Bell remarked,

The visual media—I mean here film and television—impose their pace on the viewer and, in emphasizing images rather than words, invite not conceptualization but dramatization. In the emphasis television news places on disasters and human tragedies, it invites not purgation or understanding but sentimentality and pity, emotions that are quickly exhausted, and a pseudo-ritual of a pseudo-participation in the events.[35]

Michael Ignatieff, who argues that "the moral life is a struggle to see—a struggle against the desire to deny the testimony of one's own eyes and ears," went even further in his criticism: "News is a mythic narrative of social identity constituted from commodities bought and sold on the international market."[36]

The power of visual media to shrink the world we live in, however, does not account for the heterogeneous faces of suffering that pervade our world. In some elemental way, we moderns have irretrievably opened ourselves to suffering. Herbert Spencer was correct: as pain diminishes, sympathy increases. The general improvement of our standard of living, coupled with an associated medicalization of pain and death and an expanding desire for pleasure and self-fulfillment, have made us, as I argued in chapter 7, not less but indeed more sensitive to suffering.[37] To paraphrase Malthus's law: as our pain decreases mathematically, so our desire for pleasure increases geometrically. Increasingly, we members of modernized societies understand anything that threatens our happiness—real and potential—as a form of suffering. We insist that our suffering be taken seriously, be considered a matter of government and law. Accordingly, public responsibility and civil liability have expanded immensely during the past two centuries.

Of the bountiful examples of this latter point, none is as a stunning as a horizon of new liability cases gathered around the most dubious and absurd principle of "wrongful life."[38] In these cases we have litigants attempting, so far unsuccessfully, to sue their parents or doctor or both, not for defects that they suffered at birth, but for having allowed them to be been born at all. In effect, they stand before a judge asking for compensation for having been allowed to exist. They argue that it was better that they were not born at all. Expanding legal conceptions of what constitutes harm and damage and broadening conceptions of liability and responsibility have joined in supporting the growing utopian notion that there should be neither pain nor suffering in human life at all, and that when they do appear someone is responsible to remedy or compensate for them. Victims, compensation, and reparations multiply as we assume, as no peasants ever would have, that the world should be without suffering and pain.

Our expanding responsibility for human suffering has been roughly paralleled by a growing concern for euthanasia and the formation of euthanasia societies and a broadening empathy for animals and plants. Presently emerging in certain quarters of the middle class of especially—but not exclusively—the Anglo-American world is an ecological conscience that voices not only empathy but even responsibility for the "bioregion" itself. More has been written on the subject of animal status in the past twelve years than in the past three thousand. Organizations are proliferating wildly. According to *Newsweek*, "Today there are some 7000 animal protection groups in the United States, with combined membership of ten million and total budgets of some fifty million."[39]

This conscience holds mankind collectively responsible for all planetary life. While traditional animal rights groups continue to exert their influence by calling our attention to human abuse of domestic and wild animals, newer organizations—spurred on in the 1950s and 1960s by a deepening sensitivity to nature, on the one hand, and an awareness of man's expanding power over nature, on the other—seek to fashion a new conscience for what seems a smaller and more fragile world. These voices can be shrill. The little-known Animal Liberation Front, which supposedly burned a furrier in Santa Rosa, California, phoned the Associated Press to warn that "ALF will continue its war against this Nazism (of making and selling fur coats) until the bloody fur trade is abolished forever."[40] Animal representatives can also use the same skills the medieval beggar did in search of alms. On an envelope from the Whale Rescue Project, it says, "When pilot whales are butchered alive, they scream in agony." Stamped in bold red letters on an envelope from the World Wildlife Fund is: *"JAGUAR ALERT!"* On an envelope from the Wildlife Conservation Fund, I read, "The snow leopard needs our help before it's too late." The cover of an envelope from the Whale Adoption Project tells me "To adopt the whale of your choice . . . just send this back to Cape Cod." Likewise, the International Fund for Animal Welfare has images of a sorrowful dog and cat staring out at me, while the envelope from the Defenders of Wildlife, carrying a picture of an independent wolf, cautions, "Alaska wolf killings will continue. Your help is needed immediately." As Barrington Moore points out in the context of sympathy-inducing bulk mailings, "It is even possible to gauge one's rage by the size of [one's] check."[41]

In the last few decades, philosophers have created a significant body of literature around the suffering and the rights of animals and plants.[42] As an example, Peter Singer, revealing a connection between earlier animal rights movements and the present, has argued explicitly on the basis of Bentham's notion that our kindredness with the animals is based on our mutual capacity to suffer: "We extend to other species," he wrote, "the basic principle of equality that most of us recognize should be extended to all members of our own species."[43]

Ecological discussions have not in all cases been conducted separately from consideration of increasing human population as well as the tendency to see man in all instances (even as unborn fetus) as victimizer and animals as always victims.[44] In light of what appeared to be an absolute world food shortage ahead and what they took to be the long-term good of both nature and man, some ethicists have argued for the need to allow humans to die. Garrett Hardin, a militant proabortionist and plants rights activist, drew several radical conclusions. Hardin rejected arguments that make the right to life or the right to escape unnecessary suffering as elemental rights of the individual and to be included among the first duties of government. Additionally, he spurned the "Marxist argument" made by the poorer nations that they have the right to reproduce and we have the responsibility to feed them.[45] The morality of act, he argued, is *a function of the state of the system at the time the act is performed—this is the foundation stone of situationists, ecological ethics.*[46] He argued for the need for a cosmic triage system: "In an uncrowded world there may be no ethical need for the *ecological concept of carrying capacity.* But ours is a crowded world. We need this concept if we are to minimize human suffering in the long run (not such a very long run at that)."[47] The increasing interdependence of humans and animals and issues of animals' rights and their suffering surfaced in a recent meeting of Berkeley's Citizen's Humane Commission. They had a spirited debate "on whether to exempt Chinese potbelly pigs—miniatures sold as household pets—from an ordinance that effectively bans barnyard pigs from town."[48] The issue was debated not in terms of do pigs run and stink but, in the words of one participant, "whether it is humane to impose domesticity on yet another animal."[49]

A growing number of advocates for special victims, including plants and animals, add to the river of diverse, heterogeneous, and perplexing forms of suffering against which we measure our responsibilities. Identifying with and representing suffering (of course, stylized, classified, and dramatized) is for growing numbers their home and purpose in what they find is a homeless and purposeless world.[50] Suffering (as the romantics fashionably made it) is their language of seriousness; it also serves them as a means of asserting their rights and taking power. Modern ideologies (of both the right and left) shape their most serious claims in reference to suffering, blood, and sacrifice. Regis Debray, who once served the causes of Communist revolution in Latin America in the 1960s, perceptively wrote:

Redemption through suffering, salvation in death and expiation of the past . . . are dressed up in a Marxist-Leninist vocabulary that would have left Marx and Lenin quite bewildered. . . . National revolution as the *redemption* of the poor, the revolution as *rebirth,* commitment as a *vocation,* discipline as *devotion, el hombre neuvo,* as the vanquisher of the Old Adam—all these themes figure prominently in the early Havana manifestoes (1960–1962) and are still the common language of those who fall in armed struggle in Central America. Blood is the seed of nations—an image common to Tertullian and our funeral orations—and dying for the cause is the supreme reward.[51]

If clashing claims to suffering's rights constitute one reason for our confused and divided responsibilities, diffuse and vague senses of guilt about inequality are another source. The modern state, so activist by its nature, seduces us to believe that everything unwanted is a political problem that merits a political response.[52] Democracy invites comparison. Some people are seen to do well, others are not. Often joined to this basic sense of justice is the additional moral sense that well-being is purchased at the expense of others. Although peoples of the Western World are invited to be proud of the material benefits they enjoy, wealth has also meant—at least for the most susceptible—guilt: the guilt of having what others do not and the guilt of having it at the expense of others. People of the developed world are commonly reminded of what share of the world's resources they enjoy in contrast to members of the underdeveloped world.[53]

In cyclic but spreading and intensifying scales, the sense of being responsible for the world's suffering has affected Western sensibility since the eighteenth century. Without seeking to establish a cause-and-effect connection between events, trends, ideas, and feelings in society, I note that this sensibility both preceded and followed from the spread of nationalism and industrial capitalism. American society of course, displayed the convulsive power of this sensibility in the 1960s, as American confidence and power at its apex met failure and frustration in Vietnam.

This highly contagious sensibility (to which the political left is nearly altogether without emotional or rhetorical immunities) associates everything bad with one's own nation—what one's nation has done, allowed to be done, or not done. The logic of this indictment leads back and forth from nation to self and self to nation; guilt and accusation are the emotional dynamos of this self-punishing process.

Once infected by this sensibility, one rarely escapes running a low-grade fever that confuses all suffering with nation and self. Wise words, like those offered by American statesman and elder George Kennan, have no antidotal power for the infected:

Despite frequent assertions to the contrary, not everyone in this world is responsible, after all, for the actions of everyone else, everywhere. Without the power to compel change, there is no responsibility for its absence. A first step along the path of morality would be the frank recognition of the immense gap between what we dream of doing and what we really have to offer, and a resolve, conceived in all humility, to take ourselves under control and to establish a better relationship between our undertaking and our real capabilities.[54]

Using one's own nation as the means by which one imaginatively associates with and legislates for the world at large is the expected and common act of a citizenry. After all, nations are the most generalized form of human will. This is especially true if one belongs to a powerful nation. However, concealed within this assumption there is a fallacy, one in which we Americans are well versed. The fallacy is confounding the world with our nation, and our nation with our power and responsibility.

Confusion about the means of carrying out our responsibilities to victims are further compounded by not having a national consensus upon which to judge and act. John Kekes is correct when he contends "the salient fact [of our time] is not immorality, but moral confusion."[55] Whether this confusion is a consequence of the loss of older values or of the conflicts inevitable in an increasingly pluralistic society, the fact remains that we are uncertain about the suffering to which we can and should respond. Our multiple identities and loyalties as believers, citizens of a nation, members of an emerging world community, as well as species, intensify our confusions about the possibilities of our power and thus the nature and exercise of our responsibility.

Forming the core of our uncertainty as Americans is our ambivalence about power and the state itself. The very government to which we look for help for ourselves and humanity is equipped by weaponry to destroy us and the rest of humanity. We fear that the "beast" who feeds us today will eat us tomorrow. This ambivalence, which cuts to the quick of our identity with the nation, is true also of our larger economic and scientific and technological institutions: with them there is no gift free of problem, no hope without dread. To generalize our goodwill toward innocent suffering through our government, even if it represents our greatest chance of doing anything, is never done without ambivalence. Problems are often solved only at the cost of more problems; cures frequently prove worse than diseases.[56]

Even when we have determined we are confronting a face of innocent suffering that requires action, there still remains a host of perplexing questions about means. The horizon of our choices reaches us from the solitary act of bearing witness to the full use of governmental power, from an impeccable commitment to nonviolent action to using all means necessary to secure one's cause. The contestability of choices of means adds to the diffuse guilt and frustration we experience in our attempts to be our brother's keeper.

A WORLD WITHOUT BOUNDARIES

The public world is not contiguous to, but in fact is sharply discordant with, the world of order we idealize. No matter how much we believe in the democratic process, things out there just don't seem to make sense. They are not fair; they are out of tilt; they are not just.

They don't square with our sense of community. Like the most primitive people (discussed in early chapters of this work), we want to know the value of our suffering and sacrifices. It is important to know what suffering to take seriously; we need to know when to wail, mourn, and sacrifice, when to turn to soldier, doctor, or priest. But we do not know.

As twentieth-century politics and literature testify, there is in the breast of the contemporary person an immense longing for community. As the world opens itself to its own diversity and grows smaller, as differing groups come into contact with one another, more and more people give themselves and even more tragically, their politics, over to nostalgia. Theodore Zeldin is not alone in arguing that nostalgia commands us far more than a belief in progress.[57] This longing for community conceals a valid quest to organize a coherent world in which values, experience, and suffering have an order. We need to declare our own shrines, heroes, martyrs; we need to honor our own dead and, with no blasphemy intended, describe the suffering of our own gods. If, in any sense, we are going to be whole, we have got to tell our own stories, relay our own accounts of our sufferings. We cannot stand nude before the suffering (present, past, and possible, real and feigned, individual and ideological) with which the modern world confronts us, suffering which at so many points exceeds our comprehension and defies our ability even to imagine how to minister to it. We cannot be asked to be the doctor of all and yet be given no medicine.

The limits of our ability to articulate a moral order for the public world at large is one factor among many others explaining why we become more intensely patriotic in our local world as the world becomes more planetary, why we become more nationalistic as the world increasingly turns on international relations.[58] The world is organized more easily at the level of the microcosm. In a smaller world, one can better organize the meaning and values of one's own experience. There one can better measure the worth of one's pain and know one's own sacrifices. A calculus of pain and suffering might not exclude, to use a phrase of Peter Berger, "a calculus of meaning."[59]

The human need for a meaningful order helps explain the profound staying power of the family. In the family (as awful as it can be) we make and recognize the sacrifices that matter most. In most instances, our public altruism and philanthropy is superficial by comparison to the sacrifices we make within our families. In the family we exchange the goods which most embody our lives. There we experience our sharpest pain and suffering. Consequently, the family is the object of the strongest feelings of love, hate, gratitude, and resentment. The family, too, is the home of our own dead. Like Greeks and Romans of old, the family remains the first religion of the majority. This remains true even in this age of mass and national cultures.

This disjuncture between public and familial realms explains a good deal of twentieth-century politics. While intellectuals and politicians carry on their abstract discourses about nation, world, and humanity, the majority of people know their interests and value their suffering more concretely at home and in their neighborhood. It is there they know, at least more or less, what they do and what is done to them; they know what they give and what they are given; they work and suffer and they see the work and suffering of those around them. What is decent, fair, and just is filtered (as one could only expect it to be) through what they experience and value. The world itself is too vast, heterogeneous, and complex for their deliberations. People willingly accept their ignorance of it or, more quickly, adopt the words, slogans, formulae, and ideas (as half-baked, fictitious, and simplistic as they are) that intellectuals and national politicians provide them. But what they value most is at home or nearby.

The great majority of people know vividly what their family did to get where it is, and in most instances the story of any given family contains memories of sacrifices. The family got where it did not by theft and corruption, intelligence or luck, but by work, endurance, and sacrifice. Stories of suffering and sacrifice are the family's moral identity and entitlement. Perhaps only a small percentage of youth separates itself, and then only temporarily, from its family stories.

It is this sense of moral worth that often puts society in general at odds with intellectuals and politicians and places ethnic peoples in direct conflict in the United States with the new left, liberalism, and proponents of affirmative action. Each of these groups was heard by ethnics to say in one way or another, "Your moral identities aren't valid. They are flawed by ignorance, intolerance, racism, and sexism." Beyond this, ethnics heard the history of their suffering and sacrifices repudiated; they were told that they didn't deserve what they had. These insults were felt most sharply when they came in the form of compulsive legislation that adversely affected their jobs, communities, and families, and when it came from the hands of the righteous and wealthy representatives of their government.

They experienced these insults also as an attack upon their nation and religion. For the lower classes, especially of the first, second, and third generations, America was understood as a place of opportunity and fairness—a place where one's work, suffering, and sacrifices earned one respect and improvement. The family stories of immigrants become inseparable from their views of America. Attacks upon America were understood, as conservative politicians argued, to be attacks upon them.

Described in its simplest terms, a major part of American political discourse in the 1960s, 1970s, and 1980s amounted to liberals and radicals accusing the United States of causing suffering. Another group, led by a range of conservatives, stressed America's past and present goodness. Ever greater numbers of Americans, far too intelligent for this simpleminded moralistic debate and realizing they could do little to influence the world at large, turned yet more earnestly to matters of their family, work and, in many instances, local community and church. There they could feel that their interests and sacrifices had value.

Other reactions also signal retreat in the face of an increasingly complicated world, in which personal pleasure and fulfillment are ever more possible on the one hand and complex and contradictory issues abound on the other. Many critics, from Ortega y Gasset and his analysis of mass man in the 1920s to Hannah Arendt in the 1950s, have contended that there has been a tendency in mass democratic society to reduce the autonomy and complexity of the public order to the simplifying needs of the domestic-economic order.[60] More recently, a number of critics, such as Christopher Lasch and Richard Sennett, restating an older classic criticism of contemporary democracy as failed republican life, have argued that a growing reaction to our complex world is the abandonment of the public order altogether for the sake of a private realm of tranquility, pleasure, and fulfillment.[61] For the expanding middle class, according to these critics, the truism, "There is no place like home," has justified a full-scale retreat from the public good. Historian and critic Christopher Lasch describes what he believes to be a growing flight from public life in reference to an advancing hedonism and narcissism. This flight from the public realm, according to Lasch, finds its ideological support from psychologists, social workers, and others who reduce the public order to the psychological categories of frustration and fulfillment.

From whatever perspective this flight from the public order is surveyed, there are limits to it. Nations, governments, and bureaucracies are ever more powerful. Economies are increasingly global. Outside institutions, ideologies, and communications now penetrate the most remote communities, the most insulated cultures, and the most traditional households. As mounting evidence from all fields of the natural sciences demonstrates, globally we cannot ecologically escape the consequences of one another's activities. Simply put, we have all become matters of one another's suffering and happiness, and the primary way we have to generalize our wills towards each other—as we must—is through our respective governments.

INESCAPABILITY OF POLITICS

Our concern for our own suffering and the suffering of others drives us to politics. The most obvious reason for this is that states are immensely powerful. They determine our well-being. Any general issue of happiness or misery is considered to be—correctly or incorrectly—a matter for the state. Our identities are inseparable from national states and what they do. States are important in defining who we are and what happens to us. Consequently, the value of our suffering and our responsibility for the suffering of others turns on them.

Second, by virtue of being modern, we expect to be happy. Only grudgingly do we moderns concede failure and tragedy a place in our understanding of life. As much as we might criticize and despair of the nation-state, it is our primary agent of collective change. (The worth of democracy is not easily divided from our belief that our improved lot is a matter of collectively soluble problems.)

Third, almost everywhere, there has been assent to the proposition that the nation-state is the fundamental instrument for realizing human potential and social justice. And to this has been joined the assumption, one that emerged in the eighteenth century, that the state should and can do good. Modern political discourse invariably raises questions of who benefits and who suffers. This debate, which can on occasion reach high levels, is more commonly coarse and banal, belonging to the modern condition and identity. Nevertheless, this debate forms a sort of common culture for us, as spiritually deprived as it is. Politics has become the religion of this secular age.

It is important to determine what dangers ideologies of suffering hold for the political process and, conversely, what dangers the political process holds for communities based on loyalty to traditions of suffering and sacrifice. Ideologies of suffering, be they of the political right or left, endanger the political process in many ways. For instance, ideologies of revolution usually expropriate past sufferings in order to justify their present rage as well as unlimited activism, neither of which have any place in a political community. Often equally insidious, other ideologies use constituencies of victims to conjure a sense of guilt in their opponents, making them more easy to manipulate. In some instances, certain ideologized victims become a matter of standing rhetorical traditions and entrenched bureaucracies, which sustain emotions, resentments, and claims generations after the victims have disappeared and their heirs have begun to prosper. Then, too, there are those ideologues who, as predictably as society changes its tastes and fashions, find new victims in whose names they can lacerate themselves and attack "the system" at will.

No doubt, modern society has permitted us in the West the luxury of choosing our favorite victims. "Savages" and "the under classes" are no longer to be feared but now, almost powerless, they are transformed into objects of pity, compassion, and even advocacy. Victims become not only justification for indicting civilization in whole or in part, but victims even become a matter of good taste. One chooses one's favorite victim, with an eye to being morally fashionable. Suggesting how the increasing promise of happiness sharpens, differentiates, and multiplies our awareness of the misery of others, Stephen Mennell in *All Manners of Food* pointed out that "slowly there developed greater sensitivity of feelings towards inequalities in nourishment as towards social inequalities . . . [so that] by the late twentieth century, however, it was generally considered good to express and even to feel shock and horror at hunger not only in one's own society but in the Third World too." [62]

Finally, ideologues bring to the political process claims on behalf of such an immense, tragic, and even cosmic suffering that there can be no political response to them. The harm and the remedy they set forth exceed the power of any legislature to remedy; the only adequate responses could come, if at all, from either philosophy or religion. They seek, indeed often demand, compassion, mercy, forgiveness, and love, human responses not common to any work-a-day democratic politics.

Ideologues of suffering and victims have grown bountiful in this century of warfare and revolution. In competition with one another for public attention and power, they escalate their claims, threatening at points the political process itself. Some, indeed, paradoxically enough, assert their claims beyond compromise and compensation. They prove that a claim to innocence is not necessarily an innocent act. [63] In the name of their innocent dead, radical groups sentence innocent hostages to death.

Allies of democracy must contend against those who seek to bully democracy with their victims of class, race, history, sex, and tradition. Some radical groups reduce public discourse to aggressive and irrational moralizing. They would be as quick as any with the powers of state in their hands to use it against individuals and groups. Our opposition must rest on the simplest of principles. We must start with the notion that the public realm is no one group's moral kingdom. While, of course, all claims of suffering are not equal, nevertheless, all substantive claims deserve consideration of some sort. Torture is torture; death by poison gas is death by poison gas. There can be no democracy if the claims of suffering of one group are taken seriously, simply because they are who they are, while the claims of others are disregarded simply because they are who they are. This moral Manicheanism that divides the world between victim and victimizer should have no place in a constitutional democracy.

Claims of suffering demanding public recognition and compensation should be subject to rational examination and critical debate. They should not only be carefully scrutinized, but they also should be examined in reference to their practicality as well as their fairness.

Legislators should be careful about permitting into the political process claims about suffering that exceed identifiable political remedies. Otherwise the door is opened to endless compensation for the injured, ever expanding bureaucracies representing these incompensable victims, and a language that drowns out all others. Legislators should not even seek to satisfy those who set forth insatiable claims. To try to deal with those who claim they are beyond "dealing" is to feed moral monsters. Their righteous discontent will be increased with each attempt to satiate them.

As minority compensation in the United States has shown, victims breed victims. In a society with an improving standard of living, claims to being victimized increase and the claim to be a victim becomes a common moral posture of those who want benefits. Frequently, claimants to suffering's compensation compete and collaborate with one another. They even form political parties and wings of political parties, encouraging the factionalization of the political system.

Although legislators must recognize that they cannot prima facie ignore claims of suffering, in fact must give them special attention, they, nevertheless, must recognize that certain forms of suffering often exceed the political process's capacity to remedy them. In many of its forms, the demands and language of victims and their suffering not only transcends the political process but threatens it.

Claims of victims' suffering from the past cannot be allowed to shadow the present. These claims, if admitted fully into the political discourse, put the living in the service of the dead. The democratic legislator must be leery of claims that exceed his everyday understanding and practice. As European politics of the 1920s and 1930s demonstrated, to choose only one example, a politics of suffering can produce parties of blood, resentment, and violence. Politicians, no doubt, need to speak about suffering, sacrifice, and victims, for they are irreducible, often composing, elements in any discussion of fairness and justice. The legislative process and the courts should, and have no choice but to, remain open to claims of wrong. Yet they must be cautious, for there are always abundant victims and nothing guarantees that today's victims won't be tomorrow's victimizers. Citizens do not reason well about blood, sacrifice, and martyrs. Myths become prisons for political thought and action. Democracies can fail when they speak mystical languages.

If politicians have reason to fear the representatives of suffering and victims, so, also, do representatives of suffering have reasons to fear politicians. Politics, at its best, is not a precise process. It weighs things in the rough. It lacks a fine balance. It is a matter of fad and fancy; it is determined by expediency, the give and take of compromise, anything but a fair and deliberative process. Victims have a changing worth on the political agenda. Available money, changing sensibilities, pressing problems all shape the vagaries of politics. It would take more than a little magic to know which group—be it the black, poor, veterans, Indians, alcoholics, or prisoners will be given legislative attention.

Politics invariably strives to enroll the living in its community. It is—and all who care about the past and the dead should note this—more about forgetting than remembering; it is more about establishing functional images and symbols of community rather than dwelling on the painful, tragic, and insoluble truths of past tragedies. This also means that politics has little concern for the suffering of little individuals and small groups—and may even be antagonistic to them if they contradict official identities and images or present interests and expediencies. Politics, at its best, seeks to get on with things. Its interest is not commemoration or justice. First and foremost, its metaphors and sacrifices serve the national community.

Day-in-and-day-out politics is more about preserving the remains of its official heroes than finding the bodies of its unknown victims. Nowhere is this as clear as in the main square in Buenos Aires. There, in the square where the cathedral keeps the remains of San Martin, the mothers of the disappeared *(las madres de los desaparecidos)* still march once a week. They ask where are their missing children, whose exact fate at the hands of the dictatorship are unknown and whose bodies have not been returned.

Ultimately, politics demands suffering that it cannot redeem. It asks (especially during times of war or economic crisis) sacrifices without being able to give them ultimate meanings. Governments invariably ask their subjects to sacrifice themselves against their familial and personal interests. The nation, which asked a generation to fight a war, will when the war is over erect some monuments and build some hospitals and forget about its "martyr-soldiers" in the name of a new cause. Politics is fickle. It can be precise, but it cannot be personal. Veterans and their associations always look for gratitude and honor but usually become resentful. A great deal of this century's most extreme politics turns on resentment about unacknowledged suffering.

Gratitude and resentment are powerful but imprecise human emotions. They are malleable to political rhetoric. Shaped by such coarse ideologies as utilitarianism, Marxism, and democratic egalitarianism, not to mention nationalism, racism, and other ideological languages, political language invariably distorts what it represents and conveys. With its ends being recruitment, compromise, justification, or domination, political language rarely serves truth and is often antithetical to justice.

Yet there are other factors that should dissuade the representatives of suffering and victims from seeking consolation in the political arena. Among the most obvious factors is that all suffering is not easily defined to self or world. It lacks equivalencies. Often it has no clear place in laws and treaties and even defies any attempt to define wrongs suffered: who precisely, directly or indirectly, immediately or across generations, suffered the wrongs, and who perpetrated the wrong, and who, if any, were its beneficiaries. Matters of death, tragedy, and calamity ultimately defy calculation and may be by definition incompensable. Some suffering is too personal to have any relation to the political and legal process. The betrayal of a friend, the disappointment of a lifetime's work, an inopportune death, a long disease—none of these belong to the political process. Likewise, the suffering from the biological, cultural, and religious orders should not be confused, even though they commonly and tragically are, with the political order.

Few people are as pathetic as those deluded individuals who confuse their personal suffering with politics. Such confusions can, as contemporary Iran illustrates, overtake the consciousness of entire societies, and such confusions are, as twentieth-century Western experience shows, never altogether absent from everyday politics. Democracy teaches people to compound their identities with their nations: one of the inescapable consequences of this process is the creation of mass delusions about the power of politics either to cause or relieve suffering. Men and women turn to their governments like once they did with their sacrifices to their gods of old.

In yet a more profound way, suffering and sacrifice come from the most intimate levels of the person. How we endure our suffering invariably transcends the political process. It is a matter of the deepest levels of the human spirit; it is about prayer and things hoped for. Who we suffer with and who we sacrifice for define the communities that we value most. These communities, which include the living with the dead and the unborn, are not and cannot be made contiguous with the secular political community without great distortion. There is—and here I defy a most common assumption of the modern world—much suffering that does not have, and should not have, a political equivalence. There are things greater than politics. We cannot trust our most important loyalties to politicians or ideologues.

A NEW CONSCIENCE?

It is not satisfactory to conclude this chapter defending the political process against the ideological representatives of suffering or defending valid traditions, communities, and individuals of suffering against processes of politicization.

Beyond attempting to purify our consciences from the compelling ideological impulses of our era, there is a need to formulate a conscience that goes beyond the rigid moral boundaries of class, sex, nation, and other fixed traditions. This conscience must be responsive to the victim-strangers of the world. I take this to be the central quest of Michael Ignatieff's *The Need of Strangers*.

Flawed by an all too common impulse to have consciousness and ethics directly correspond to changing historical reality, Ignatieff's arguments seek a new conscience for what Ignatieff takes to be a new age. Ignatieff defines our age not in terms of its expanding aspirations to overcome all pain, suffering, and limits, but in reference to the great tragedies that have overcome humanity in this century. He revealingly wrote:

In the twentieth century, the idea of human universality rests less on hope than on fear, less on optimism about the human capacity for good than on the dread of human capacity for evil, less on a vision of mankind as a maker of history than of man the wolf towards his own kind. The way stations on the road to this internationalism were Armenia, Verdun, the Russian front, Auschwitz, Hiroshima, Vietnam, Cambodia, and Lebanon. A century of total war has made victims of us all, civilians and military, men, women, and children alike. We no longer live in a time when violence is distributed and pity and compassion too—along the lines of tribe, race, religion, or nation. If new technology has created a new form of war and a new crime—genocide—we have also witnessed the creation of a new kind of victimhood. War and genocide have overturned the moral boundary-markers of citizenship, race, and class which used to allocate responsibility for the relief of suffering. If we take it for granted now that the Ethiopians are our responsibility, *it is because a century of total destruction has made us ashamed of that cantonment of moral responsibilities by nation, religion, or region,* which resulted in the abandonment of the Jews. Modern universalism is built upon the experience of a new kind of crime: the crime against humanity.[64]

In Ignatieff's view we are all potential victims. The possibility of nuclear war assures that. Furthermore, given the power of the state to destroy and the power of the media (especially television) to relay images, anyone of us can be uprooted from all our local environments and stripped of all support from traditional groups to which we belong. We will be left entirely dependent on the help of distant strangers before whom we appear not in person but as fleeting images. The condition of many—the potential condition of us all—is to be thrown on "the charity of strangers."[65] "In this sense," Ignatieff contended, "human brotherhood is a myth made actual and concrete by the history of twentieth century horror: it is a myth with a history, a necessity only history can give."[66] Upon this basis Ignatieff concluded that "an ethic of universal moral obligation among strangers" is "a necessity for the future of life on the planet;" without such an ethic, "the universal victim will find no one beyond the wire to feed him."[67]

Leaving aside a certain melodramatic rhetoric, which understandably is common to those who write on the twentieth century, Ignatieff's quest for a new ethic is not naive. He realizes such an ethic is not easily separated from the fashions in morality, stylish victims so to speak. "There are fashions in morals as there are fashions in clothes," he wrote.[68] He understands, given the topsy-turvy character of the modern world, that there are great temptations to indifference. He also understands that the representatives of victims must compete in a public world lacking established frames of reference and argued upon judgments. They must make their case in the news which, in Ignatieff's words, constitutes "a market in images of horror as there is a market in grain or cameras, and there are those who specialize in the production and specialization of such images."[69]

Further compounding the problem of formulating such a conscience for our era is the ideological character of contemporary society. Ignatieff praises such recent groups, born after the Second World War, as Amnesty International, Care, Save the Children, Christian Aid, Oxfam, Medicins sans Frontières, as well as such ecologically committed groups as Greenpeace and World Wildlife Fund. These groups strive to create a world constituency for their causes independent of the political right or left. Seeking to articulate the core sense or impulse of a new conscience adequate for our time, Ignatieff favorably cited the words of British war photographer, Don McCullin, who in his introduction to a collection of some of his photographs of Biafra, Bangladesh, and Vietnam, wrote: "But what are my politics? . . . I am so defeated by it [political theory] I don't even vote. I've tried to be a witness, an independent spectator, with the result I can't get beyond the facts of what I've seen. I've experienced too much suffering. I feel in my guts, at one with the victims. And I find there's an integrity in that stance."[70]

The highest conscience, I read Ignatieff to say, will bear witness to individual victims. This conscience will compel us to witness and serve their suffering.

I believe Ignatieff would concur that such a conscience proves rare. Multiple groups of victims have to compete for limited sympathetic attention in a world that, not just by its tragedies but by its aspirations, produces more and more victims. Victims multiply more rapidly than the number of people capable of empathy: sufferings and tragedies are greater than the number of audiences that can be assembled.

Inescapably we must establish hierarchies of victims. We must compare victims to one another. It is not easy to determine and, even more difficult to establish, a consensus regarding whose suffering and what kind of suffering should count the most in our minds—animal or human; victims of political acts or natural disasters; peoples who have suffered great things, are suffering great things, or will suffer great things. This consideration is never conducted entirely free of our prejudices, stereotypes, and predispositions. There are required additional considerations involved in determining the assignment of responsibilities for victims and the means necessary to respond to them. Each of these considerations brings into play ideologies as well as cultural myths and religious values. In our divided and bipolar world, victims who escape death by indifference might suffer annihilation by ideology—the great contaminant of modern society.

Different types of victims awake different types of sympathy. There are victims, like the native peoples of North and South America, Asia, and Africa, as well as the peasant cultures of the world, who have perished or are on the verge of extinction. They do not produce any claim to political action. They only evoke in us, when thought of, a profound sorrow; they are being slaughtered by the forces of modernity and nothing can be done about it. We are losing forever living human voices. No set of flags or bureaucracy will spare them from their obliteration. We can only commiserate.

The plight of many victims goes beyond our ability to act and exceeds our capacity to redeem. Not to recognize this is irreverent. To use our dead, for instance, to assault and negate the entire present, as tempting as this can be, is wrong. It is only another moral nihilism, of which so many abound. Our obligation to such victims can only be commemorative and prayerful.

We cannot remember all the dead and dying. We haven't their names or even time to say them all. We must make our wishes collective; as masses have throughout the ages, we can only ask for collective blessings for all those who are hungry, who are injured, who suffer injustices, who despair. The litany of victims is long. On their behalf we must not only have courage to act but the compassion to remember—and we must not venerate, as if we are some sort of Buddha or Christ, our own compassion.

Our hearts are too small and fragile to contain the world's victims. In truth, our memory does not suffice to hold their history; our sympathy cannot compass their condition; our imagination fails to espy their cure. Our humility before their suffering can be great yet we must not surrender our reason to their soulful fates.

NOTES

1. For a useful introduction and excerpts of thinkers concerned with the importance and even primacy of sympathy for an ethical life, see Christina Hoff Sommers, ed., *Vice and Virtue in Everyday Life* (New York: Harcourt Brace Jovanovich, 1985), 1–66.

2. See David Hume's *Treatise of Human Nature* (1739–40), ed. Ernest Mossner (Baltimore: Penguin Books, 1969) and *An Inquiry Concerning the Principles of*

Morals (1752), ed. Charles Hendel (Indianapolis: Bobbs-Merrill, 1957) and Adam Smith's *The Theory of Moral Sentiments* (1759), (Indianapolis: Liberty Classics, 1969). Also useful is J. D. Campbell's *Adam Smith's Science of Morals* (Totowa, N.J.: Rowman and Littlefield, 1971).

3. For a complex argument, verging on contradiction, which argues that future generations have no rights and we have no obligations to them even though future generations represent a value we might choose to serve, see Richard DeGeorge, "Do We Owe the Future Anything?," in *Morality in Practice*, ed. James Sterba (Belmont, Calif.: Wadsworth, 1988), 108–15. For an argument that both distant peoples and future generations have a right to life and fair treatment, see Frank Sterba's "The Welfare Right of Distant Peoples and Future Generations," ibid, 115–27. In "Abortion, Distant Peoples, and Future Generations," ibid., 177–83, James Sterba correctly points out the common and widely shared contradiction of many ecologists who advocate the rights of future generations, while denying altogether the right of the unborn child to life itself.

4. Cited in Agnes Heller, *Beyond Justice* (Oxford: Basil Blackwell, 1987), 24.

5. Ibid., 25.

6. André Béjin, "The Decline of the Psychoanalyst and the Rise of the Sexologist" and "The Influence of Sexologists and Sexual Democracy," in *Western Sexuality*, ed. Philippe Ariès and André Béjin (Oxford: Basil Blackwell, 1985), 181, 200–217.

7. George Church et al. "The U.S. and Iran," *Time* (November 17, 1986): 24.

8. Cited in Geoffrey Hartman, ed., *Bitburg in Moral and Political Perspective* (Bloomington, Ind: University of Indiana Press, 1986), xiv.

9. Ibid.

10. Ibid., xv.

11. For one short guide to the Holocaust, see Yehuda Bauer, *The Holocaust in Historical Perspective* (Seattle: University of Washington Press, 1978).

12. George Kren and Leon Rappoport, *The Holocaust and the Crisis of Human Behavior* (New York: Holmes and Meier, 1980), 93.

13. For one recent Christian examination, illustrating the sensitivity of a discussion of the United States' obligation to Israel, see Robert McAfee Brown, "Speaking About Israel," *The Christian Century* (April 6, 1988). Brown comments, "Love is our only valid passport into the territory of discussion about Israel," 340.

14. For an example of a Gentile willing to sound the alert of resurgent anti-Semitism, see Abigail McCarthy's "An Ugly Resurgence: Hate Calls Out Hate," *Commonweal* (December 17, 1982), 678–79, and a reply by Thaddeus Radzilowski, "Prejudicial Images," *Commonweal* (March 11, 1983): 130.

15. Phillip Lopate, "Resistance to the Holocaust," *Tikkun* 3, no. 4 (1989): 63–64.

16. Israel Shahak criticizes Timothy Ash and Claude Lanzmann, the producers of the lengthy film *Shoah, Polish Jew*, for their harsh judgment of Poles for not intervening at every point and in every way to prevent the Nazi atrocities against the Jews. He claims that they overlooked the essential "fact that Jews, Poles, and everybody else so far as we can know . . . behave in about the

same way (they sympathize but continue as best they can their own lives) and such behavior is part of something that we may call human nature," *New York Review* (January 29, 1987): 45.

17. Lopate, "Resistance to the Holocaust," 55–65, and Yehuda Bauer, "Don't Resist: A Critique of Phillip Lopate," *Tikkun* 3, no. 4 (1989): 65–69.

18. For an example of the passion aroused by the question to whom does the Holocaust belong, see Henrijk Grynberg's "Appropriating the Holocaust," *Commentary* (November 1982): 8–9, and the range of letters to the editor it provoked, ibid. (April 1983), 6–9.

19. For a reference to Jewish collaborators in Poland, see Richard Lukas, *The Forgotten Holocaust: Poles under German Occupation* (Lexington, Ken.: University of Kentucky Press, 1986), 118, 251. For two pieces that argue that Jews should be judged by standards different than Poles for cooperation with Nazis or Jews should be exempted altogether from judgment, see respectively Lucy Dawidowicz, *The Holocaust and the Historians* (Cambridge: Harvard University Press, 1981) and Jacob R. Ginson, "Holocaust," part 2, "Behavior of the Victims," in *Encyclopedia Judaica*, 16 vols., (New York: Macmillan, 1972), vol. 8, 890–902.

20. "Elie Wiesel Receives the Nobel Prize," Elie Wiesel quoted in article *Martyrdom and Resistance* 13, no. 3 (Jan./Feb. 1987), 1; for a description of Wiesel, see Lopate, "Distance to the Holocaust," 56.

21. Czeslaw Milosz, *Nobel Lecture* (New York: Farrar, Straus, Giroux, 1980), 16.

22. For a short review of how the Holocaust stands at the center of German historical self-interpretations, see Karen Winkler, "German Scholars Sharply Divided over Place of Holocaust in History," *Chronicle of Higher Education* 33, no. 37 (May 27, 1987): 4–5. For a single example of the complex legal issues surrounding the question of the United States' responsibility to act against former Nazis, see Stephen J. Massey, "Individual Responsibility for Assisting Nazis in Persecuting Civilians," *Minnesota Law Review* 71, no. 1 (October 1986): 97–170.

23. For a discussion of American-Israeli relations and the pro-Israeli lobby, see Edward Tiunan, *Jewish Political Power and American Foreign Policy* (New York: Simon and Schuster, 1987).

24. Rabbi Daniel Landes heatedly accuses the pope of "hijacking the Holocaust" with the establishment of a Carmelite convent in Auschwitz and by canonizing saints who, though perishing at the hands of the Nazi, are used to represent the promise of the cross and resurrection. This, according to Landes, hides the indictment the Holocaust makes of the world's "cruelty, cowardice, and apathy" and the horrible death of these true Jewish martyrs who died bitterly distant from "the eternal construct of Judaism that includes the promise of the afterlife." Daniel Landes, "The Pope's Assault on the Jews," *Tikkun* 2, no. 4 (Sept./Oct. 1987): 47–51. In a following issue of *Tikkun* (Jan./Feb. 1988):77–78, Catholic Eugene Fisher's attempt to placate Landes by arguing that neither pope nor church were seeking to Christianize the Holocaust, failed. In the same issue, Landes replied, "If other religions want to treat death differently, it is their prerogative. But let our remains lie in peace. It is immoral to recycle them for fuel to run some devotional machine. It is blasphemous to utilize our dead for the victory of a religion which helped destroy them," 79.

For more recent twists of the affair, see Catholic William Pfaff's insightful but confused conciliatory piece, "Nazism's Victims in Painful Clash," *Minneapolis Star Tribune* (August 27, 1989): 28A.

25. Terrence Des Pres, *The Survivor: An Anatomy of Life in Death Camps* (New York: Pocket Books, 1976), 45. According to Des Pres, the remembrance of suffering is the sustaining and compelling force of the survivor. Survivorship is a way of being in this century. The survivor remembers and retells, never forgetting that we live in a world of endless suffering and mutual sacrifice.

26. Gene Oishi, "Exhibit Launches Personal Journey for Camp Veteran," *Minneapolis Star Tribune* (August 2, 1988): 9A.

27. Non-Europeans often conclude, even in the matter of the Holocaust, that white Europeans only take their own sufferings seriously. This sentiment surfaced strongly, especially among those sympathetic to Algerians who suffered at French hands, at the trial of Gestapo officer Klaus Barbie in Lyons in 1987. Diana Johnstone, "Barbie Trial: Response to Ugly Past Reveals Contradictions of the Present," *In These Times* (July 22–August 4, 1987): 8–9.

28. For a recent discussion of the controversial gift of a conservative synagogue to a black arts group in light of black suffering after the death of Martin Luther King, see Hillel Levine and Lawrence Harmon, "Profit and Prophets: Overcoming Civil Rights in Boston," *Tikkun* 3, no. 4 (July/August, 1988): 45–48, 94.

29. Czeslaw Milosz, *Nobel Lecture*, 20.

30. Cited in Lance Morrow's "The Morals of Remembering," *Time* (May 23, 1983): 88.

31. British scholar Norman Davies—one of Europe's foremost scholars of Poland—was denied by fellow faculty a chair at Stanford University by a twelve to eleven vote because his recently published and award-winning book, *God's Playground: A History of Poland*, 2 vols. (New York: Columbia University Press, 1984), was found to be unacceptably defensive of Polish relations to Jews during the Second World War. Stanford University, taking the side of the majority, argued in its defense of the faculty's politically motivated judgment, that, indeed, in the case of subjects like history, political persuasions could validly be scrutinized in assigning appointments. Leaving aside the bitter accusations that marked the debate, several profound historical-moral questions came into play regarding not only Polish collective responsibility for the fate of the Jews but the right of Poles to write a history of their own suffering as an immense tragedy. This debate, which covers a complex range of historiographical matters about cause, motivation, and responsibility, does not escape, on the one hand, consideration of the twenty to thirty million humans who lost their lives in eastern Europe during the Second World War and, on the other, the need for all parties to tell stories of their own martyrs and heroes. For a clear expression of the ideological issues that underlay the debate, see Norman Davies's and Abraham Brumberg's exchange of letters, "Poles and Jews: An Exchange," *The New York Review* (April 9, 1987): 41–44.

32. Illustrative of the mentality of righteous innocence, Minnesota U.S. Senate Democratic candidate Polly Mann announced herself in her campaign literature to prospective voters as a person who had undergone a moral conversion to the side of good:

Dear Friend: I could credit my high school history teacher [a real person or a fictive person standing for ignorance?] for my early misconceptions about the United States. But she was a victim as I was—she believed what she'd been taught: that the U.S. had the most noble, generous, and unselfish government in the history of the world, that it had never knowingly done anything wrong; and that its people received equal treatment under the law. It took a good amount of study and personal experience, including a year and a half in a foreign country, to shake me loose from my views!

Polly Mann for U.S. Senate (Jan./Feb. 1988), 1.

33. Exemplary of the vast literature on victims is Kurt Glaser and Stefan Possony, *Victims of Politics: The State of Human Rights* (New York: Columbia University Press, 1979); John Bodley, *Victims of Progress* (Menlo Park, Calif.: Cummings Publishing Company, 1975); Peter Berger, *Pyramids of Sacrifice: Political Ethics and Social Change* (Garden City, N.Y.: Anchor Books, 1976); Gil Elliot, *Twentieth Century Book of the Dead* (New York: C. Scribner, 1972); Barrington Moore, *Reflections on the Causes of Human Misery and Upon Certain Prosposals to Eliminate Them* (Boston: Beacon Press, 1972), and Aleksandr Solzhenitsyn, *The Gulag Archipelago*, 3 vols., (New York: Harper & Row, 1974, 1976).

34. For a thoughtful but impressionistic exploration of the claim of the stranger upon us, see Michael Ignatieff, *The Needs of Strangers: An Essay on Privacy, Solidarity, and the Politics of Being Human* (New York: Viking, 1985).

35. Cited in Patrick Brantlinger's *Bread and Circuses: Theories of Mass Culture of Social Decay* (Ithaca, N.Y.: Cornell University Press, 1983), 286.

36. Michael Ignatieff, "Is Nothing Sacred? The Ethics of Television," *Daedulus* (Fall 1985); 57–78.

37. Herbert Spencer wrote, "The great factor in progressive modification is shown to be sympathy," *Principles of Ethics*, 2 vols. (New York: D. Appleton Company, 1898), vol. 1, vi; also see, ibid., vol. 2, 431–33. For a study of the close connection between sympathy and the modern mentality, see Daniel Lerner, *The Passing of Traditional Society: Modernizing the Middle East* (New York: Free Press, 1958), esp. 19–75.

38. For examples of wrongful life cases, see *Simin v. Hickman and Chris A. Hickman v. Group Health, State of Minnesota Intervenor*, No. C2-85-2013, Supreme Court of Minnesota (Oct. 24, 1986) and *Sharon E. Berman, Paul A. Berman, and Shirley A. Berman v. Ronald Allan and Michael V. Attardi*, Supreme Court of New Jersey (June 26, 1979).

39. Geoffrey Cowley, et al., *Newsweek* (December 26, 1988): 50.

40. Cited ibid., 52.

41. Barrington Moore, *Injustice* (New York: M. E. Sharpe, 1978), 501.

42. For examples of the emerging literature on animal and plant rights, see John Rodman, "The Liberation of Nature?" *Inquiry* 20 (1977): 83–145; Stanley Goddovitch, Roslind Goddovitch, and John Harris, eds., *Animals, Men, and Morals* (New York: Tarplinger Publishing Company, 1971); Christopher Stone, "Should Trees Have Standing?—Toward Legal Rights for Natural Objects," *Southern California Law Review* 45 (1972), 450–501; Laurence Tribe, "Ways Not To Think About Plastic Trees: New Foundations for Environmental Law," *The Yale Law Journal* 83 (June 1974): 1315–48. Also of critical interest is R. G. Frey, *Rights, Killing and Suffering: Moral Vegetarianism and Applied Ethics* (Oxford: Basil Blackwell, 1983) and Joel Feinberg, "The Rights of Animals and Unborn Genera-

tions," in *Rights, Justice, and the Bounds of Liberty,* ed. Joel Feinberg (Princeton, N.J.: Princeton University Press, 1980), 159–83.

43. Peter Singer, "All Animals Are Equal," *Applied Ethics* (Oxford: Oxford University Press, 1986), 216; for use of Bentham, ibid., 221.

44. Of course, in the case of domestic pets the reverse is also true: while in the United States 415 human babies are born every hour, 2000 dogs and 3500 cats were born on the average every hour to a total population of 56 million cats and 54 million dogs. Last year, animal shelters took in 22 million dogs and cats, as cited in Geoffrey Cowley, et al. "Of Pain and Progress," *Newsweek* (December, 1988), 59.

45. Garrett Hardin, "Carrying Capacity as an Ethical Concept," in *Lifeboat Ethics,* ed. George Lucas et al. (New York: Harper and Row, 1976), 121.

46. Ibid., 132; emphasis is mine.

47. Ibid., 134.

48. Ken Wells, "Going Berserkeley," *The Wall Street Journal* (January 11, 1989).

49. Ibid.

50. Regis Debray, *Critique of Political Reason* (Norfolk: Thetford Press, 1983), 333.

51. Debray, Critique, 5–6.

52. The temptation to reduce reality to politics is well articulated by Jacques Ellul's *The Political Illusion* (New York: Vintage Books, 1967) and keenly set forth in Peter Berger's *Pyramids of Sacrifice.*

53. The ethical dimension of global equality in a changing world is well explored by Raymond Aron, *Progress and Disillusion: The Dialectics of Modern Society* (New York: Mentor Books, 1968).

54. George Kennan, "Morality and Foreign Policy," in *Best American Essays 1986,* ed. Elizabeth Hardwick (New York: Ticknor and Fields, 1986), 195.

55. John Kekes, "Is Our Morality Disintegrating?" *Public Affairs Quarterly* 1, no. 1. (January 1987): 82.

56. For a short piece on anarchist persuasion, see my "Freedom, Fatalism, the State," *The Phoenix* 9, nos. 7 & 2 (1983): 5–27.

57. Theodore Zeldin, *Intellectual Taste and Anxiety,* vol. 2 of *France: 1848–1945,* 2 vols. (Oxford: Oxford University Press, 1977), 1083.

58. Debray makes the point that as the world becomes ever more one, it becomes ever more fragmented, ever more planetary, ever more patriotic, suggesting an interplay between globalization and tribalization, *Critique of Political Reason,* 341. All this has to be considered in detail and understood in light of how recent all translocal institutions and identities are for the majority of humanity.

59. Peter Berger, *Pyramids of Sacrifice,* 8.

60. See Ortega y Gasset, *Revolt of the Masses* (New York: Norton, 1932) and Hannah Arendt, *The Human Condition* (Chicago: University of Chicago, 1958).

61. See Christopher Lasch, *The Culture of Narcissism* (New York: Norton, 1979) and Richard Sennett, *The Fall of Public Man* (New York: Vintage, 1977).

62. Stephen Mennell, *All Manners of Food: Eating and Taste in England and France from the Middle Ages to the Present* (London: Basil Blackwell, 1985), 322–23.

63. For a keen comment on innocence as a matter of entitlement and power,

see Shelby Steele, "I'm Black, You're White, Who's Innocent?," *Harper's* (June 1988): 47.

64. Ignatieff, *The Needs of Strangers* and "Is Nothing Sacred? The Ethics of Television," *Daedalus* (Fall, 1986), 64–65. Also of use for Ignatieff's critical concern for the suffering of others is his *The Needs of Strangers*.

65. Ignatieff, "Is Nothing Sacred?," 65.

66. Ibid., 65–66.

67. Ibid., 66.

68. Ibid., 68.

69. Ibid., 71.

70. Ibid., 68.

Conclusion: To Tell the Story of One's Own Sufferings

A people without history is like wind upon the buffalo grass.
Old Teton Sioux Saying

Let everyone tell his own story, his own way.
Ignazio Silone, *Fontamara*

Moral stories are often about worthy suffering. They tell of suffering that merits honor. They define human meaning.

A person without his or her own moral stories to tell is hardly a person at all.[1] In "The Story-Telling Animal," Alasdair MacIntyre wrote, "There is no way of founding my identity—or lack of it—on the psychological continuity or discontinuity of the self. The self inhabits a character whose unity is given as the unity of character."[2] The self must be found in the stories it tells or allows to be told about itself.

Elsewhere in that essay, MacIntyre suggested we belong to a community of stories: "I am part of their story, as they are part of mine. The narrative of any one life is part of an interlocking set of narratives. . . . The unity of a human life is the unity of a narrative quest."[3]

Stories constitute identities. They are our most common way to establish ourselves in time, in community, and in value. Indeed what are humans but their stories? ("God made man because he loved stories", wrote Elie Wiesel.[4]) Individuals are stories. Families are stories. Peoples are stories. Nations are stories. Religions are stories. Events insist upon stories.

Stories are the moral center of our human experience, for they re-count what we have done. Out of them we construct ourselves. They tell of the exchange of gifts and the carrying out of deeds. They mea-sure inheritances, accomplishments, luck, and failures. Without stories generosity, gratitude, and fairness cannot be recounted; greatness and meanness go unexpressed.

Nothing so denies us and our stories, as the denial of our sufferings and sacrifices. If we have no sufferings or sacrifices to call our own, we have no story to tell, and with no story to tell, we are no people at all. (Perhaps this recognition and the indignation it supports that more than anything else recently turned great numbers of ethnic Americans against what is called the liberal wing of the Democratic party.)

There are many enemies of our suffering and sacrifices and our sto-ries about them. Many of them are inseparable from how we experi-ence the modern world. We encounter the modern world as richly var-iegated, unmeasurably disjointed, and overwhelmingly crushing. Next to it our stories seem puny. We find ourselves devoid of stories capable of matching the range of the accomplishments, aspirations, feats, and tragedies of the humanity we increasingly come to know. We cannot help but feel that we and our stories are mere straws in the mighty rivers of contemporary history.

As a first enemy would have us not take our suffering seriously—even tempt us in some way, like the peasant of old, to steel our hearts against our own feeling—a second enemy of our suffering who so in-undates us with the sufferings of others we can have no stories of our own sufferings. This enemy would make our hearts throbbing, aching residences for all imagined hurts. No pain, no plea for sympathy, would escape our open hearts. It would have us, if it had its way, suffer all suffering. He would spare us no pain, no misery, real or imagined, past or future. He would transform our consciousness into a pitiful mess of confused and pretended sympathies; we would take our compassion to be without boundary, fathomless, and he invites us to live the sham of imagining ourselves to be none other than an all-feeling and merciful God, while in fact we are pitiful wrecks, driven by the unassuageable guilt of knowing that our hearts can never encompass the world's mis-ery. This enemy sentences us to the pretense of believing we have the inexhaustible capacity to care. It would be as if the morbid protagonist of Chekhov's "Gooseberries," who hates the happy man, would finally have his way:

Behind the door of every contented, happy man there ought to be someone standing with a little hammer and continually reminding him with a knock that there are unhappy people, that however happy he may be, life will sooner or later show him its claws, and trouble will come to him—illness, poverty, losses, and then no one will see or hear him, just as now he neither sees nor hears others.[5]

Aside from various cults of the mindless, who preach perennial happiness or its possibilities, and that growing number of psychologists who forever promise a new road to bliss, there are other enemies of our stories and suffering: the "utilitarians," who reduce all suffering to calculable pain and attribute only negative meaning to it, and the dominators of suffering, who seek to give an exclusive meaning to suffering. These enemies dislike stories equally, for stories exceed their reductionism and their attempts to calculate or monopolize meaning.

While the utilitarians (among whom we include all those diverse moderns who reduce suffering to pain and subordinate pain to pleasure) subvert our stories by denying all intrinsic and transcendental meaning to our suffering, the manipulators of suffering are in many ways more insidious. While boldly asserting the value of suffering and sacrifice, they seek to make themselves the rulers of suffering. They wish to define its meaning and control its value.

The manipulators of suffering, who in their most concentrated, ideological forms, lead revolutions and run states, arrogantly insist upon the singular validity of their moral worlds. They are not dumb about power; they know it pays to have right on their side. They do not hesitate to divide the world cleanly into two moral groups, those who suffer and those who cause this suffering.

Believing in the singular worth of one's own suffering, sacrifices, and stories is as old as human history itself. However, in the course of the nineteenth century, nationalism enrolled ever greater numbers of people in exclusive and totalistic myths. In the case of the most extreme forms of nationalism, imperialism, racism, and anti-Semitism, groups were equipped with the right, and even the duty, to inflict suffering upon one another. Marxist doctrines of the inevitability and the propriety of class warfare, as well as Darwinian contentions about the need and the good of struggle within and between species, further poisoned the public discourse by contending that one class or race had the right to liquidate another. The great wars and revolutions that greeted the twentieth century produced veritable legions of people and industries of propaganda committed to asserting the exclusivity of certain forms of suffering and its entitlements. (No one else's heroism, innocence, or suffering was considered comparable; nor was there any admission on the limits of their claims on either theoretical or practical grounds.) Stories of bloody suffering, betrayed innocence, and unforgettable sacrifice took hold of the twentieth century. Innocent blood became the moral treasury of legionnaires and revolutionists alike; every cause of both political right and left had its martyrs. Domestic and international discourse became a matter of irreducible and irreconcilable moral claims about suffering, sacrifice, and victims. Tolerance was discounted altogether.

The representatives of sacred suffering bring to twentieth-century liberal and democratic politics impossible claims. They not only assert their public right to tell and benefit from their stories, but paradoxically, they don't want their holy stories either publicly debated, challenged, or, most of all, politicized so that the claims their stories contain can either be satisfied or, judged unsatisfiable, set aside. While wanting to bring their stories forward, they wish to insist that their suffering is singularly unique and forever beyond compensation. They want their stories to retain religious sanctity (to be a matter of pure and uncompromised suffering), but be publicly known and politically effective.

The greatest zealots intimidate others into silence. They would dominate all in the name of the suffering of their preferred innocent victims. With their bloody tales, they seek to bully the political process and justice itself, deciding the issue of right and wrong in advance of all deliberation. This behavior only surprises those of us who mistakenly believe ourselves and our contemporaries to be too modern to transact our moral and ethical business in reference to victims, blood, and sacrifice.

In this century, our personal and familial stories are often swallowed by the scale of public life and the pervasive penetration of the media. Most of our stories seem to be few and insignificant when compared to the dramatic and mass events of this century. In turn, our stories are commingled with the stories of mass society, nations, and their institutions. Their stories—be they official histories, coarse ideologies, or vague myths—become ours. Our stories, as our lives themselves, become annexed to theirs. We cannot have landed, so to speak, on the beaches of Normandy, suffered the Great Depression, or been moved by a terrorist act against fellow citizens without our personal stories becoming part of our nation's history.

In the contemporary world our stories are increasingly circumscribed by, grafted to, and swallowed by the stories of class, nation, and the world at large. We tell their stories as our own. And in telling them, we join ourselves to new communities. We emplot ourselves in new stories, fill out new narratives, and in so doing, take upon ourselves new identities.[6]

We keep losing ourselves and values in the stories of others. Our "village" is shattered, yet the shattering world is no new village. We sense that we have been transformed into perpetual spectators at a theatre of unending performance and incalculable consequences. Television in particular has made us feel that, at most, it is our fate merely to observe the experience of others. Our moral worth is reduced to merely considering our reactions to the experiences of others. Life itself becomes another movie we go to and talk about.

We find ourselves compelled to struggle with all our might to maintain our own stories. More and more we resemble the elderly rural storyteller who can find no one—not even his own children—to listen to his tales. It seems somehow his stories and, therefore, his life count little if they do not meet, as they never do, the bountiful leisures and the Benthamite calculations of the world around them. He, like each of us, is worth only so much pleasure and so much pain—and beyond that he should shut up, go about his business, and if not up to that, quietly die or graciously accept our institutions for the old. There is, the romantic within us observes, a mechanical and predictable grimness in our well-organized and "painless" world. Too few stories are told.

At times, we sense we have been betrayed. We have been lured into the modern world by goods, education, the promise of a better life. And now we, its prisoners, are subject to its alien power, ideas, morals, traditions, and stories. Over generations our families struggled and sacrificed to get a national identity—and now that very identity we so earnestly sought leads us into a distant and alien world whose suffering and sacrifice, victims and victimizers are not ours.

We cannot easily differentiate ourselves from either nation or world. With our moral imagination vastly extended by the range of our power and sympathies, we lend ourselves to the most distant and diverse roles of victim and victimizer. We find ourselves playing all moral parts in the broken worlds that surround us. We do not know where the stories around us begin and end.

Given the consequences of twentieth-century politics, we can no longer presume that the extension of human power is good. Since we do not know with certainty either the consequences of, our responsibilities for, our vast political and economic agencies that we by citizenship rule and from which we by consumption benefit, our moral position vis-à-vis the world's suffering is ambiguous.

With surrounding powers so great and moral boundaries so unclear and ambiguous, our inner forums are confused. Some of us go as far as to hold ourselves responsible for such an abstraction as the collective fate of humanity itself and all sensate creatures as well as the existence of the world itself. Beyond the imagination of the boldest philosophes, we make ourselves God—responsible for nothing less than the world's suffering and the redemption of humanity itself.

So the enemies of our stories are great. Yet suffer, sacrifice, and tell stories we must. There is no human action without sacrifice; no human life without having to suffer and to cause suffering. Through sacrifice alone we become lucid to ourselves.[7] A lifetime is a matter of sacrifices, and its meaning can only be rendered by stories of sacrifices. A family, a religion, a community—each is a collection of stories, of which the most important are about suffering and sacrifice. Even if the heavens are deaf, we continue to value things beyond life itself.

Our sacrifices define the moral order of things. In relation to them we define friend and foe, god and demon, alike. Sacrifice is a matter of our first transactions, those pertaining to blood and lives.

Some of us may still wish to conduct traditional sacrifices.We may wish to tell stories that do not conform to the official and popular myths, metaphors, and heroes of the era. We cling to stories that pale in significance by the measure of present powers and the faithless flux that prevails. Nevertheless, we make our sacrifices and tell our stories as best we can.

Sacrifices cannot be reduced to self-interest or utility. Nor can they be reduced to moral judgments of character. Suffering is not only a necessity and a test, but it is also—especially when concentrated as sacrifice—our risk for the good. Sacrifice defines our moral territory. It measures our freedom and loyalty. It is the singular means by which we, with a part or a whole of our being, choose one thing over another.

Until a person sacrifices his or her life for something, nothing—not word or love or truth—can be said to be more valuable than having life itself. Sacrifice is the cornerstone of the moral person and community.

As in most serious human matters, we must act and hope, never ultimately knowing the depths of ourselves, or the outcome of our actions. We are the blind kings of our own sacrifices. We do not fully know what we give or receive. Michael Weinstein wrote, "The sense that we are always sacrificing ourselves and others, and that our sacrifices have no justification, yet are necessary, is the moral predicament and the moral motive."[8]

Our trust, loyalty, fidelity, and love itself find their primary expression in sacrifice. Mutual sacrifices testify to our highest communities and meanings.[9] Beyond sacrifice there is only hope for a meaning that we cannot assure. It is that meaning our most intimate stories preserve. We must struggle to preserve these stories, as modest, inadequate, and insignificant as they are, against contemporary events and ideologies and those who would seek to dominate all experience and suffering.

Let men and women tell their stories of suffering and sacrifice as they will. We and our democracies will all be richer for this—and philosophy, which has never had much room for stories—none the poorer.

Man is a story telling animal.[10] Stories are the scripts by which we place ourselves in time and society, define our virtues and vices, and tell histories—histories that may interest God himself—about how we suffer this world and how, on rare and blessed occasions, we sacrifice ourselves to meanings we value but cannot secure. Stories are our most important inheritance; the heart and the blood of our moral life. We should not surrender our stories any easier than we would surrender our freedom.

NOTES

1. I developed the theme of story as creator of the person and human institutions in my recent book, *When Father and Son Conspire: A Minnesota Farm Murder* (Ames, Iowa.: Iowa State University Press, 1988), esp. 205–9; also, see my "Parents and Grandparents: We Are All Migrants and Immigrants," *Great Lakes Quarterly* (Winter 1976): 27–42.

2. Alasdair MacIntyre, ed., "The Story-Telling Animal," *Twenty Questions: An Introduction to Philosophy* (New York: Harcourt, Brace, & Jovanovich, 1988), 362.

3. Ibid., 362–63.

4. E. Wiesel, *Gates of the Forest* (New York: Holt, Reinhart & Winston, 1966).

5. Anton Chekhov, "Gooseberries," *The Portable Chekov,* ed. Avram Yarmolinsky (New York: Penguin Books, 1978), 381.

6. Theodore R. Sarbin, "Emotions as Narrative Emplotments," in *Entering the Circle: Hermeneutic Investigation in Psychology,* eds. Martin J. Packer and Richard B. Addison (Albany: State University of New York Press, 1989), 185–201.

7. Useful for a discussion of this is Michael Weinstein, *Structure of Human Life: A Vitalist Ontology* (New York: New York University Press, 1979), esp. 128–68 and Emmanuel Mounier, *Personalism* (Notre Dame, Ind.: Notre Dame University Press, 1970).

8. Weinstein, *Structure of Human Life,* 150.

9. This conclusion is shaped by French Catholic personalist, Emmanual Mounier, who is the subject of my *Mounier and Maritain: A French Catholic Understanding of the Modern World* (Tuscaloosa, Ala: University of Alabama Press, 1975).

10. Alasdair MacIntyre, "The Story-Telling Animal," 361–63.

Bibliographical Essay

I hope that this work, in the best sense of the word, is interdisciplinary. Its underlying premise is historical. I assume that we best understand what our individual and collective conditions are by knowing what we have inherited. My historicism is, however, tempered, for I do not believe that our ethical inheritance is devoid of truth and transcendence.

For general works in ethics and moral theory, see Abraham Edel, *Morality, Philosophy and Practice: Historical and Contemporary Readings and Studies* (New York, 1989); Milton Gonsalves, *Right and Reason: Ethics in Theory and Practice* (Toronto, 1989); Louis Pojman, *Ethical Theory: Classical and Contemporary Readings* (Belmont, CA., 1989); and George Sher, *Moral Philosophy: Selected Readings* (New York, 1987).

Aside from David Hume, *An Inquiry Concerning the Principles of Morals* (1752) and Adam Smith, *The Theory of Moral Sentiments* (1759), for works in ethics illustrative of the growing interest in character and virtues on the one hand and sympathy on the other, see Michael Bayles and Kenneth Henley, *Right Conduct* (New York, 1983); Lawrence Blum, *Friendship, Altruism, and Morality* (Boston, 1980); Robert Kruschwitz and Robert C. Roberts, *The Virtues: Contemporary Essays on Moral Character* (Belmont, CA., 1987); Alasdair MacIntyre, *After Virtue* (Notre Dame, 1981); and Christina Sommers, *Vice and Virtue in Everyday Life* (New York, 1985).

For suggestive works on pain and suffering, see David Bakan, *Disease, Pain, and Sacrifice* (Boston, 1968); Paul Chauchard, *La Douleur* (Paris, 1974); Fyodor Dostoyevsky, *The Brothers Karamazov* (1880); Sigmund Freud, *Civilization and its Discontents* (1930); Freud, *The Future of an Illusion* (1927); Erving Goffman, *Stigma: Notes on the Management of Spoiled Identity* (Englewood Cliffs, NJ., 1963); C. S. Lewis, *The Problem of Pain* (London, 1949); Jonathan Miller and Hubert Marcuse, *An Essay on Liberation* (Boston, 1969), *The Body in Question* (New York, 1982); Blaise Pascal, *Pensées* (posthumously published, 1670); Edward Peters, *Torture* (Oxford, 1985); Dorothy Rowe, *The Construction of Life and Death* (New York, 1982); Elaine Scarry, *The Body in Pain* (New York, 1985); Edwin Schneidman, *Deaths of Man* (Baltimore, 1974); Thomas Szasz, *Pain and Pleasure* (New York, 1975); Richard Taylor, "Arthur Schopenhauer," *Nineteenth Century Religious Thought In the West* (Cambridge, 1985), 157–80; Michael Weinstein, *Structure of Human Life* (New York, 1979); Matisyohu Weisenberg, *Pain: Clinical and Experimental Perspectives* (St. Louis, 1975); Hans Wenke, *Pain: Its Meaning and Significance* (London, 1963); and Corrine Wood, *Human Sickness and Health: A Biocultural View* (Palo Alto, 1979).

As suggested by the following works, cultures value our pain, work, and suffering; they prescribe our punishment and define our sacrifice. Ernest Becker, *The Denial of Death* (New York, 1973); John Bowker, *Problems of Suffering in the Religions of the World* (Cambridge, 1970); Joseph Campbell, *The Hero with a Thousand Faces* (New York, 1956); Jacques Choron, *Death and Western Thought* (New York, 1963); Stanley Diamond, *Primitive Views of the World* (New York, 1960); Mary Douglas, *Purity and Danger* (London, 1966); Mircea Eliade, *Rites and Symbols of Initiation* (New York, 1958); Peter Farb, *Man's Rise to Civilization* (London, 1971); Herman Feifel, *The Meaning of Death* (New York, 1965); Martin Foss, *Death, Sacrifice, and Tragedy* (Lincoln, NE., 1966); René Girard, *Violence and the Sacred* (Baltimore, 1977); Jean-Louis Golin, *Les misérables dans l'Occident médiéval* (Paris, 1976); Edward Hall, *Beyond Culture* (New York, 1976); Marvin Harris, *Cannibals and Kings: The Origins of Kings* (New York, 1977); Joseph Henninger, "Sacrifice," vol. 12, *Encyclopedia of Religion*, ed. Mircea Eliade (New York, 1987), 544–47; Gary Hogg, *Cannibalism and Human Sacrifice* (New York, 1966); H. Hubert and Marcel Mauss, *Sacrifice: Its Nature and Functions* (Chicago, 1964); E. O. James, *Comparative Religion* (New York, 1961); Vittorio Lantenari, *La Grande Festa* (Bari, Italy, 1976); Arien Mack, *Death in American Experience* (New York, 1973); B. Malinowski, *Crime and Custom in Savage Society* (Totowa, NJ., 1972); Anne Marie Malejjt, *Religion and Culture* (London, 1968); Calvin Martin, *Keepers of the Game: Indian-Animal Relationships and the Fur Trade* (Berkeley, 1978); Barrington Moore, *Injustice* (New York, 1978); Marcel Mauss, *The Gift: Forms and Functions of Exchange in Archaic Societies* (New York, 1967); Walter Moberly, *The Ethics of Punishment* (Hamden, CT., 1968); A. R. Radcliffe-Brown, *Structure and Function in Primitive Society* (New York, 1965); Claude Levi-Strauss, *Tristes Tropiques* (New York, 1969); G. Van Der Leeuw, *Religion in Essence and Manifestation*, 2 vols. (New York, 1963); Arnold van Gennep, *The Rites of Passage* (Chicago, 1960); Hans von Hentig, *Punishment: Its Origin, Purpose and Psychology* (London, 1937); Michel Vovelle, ed., *Mourir autrefois: Attitudes collectives devant la mort aux XVIIe et XVIIIe siècles* (Paris, 1974); and Max Weber, *The Sociology of Religion* (Boston, 1963).

As the polis became the center of Greek social life, fourth- and fifth-century Greek philosophers, mirroring this transition, sought to carry out an equally profound revolution. If they were to have their way, human reason and will would replace religion and sacrifice as the means by which humanity would define its place in the cosmos. Aside from classic texts of Plato, Aristotle, Epicurus, Epictetus, etc., useful secondary works include: Hannah Arendt, *The*

Human Condition (Chicago, 1958); Jonathan Barnes, *Early Greek Philosophy* (New York, 1987); F. M. Cornford, *From Religion to Philosophy* (New York, 1957); Stanley Diamond, *In Search of the Primitive* (New Brunswick, NJ, 1974), 176–202; M. I. Finley, *The World of Odysseus* (New York, 1978); H. Frankfort and H. A. Frankfort, "The Emancipating of Thought from Myth," in *The Intellectual Adventure of Ancient Man*, ed. H. Frankfort, et al. (Chicago, 1977), 363–88; William Greene, *Moira: Fate, Good, and Evil in Greek Thought* (New York, 1963); Werner Jaeger, *Paideia: Ideals of Greek Culture*, 2 vols. (New York, 1965); Alasdair MacIntyre, *A Short History of Ethics* (New York, 1966), 5–109; and Erich Voeglin, *The World of the Polis*, vol. 2 of *Order and History* (Baton Rouge, LA., 1957).

Christianity made sacrifice of self the highest measure of conscience. In addition to a range of articles on such topics as sacrifice, blood, saints, the sacred heart, and martyrs found in the *Encyclopedia Judaica*, 16 vols. (New York, 1972); the *New Catholic Encyclopedia*, 16 vols. (New York, 1967); and the *Encyclopedia of Religion and Ethics*, 12 vols. (New York, 1908–1927), a few useful books on the power of sacrifice in Christian thought are Søren Kierkegaard, *Fear and Trembling* (Garden City, NY., 1955); Karl Löwith, *Meaning in History* (Chicago, 1949); Jaroslav Pelikan, *Jesus Through the Centuries* (New Haven, CT., 1985); and Pelikan, *The Christian Tradition*, 4 vols. (Chicago, 1971–1984). Suggestive of how medieval Christianity built a system of transacting suffering, sacrifice, and grace around Christ and his martyrs and saints, are Peter Brown, *The Cult of the Saints: Its Rise and Function in Latin Christianity* (Chicago, 1981); Brown, *Society and the Holy in Late Antiquity* (Berkeley, CA., 1982); Caroline Bynum, *Holy Feast and Holy Fast: The Religious Significance of Food in Medieval Women* (Berkeley, CA., 1987); Jacques LeGoff, *The Birth of Purgatory* (Chicago, 1984); and Jonathan Sumption, *Pilgrimmage, An Image of Medieval Religion* (Towota, NJ., 1975). Aside from Luther's and Calvin's writings, useful to understand Protestantism's internalization and privatization of faith and suffering (undercutting the Communion of Saints, prayers for the dead, and purgatory), is John Bossy, *Christianity and the West* (Oxford, 1985). However, as is shown by William Monter, in *Ritual, Myth and Magic in Early Modern Europe* (Athens, OH., 1983) and Jean Delmeau, *Catholicism Between Luther and Voltaire* (Philadelphia, 1977), neither the Reformation nor the Counter-Reformation spelled the end of beliefs in the supernatural efficacy of saints, sacrifices, and suffering.

Of course, it was the Enlightenment, as a movement of high culture and emerging middle class reformist culture, that directly attacked the notion that suffering in any form was a good and that sacrifice was a necessary medium by which humanity transacted its relations with the dead and God. In addition to many representative articles on grace, providence, miracles, saints, and sacrifices, which fill Pierre Bayle's *Dictionnaire historique et critique* (1697) popularly available in English, *Historical and Critical Dictionary*, ed. Richard Popkin (Indianapolis, 1965); Voltaire's *Dictionnaire philisophique* (1764) in English, *Philosophical Dictionary*, ed. Theodore Besterman (New York, 1972); and Denis Diderot, ed., *Encyclopédie; ou, Dictionnaire raisonné des sciences, des arts, et des métiers* (1751–1772; publisher and place of first two editions unknown), there are the writings of such philosophes as Voltaire, Hume, Paine, D'Almbert, Helvétius, Beccaria, and Bentham. For a few useful secondary works, accenting the secular and immanent thrust to Enlightenment thought, see Carl Becker's classic *Heavenly City of the Eighteenth Century Philosophers* (New Haven, CT, 1932); Ernst Cassirer, *The Philosophy of the Enlightenment* (Boston, 1955); Elie Halevy, *The Growth of Philosophical Radicalism* (Boston, 1955); Eric Voegelin, *From the Enlightenment to the Revolution* (Durham, NC., 1975); and Peter Gay, *The Enlightenment: An Interpretation* (New York, 1966). For works that help show that the Enlightenment was more than the abstract proposals of a handful of thinkers but also involved, at least on some level, a change of world views and attitudes, see Elinor Barber, *The Bourgeoisie in the Eighteenth Century* (Princeton, NJ, 1955); Crane Brinton, *A History of Western Morals* (New York, 1959); Robert Darnton, "In Search of the Enlightenment: Recent Attempts to Create a Social History of Ideas," *Journal of Modern History* 43 (March 1971): 113–32; Steven Kaplan, ed., *Understanding Popular Culture: Europe from the Middle Ages to the Nineteenth Century* (Amsterdam, 1984); Robert Mauzi, *L'idée du bonheur dans la littérature et la pensée au XVIIIe siècle* (Paris, 1961); John McManners, *Death and Enlightenment* (Oxford, 1985); Franco Venturi, *Utopia and Reform in the Enlightenment* (Cambridge, 1971); and Guy Williams, *The Age of Agony: The Art of Healing* (Chicago, 1986).

By creation and aspiration, the nineteenth century confronted traditional resignation to pain and suffering. To examine the traditional and peasant attitudes about pain and suffering, the inevitability of which the modernizing forces of the modern world contradicted, see my "World Without Intimacy: A Portrait of a Time Before We Were Intimate Individuals and Lovers," *International Social Science Review* 61, no. 4 (Autumn 1986), 155–68; Jerome Blum, *The End of the Old Order in Rural Europe* (Princeton, NJ, 1978); Peter Burke, *Popular Culture in Early Modern Europe* (New York, 1978); Pierre Goubert, *The Ancien Régime, French Society, 1600–1750* (New York, 1973); André Varagnac, *Civilisation traditionnelle et genres de vie* (Paris, 1948); and Eugen Weber, *Peasants into Frenchmen: The Modernization of Rural France, 1870–1914* (Stanford, 1976). Works suggesting the modernizing forces and sensibilities that attacked the traditional assumptions that God wanted sacrifice and life demanded pain include Philippe Ariès, *Western Attitudes Towards Death from the Middle Ages to the Present* (Baltimore, 1974); John Burnett, *Plenty and Want: A Social History of Diet in England from 1815 to the Present Day* (London, 1966); Elborg and Robert Forster, *European Diet from Pre-Industrial to Modern Times* (New York, 1975); Gertrude Himmelfarb, *The Idea of Poverty* (New York, 1983); Edward Shorter, *The Making of the Modern Family* (New York, 1975); Edward Tannenbaum, *1900, The Generation Before the Great War* (Garden City, New York, 1976); Keith Thomas, *Man and the Natural World: A History of Modern Sensibility* (New York, 1983); William Thomas, ed. *Man's Role in Changing the Face of the Earth*, 2 vols. (Chicago, 1956); Eugen Weber, *A Modern History of Europe* (New York, 1971); Charles Wilcock, *Medical Advance, Public Health and Social Evolution* (Elmsford, NY, 1966); Guy Williams, *The Age of Miracles* (Chicago, 1985); Lawrence Wright, *Clean and Decent: The Fascinating History of the Bathroom and the Water Closet* (Toronto, 1960); and Theodore Zeldin, *France, 1848–1945*, 2 vols. (Oxford, 1973, 1977).

Romanticism, the era's dominant cultural impulse, shaped emerging middle class sensibilities. Among other things, it taught individuals to cultivate their suffering, transforming their suffering into personal and public identities. Guides to romanticism and its pervasive role in shaping Western sensibility are Franklin Baumer, *Modern European Thought* (New York, 1977); Howard Hugo, *The Portable Romantic Reader* (New York, 1957); George Mosse, *The Culture of Western Europe* (Boulder, 1988); and Eugen Weber, *Paths to the Present* (New York, 1960). For a brief guide to the romantic thinkers Marx, Dostoevsky, and Nietzsche, see my *Ethics, Living or Dead?* (Tuscaloosa, LA/Marshall, MN., 1982). For some of the expressions of philanthrophy and fellow feelings, which merged with and were given additional force by romantic sympathy, see David Brian Davis, *The Problem of Slavery in the Age of Revolution*, 2 vols. (Ithaca, NY, 1975); Norman Fiering, "Irresistible Compassion: An Aspect of Eighteenth Century Sympathy and Humanitarianism," *Journal of the History of Ideas* (April–June, 1976): 196–218; Michel Foucault, *Madness and Civilization* (New York, 1973); Shelby McCloy, *The Humanitarian Movement in Eighteenth Century France* (Lexington, KY., 1957); John Neff, *Cultural Foundations of Industrial Society* (New York, 1960); Martin Pernick, *A Calculus of Suffering: Pain, Professionalism, and Anesthesia in Nineteenth Century America* (New York, 1985); J. H. Plumb, "The New World of Children in Eighteenth Century England", *Past and Present* 67 (May 1975): 64–69; David Rothman, *The Discovery of Asylum* (Boston, 1971); E. P. Thompson, *The Making of the English Working Class* (New York, 1963); and James Turner, *Reckoning with the Beast: Animals, Pain, and Humanity in the Victorian Mind* (Baltimore, 1980).

The twentieth century, a century of war and revolution, filled public life with victims and their suffering. Also, expanding human power and accelerating aspirations, multiplied the number and variety of victims who lay claim to public attention. For the growing horizon of the rhetoric of victims, see Raymond Aron, *Progress and Disillusion: The Dialectics of Modern Society* (New York, 1968); Peter Berger, *Pyramids of Sacrifice: Political Ethics and Social Change* (Garden City, NY., 1976); John Bodley, *Victims of Progress* (London, 1975); Marshall Cohen et al., eds., *Marx, Justice, and History* (Princeton, NJ., 1980); Terrence Des Pres, *The Survivor: An Anatomy of Life in the Death Camps* (New York, 1976); Jacques Ellul, *The Political Illusion* (New York, 1967); Kurt Glaser and Stefan Possony, *Victims of Politics: The State of Human Rights* (New York, 1979); Michael Ignatieff, *The Needs of Strangers* (New York, 1985); Barrington Moore, *Reflections on the Causes of Human Misery* (Boston, 1972), and his *Injustice: The Social Bases of Obedience and Revolt* (White Plains, NY., 1978); Aleksandr Solzhenitsyn, *The Gulag Archipelago*, 3 vols. (New York, 1973, 1974, 1976); and Adam Ulam, *The Unfinished Revolution* (New York, 1960).

The language of victims, emerged as a commanding political rhetoric of post–World War II America, as much of the standard literature on American culture since 1945 testifies. See for instance, Peter Carrol and David Noble, *The Free and Unfree: A New History of the United States* (Baltimore, 1977); Erich Tuveson, *Redeemer Nation: The Idea of America's Millenial Role* (Chicago, 1968); Sacvan Bercovitch, *The American Jeremiad* (Madison, WI, 1978); Richard Nelson, "The Progressive Jeremiad, Critical Theory and the End of Republican Virtue,'" *Clio* 16, no. 4 (1987): 360–79; Henry Commanger, *The Empire of Reason* (Garden City, NY., 1977); Roy Pearce, *Savagism and Civilization: A Study of the Indian and the American Mind* (Berkeley, 1988); Michael Kammer, *The People of Paradox: An Inquiry Concerning the Origins of American Civilization* (New York, 1980); David Noble, *The End of American History* (Minneapolis, 1985); Richard Neuhaus, *Time*

Toward Home: The American Experiment as Revelation (New York, 1975); Theodore Roszak, *The Making of a Counter Culture* (New York, 1969); and Richard King, *The Party of Eros: Radical Social Thought and the Realm of Freedom* (Chapel Hill, 1972).

By the 1970s the suffering of victims became the moral capital of many groups and formed a horizon of standard rhetorics. These rhetorics were not only consciously shaped to indict official America, but they were crafted to serve groups and even to justify bureaucracies. The following works illustrate some of the elements of this insight: Alfred Crosby, *The Columbian Exchange: The Biological Consequences of 1492* (Westport, CT., 1972); Lance Liebman, ed., *Ethnic Relations in America* (Englewood Cliffs, NJ., 1982); Vine Deloria, *We Talk, You Listen* (New York, 1970); Thaddeus Radzialowski, "The Competition for Jobs and Racial Stereotypes: Blacks and Poles in Chicago," *Polish American Studies* 33, no. 2 (Autumn 1976): 5–18; Eldridge Cleaver, *Soul on Ice* (New York, 1969); Frantz Fanon, *The Wretched of the Earth* (New York, 1968); Glen Loury, "Who Speaks for American Blacks?" *Commentary* 83 (January 1987): 34–38; Shelby Steele, "Being Black and Middle Class," *Commentary* 85 (January 1988): 42–47; Boris Bittker, *The Case for Black Reparations* (New York, 1973); Betty Friedan, *The Feminine Mystique* (New York, 1963); June De Hart-Mathews, *Women's America* (New York, 1987); Jean Bethke Elshtain, "The New Feminist Scholarship," *Salgamundi*, no. 70–71 (Spring–Summer, 1986): 3–49; Jessica Benjamin, "Victimology," *Tikkun* 4, no. 2 (March–April 1989): 75–77; Kristin Luker, *Abortion and the Politics of Motherhood* (Berkeley, 1984); Nathan Glazer, *Affirmative Discrimination* (New York, 1975); James Fishkin, *Justice, Equal Opportunity, and the Family* (New Haven, CT., 1983); Thomas Sowell, *Civil Rights: Rhetoric or Reality?* (New York, 1984); Geoffrey Hartmann, ed., *Bitburg in Moral and Political Perspective* (Bloomington, 1986); Yehuda Bauer, *The Holocaust in Historical Perspective* (Seattle, 1978); Richard Lukas, *The Forgotten Holocaust: Poles under German Occupation* (Lexington, KY., 1986); Norman Davies, *God's Playground*, 2 vols. (New York, 1984); Lucy Dawidowicz, *The Holocaust and Historians* (Cambridge, MA., 1981); George Lucas et al., eds., *Lifeboat Ethics: The Moral Dilemmas of World Hunger* (New York, 1976); R. G. Frey, *Rights, Killing, and Suffering: Moral Vegetarianism and Applied Ethics* (Oxford, 1983); and Joel Feinberg, "The Rights of Animals and Unborn Generations," in *Rights, Justice, and the Bounds of Liberty*, ed. Joel Feinberg (Princeton, 1980), 159–83.

As Nietzsche contended a hundred years ago in his *Genealogy of Morals* (1886) and *Will to Power* (1883–1887) that Western humanity was being overrun by debilitating sympathy, so we might argue that today we, of far more democratic sprit, must protect both our politics and consciences from the pervasive hold of victims. No one should be allowed to command all values as well as deny the worth others derive from their work, suffering, and sacrifices. In the spirit of Emmanuel Mounier's personalism (as defined in his *Personalist Manifesto*, 1936, and *Character of Man*, 1946, and set forth in my *Mounier and Maritain: A French Catholic Understanding of the Modern World* (Tuscaloosa, AL, 1975), it must be recognized that universally—even in our advanced world—the great majority of humans must in large measure fashion the value of lives, families, and communities out of their pains, suffering, and sacrifices. Illustrating the place of

pain and the value of suffering in everyday working class life are Jonathan
Cobb and Richard Sennett, *The Hidden Injuries of Class* (New York, 1972); Pa-
tricia Sexton and Brendan Sexton, *Blue Collars and Hard Hats* (New York, 1971);
and Lillian Rubin, *The Worlds of Pain* (New York, 1976).

Subject Index

Priests, 28–30, 58–67, 84, 126
Profit, 116
Progress, 10, 83, 95, 105, 107, 119,
  122–23, 152–53, 191
Proletariat, 114–17, 159
Protestantism, 58–67
Providence, 65, 84–85
Public/private discourse, 138
Public world, 190–98
Purgatory, 53–55, 61
Punishment, 80, 92–95
Puritans, 152
Purpose, 11

Reason, 30–39, 119, 123
Redemptive myth, 151–70
Reform, 76–77, 84, 89–90, 108
Reformation (Protestant), 58–67
Relativism, 4, 23
Religion, 24, 76, 112. See also Bud-
  dhism; Christianity; Hinduism
Repression, 126
Resentment, 119, 126, 128, 138, 141,
  169, 185, 194, 197
Resignation, 37
Responsibility, 176, 185–98
Retribution, 33
Revenge, 28, 119–20, 141
Revisionism, 155
Revolution, 114–17, 121–22, 138,
  194
Rhetoric, 156–58, 197
Ritual, 23

Sacraments, 45, 59, 61, 65
Sacrifice, 23–29, 44–45, 50–51, 56,
  58–67, 75, 80, 82, 86, 90, 95, 114–
  17, 127, 137–48, 196–97, 210,
  213–14
Saints, 46–50, 59, 61–62, 64–66, 77–
  78, 86, 106, 114, 116, 118–19
Salvation, 55, 57, 58–67, 117–24
Science, 65
Secularization, 64–65, 82–83, 95,
  103–31
Self-fulfillment, 186
Self-interest, 24, 78, 151–70, 214
Self-preservation, 7

Self-sacrifice, 25, 43, 46, 114–17
Sexual enjoyment, 179
Sin, 6
Sincerity, 17
Slave morality, 126
Sorrow, 113
State, 89, 92–95, 104, 137–48. See
  also Nation-States
Story, 16, 191, 209–15
Suicide, 118–22
Suffering: of animals, 87, 109–10,
  186–87; banalization of, xvi; of
  Christ, 43–67; and Christianity,
  43–44, 57, 58–67, 117–24; as
  cleansing, 119; communal, xii, 61;
  and community, 121; compensation for, 156–71, 186, 196; confusion about, xi–xvii, 179, 185–90;
  and consciousness, 119; as cosmic,
  195; cultivation of, 111–14; definition of, 13–20, 175–201; denial of,
  57, 186, 210; elimination of, 57,
  75–97, 114–17, 178; and forgiveness, 117–24; as giver of identity,
  113–17; and God, 58–67; as God's
  calling, 58–67; and happiness, 75–
  97, 137–48; heterogeneity of, 186;
  hierarchies of, 110, 200; ideologies
  of, 137–48; and ideology, 114–17;
  inevitability of, 1, 81–82; and innocence, xvii, 87, 117, 124, 147; innocence regarding, 18, 87, 114–17,
  140; as intrinsic to experience, 81–
  82, 103–31; and language, 2–3;
  manipulators of, 137–48, 211; and
  meaning, xviii, 55, 58–67, 114–17,
  209–15; medicalization of, 105,
  186; and merit, 48–50, 53, 58–67,
  77, 90; and modernity, vi–xix, 137–
  48; nationalization of, 137–48;
  noninevitability of, 82, 106, 186;
  nonpolitical nature of, 193–98;
  and originality, 113; and pain, 15,
  115; pervasiveness of, vi, 103–31;
  as pleasurable, 127; politicalization
  of, 193–98; political response to,
  137–48; and politics, 175–201; and
  predestination, 58–67; and Protes-

Name Index

About the Author

JOSEPH A. AMATO is Professor of History at Southwest State University in Minnesota. He has served as a consultant, humanist, and evaluator for several state and national humanities projects. Frequent reviewer, essayist, and the author of several books on ethics, death, and murder, Amato's abiding interest in twentieth century thought is represented by his *Mounier and Maritain: A French Catholic Understanding of the Modern World, Ethics, Living or Dead?*, and *Guilt and Gratitude: A Historical Study of the Origins of Contemporary Conscience* (Greenwood Press, 1982).